After Postmodernism

Several of American literature's most prominent authors, and many of their most perceptive critics and reviewers, argue that fiction of the last quarter century has turned away from the tendencies of postmodernist writing. Yet, the nature of that turn, and the defining qualities of American fiction after postmodernism, remain less than clear.

This volume identifies four prominent trends of the contemporary scene: the recovery of the real, a rethinking of historical engagement, a preoccupation with materiality, and a turn to the planetary. Readings of works by various leading figures, including Dave Eggers, Jonathan Franzen, A.M. Homes, Lance Olsen, Richard Powers, William T. Vollmann, and David Foster Wallace, support a variety of arguments about this recent revitalization of American literature.

The chapters in this book were originally published as a special issue of the journal *Textual Practice*.

Christopher K. Coffman is Senior Lecturer in Humanities at Boston University, MA, USA. He is the author of *Rewriting Early America: The Prenational Past in Postmodern Literature* (2019) and co-editor of *William T. Vollmann: A Critical Companion* (2015).

Theophilus Savvas is Lecturer in English at the University of Bristol, UK. He is the author of *American Postmodernist Fiction and the Past* (2011).

'While some work on contemporary American fiction has been shaped by the crosswinds of transitory trends and superficial labels, *After Postmodernism: The New American Fiction* is a major and substantial volume that anchors its readings in a much deeper understanding of how the contemporary novel has changed over time. Alert to the influence of DeLillo and Nabokov, attuned to mainstream voices (Eggers, Franzen), whilst also bringing welcome readings of often overlooked writers (Homes, Olsen), Savvas and Coffman's collection offers fine-grained analyses of what has happened to postmodernism's key concerns – from the Jamesonian shadow cast over history and affect to its ambitions to historical greatness – alongside pioneering readings of new areas, such as genrefication and vegetarianism.'

– Stephen Burn, Reader in Post-1945 American Literature, University of Glasgow, UK.

'"Post-postmodern" has long been a broad and unwieldy designation for what's going on in US literature now, and this rich collection not only evokes the stakes of naming the contemporary but shows just how many branches of the network will lie hidden beneath any chosen term, unearthing affect, ecology, textual materialism, and much else in important recent fiction.'

– Jeffrey Severs, Associate Professor, University of British Columbia, Canada, and author of *David Foster Wallace's Balancing Books: Fictions of Value* (2017).

After Postmodernism

The New American Fiction

Edited by
Christopher K. Coffman and Theophilus Savvas

LONDON AND NEW YORK

First published 2021
by Routledge
2 Park Square, Milton Park, Abingdon, Oxon OX14 4RN

and by Routledge
52 Vanderbilt Avenue, New York, NY 10017

Routledge is an imprint of the Taylor & Francis Group, an informa business

British Library Cataloguing in Publication Data
A catalogue record for this book is available from the British Library

ISBN 13: 978-0-367-64010-1

Typeset in Minion
by Newgen Publishing UK

Publisher's Note
The publisher accepts responsibility for any inconsistencies that may have arisen during the conversion of this book from journal articles to book chapters, namely the inclusion of journal terminology.

Disclaimer
Every effort has been made to contact copyright holders for their permission to reprint material in this book. The publishers would be grateful to hear from any copyright holder who is not here acknowledged and will undertake to rectify any errors or omissions in future editions of this book.

Contents

Citation Information

The chapters in this book were originally published in *Textual Practice*, volume 33, issue 2 (February 2019). When citing this material, please use the original page numbering for each article, as follows:

Introduction

American fiction after postmodernism
Theophilus Savvas and Christopher K. Coffman
Textual Practice, volume 33, issue 2 (February 2019), pp. 195–212

Chapter 1

Vegetarianism in the Anthropocene: Richard Powers and Jonathan Franzen
Theophilus Savvas
Textual Practice, volume 33, issue 2 (February 2019), pp. 213–228

Chapter 2

The genrefication of contemporary American fiction
Alexander Moran
Textual Practice, volume 33, issue 2 (February 2019), pp. 229–244

Chapter 3

Feverish fictions: William T. Vollmann and American literary history after postmodernism
Christopher K. Coffman
Textual Practice, volume 33, issue 2 (February 2019), pp. 245–262

Chapter 4

Metaffective fiction: structuring feeling in post-postmodern American literature
Ralph Clare
Textual Practice, volume 33, issue 2 (February 2019), pp. 263–279

Chapter 5

Entropology and the end of nature in Lance Olsen's Theories of Forgetting
Alison Gibbons
Textual Practice, volume 33, issue 2 (February 2019), pp. 280–299

Chapter 6

Typical Eggers: transnationalism and America in Dave Eggers's 'globally-minded' fiction
Bran Nicol
Textual Practice, volume 33, issue 2 (February 2019), pp. 300–317

Chapter 7

Making it long: men, women, and the great American novel now
Kasia Boddy
Textual Practice, volume 33, issue 2 (February 2019), pp. 318–337

Notes on Contributors

Kasia Boddy, Faculty of English, University of Cambridge, UK.

Ralph Clare, Department of English, Boise State University, ID, USA.

Christopher K. Coffman, Division of Humanities, College of General Studies, Boston University, MA, USA.

Alison Gibbons, Department of Humanities, Sheffield Hallam University, UK.

Alexander Moran, School of English, Drama, and American and Canadian Studies, University of Birmingham, UK.

Bran Nicol, School of Literature and Languages, University of Surrey, UK.

Theophilus Savvas, Department of English, University of Bristol, UK.

INTRODUCTION

American fiction after postmodernism

Theophilus Savvas and Christopher K. Coffman

In a number of essays published between 1988 and 1993, David Foster Wallace presented a vision of contemporary American fiction that broke in some important regards from then-typical definitions of postmodernist writing. The most influential articulations of his various claims are those of 'E Unibus Pluram: Television and U.S. Fiction,' which appeared in a 1993 issue of *The Review of Contemporary Fiction* and later in his 1997 collection, *A Supposedly Fun Thing I'll Never Do Again*. In this piece, Foster Wallace argues for what he variously labels 'hyperrealism,' 'fiction of the image,' and 'post-postmodernism,' a rejection of ironic modes and attitudes, which he sees as characteristic of postmodernist literature, and for a shift in the direction of a 'single-entendre' fiction, one that finds authenticity by supplanting or supplementing the generally unproductive impulses of critique with those of constructive moral engagement and the recovery of language's referential function. While a number of reviewers, critics, and essayists commented on post-postmodernist tendencies in the decades following Foster Wallace's publication of these arguments, it took several years for them to gain traction, and critics only settled on something like a descriptor for them upon publication, in 2010, of Adam Kelly's 'David Foster Wallace and the New Sincerity in American Fiction.'[1]

Although Foster Wallace's statements are perhaps the most well-known of this sort, he is hardly the only figure to have registered that American authors of the early 1990s were producing a new sort of fiction, or to have attempted to elucidate the terms on which that fiction was unfolding. In the succeeding decades, an array of writers and critics have increasingly recognised that something different from the sort of high-postmodernism of figures like John Barth, Robert Coover, and Thomas Pynchon may be found in many of the most interesting and aesthetically successful of recent fictions. Furthermore, many have attempted to describe the nature of this shift, or at least to clarify the terms of the debate inspired by it. In most instances, these efforts conclude that contemporary fiction offers a development of or refocusing on certain neglected aspects of postmodernist literature, but not a radical break with it. Works such as Jeremy Green's 2005 *Late Postmodernism: American Fiction at the Millennium* and Jeffrey T. Nealon's 2012 *Post-Postmodernism, or, The Cultural Logic of Just-in-Time Capitalism*, for example, regard 'late postmodernist' or 'post-postmodernist' fictions as evidence of the intensification of the impact of late capitalist economies and electronic mediation on cultural production. Others, such as the authors of the essays in Alison Shonkwiler and Leigh Clare La Berge's 2012 *Reading Capitalist Realism* and James Wood (albeit less flatteringly) in his 2000 review 'Human, all too Inhuman,' suggest that fiction is, provoked by some of those same factors, undergoing a reactionary return to Realist aesthetics. On the other hand, some critics argue for a more radical break between the postmodern and post-postmodern, as does Alan Kirby in his 2009 *Digimodernism: How New Technologies Dismantle the Postmodern and Reconfigure Our Culture*. In spite of some disagreement among critics regarding the nature and degree of difference between the postmodern and the post-postmodern, there is a general acceptance of the idea that claims like Foster Wallace's are on the mark: contemporary American fiction has, since roughly 1989, increasingly valorised such seemingly naïve literary qualities as a return to mimetic verisimilitude, a display of historical awareness, and a preoccupation with the physical nature of the textual artifact as keys to the revitalisation of a constructive textual authenticity, one that reinvigorates the exchange between reader and literary text.

While the dates of the aforementioned pieces begin only in 2005, they in fact follow signs posted throughout the 1990s and early 2000s that indicate a more extensive history of thinking about the subject. Notable instances of earlier engagements include the papers of Heide Ziegler's 1991 symposium 'The End of Postmodernism,' Mark Amerika and Lance Olsen's arguments in *In Memoriam to Postmodernism* (1995) that an 'Avant-Pop' aesthetic has replaced the postmodernist one, Stephen Burn's 2000 essay 'The End of Postmodernism: American Fiction of the Millennium,' Raymond Federman's 2001 claim that postmodernism died in 1989, with the death of Samuel Beckett (and, perhaps, the fall of the Berlin Wall), and Robert McLaughlin's 2004 article 'Post-Postmodern Discontent: Contemporary Fiction and the Social World.' In spite of the at least temporary dominance of Foster Wallace's perspective, and the relatively lengthy timeline of efforts to ascertain the nature of a post-postmodern turn, there remains considerable disagreement among critics regarding a number of factors germane to the categorisation and description of such recent developments in fiction. Furthermore, the terms 'Avant-Pop,' 'post-postmodernist,' 'late-postmodernist,' 'digimodernist,' and 'New Sincerity' are themselves maligned in certain quarters as insufficient. One intervention was attempted by a number of cultural theorists who proposed 'metamodernism' as a term sufficient to both the shift in literary practice and all of the several qualities and concerns that other efforts to describe that shift have identified. The best statement of this position so far is Robin van den Akker, Alison Gibbons, and Timotheus Vermeulen's 2017 collection *Metamodernism: Historicity, Affect, and Depth after Postmodernism.* While it is possible that 'metamodernism' may win the day as a label for the best next thing after postmodernism, questions regarding the post-postmodern turn's nature and implications are hardly resolved. Indeed, the catalogues of the preceding paragraphs indicate the remarkable degree to which the critical debate surrounding the post-postmodern is ongoing, rich, and problematic. As Linda Hutcheon suggests in the epilogue to her 2002 *The Politics of Postmodernism*, the lack of clarity is a problem of some concern, for the inability to establish the terminology and general thrust of critical projects relating to contemporary literary efforts hinders not only the critical enterprise, but also, and more importantly, the dissemination of critical insights to a wider audience. The articles collected in this issue of *Textual Practice* began with a recognition that arguments about what follows postmodernism have settled into a handful of fairly stable positions, and that some stock-taking is thus overdue.[2] They each touch upon one or more familiar figures, positions, and approaches, but collectively augment and assess the implications of the ongoing conversation about post-postmodernist American literature as revealed in some of its definitive texts. In the pages that follow, we offer a brief overview of these positions and their contexts.

Recovery of the Real

Philip Roth's essay 'Writing American Fiction,' from 1961, is concerned, as one of the contributors to this issue notes, with how "the serious writer' has failed to find an appropriate strategy or form for dealing with the reality of the social and historical world.' One might suggest that US writing went on to offer two possible solutions to the problem that Roth diagnosed. One way produced 'New Journalism' and the 'Non-Fiction Novel.' The writers of these related forms – including most prominently Tom Wolfe and Truman Capote – utilised the techniques of fiction in an attempt to achieve a greater degree of verisimilitude in, and so authority for, their work. For Wolfe, such literature 'enjoys an advantage so obvious, so built in, one almost forgets what a power it has [...] the simple fact that the reader knows all this actually happened. The disclaimers are erased. The screen is gone. The writer is one step closer to the absolute involvement of the reader that Henry James and James Joyce dreamed of and never achieved.'[3] Here was a form which would, in the words of Capote, 'remove disguises,' from the representation of the 'social and historical world,' and let the facts apparently speak for themselves. Postmodernist writers took the opposite stance.[4] As Barth commented,

'A different way to come to terms with the discrepancy between art and the Real Thing is to affirm the artificial element in art (you can't get rid of it anyhow) and make the artifice part of your point.'[5] This, of course, is the credo of the metafictionists, and it begins from the premise outlined by Ronald Sukenick that 'reality is, simply, our experience and objectivity is, of course, an illusion.'[6]

Coover's 'The Babysitter' troubled the distinction between 'objective' reality and experience, by refusing to distinguish ontologically between what happens, what might possibly happen and what characters want to happen.[7] Coover establishes a narrative world in which generic conventions and television seem to generate and govern the characters' behaviour. Undercutting the distinction between artifice, fantasy, and reality means that everything we read in the story must be regarded as 'both true and false, as both happening and not happening,' in the words of Ronald Christ.[8] The 'illusion' of objectivity also governed the work of E. L. Doctorow in the 1970s and 1980s and led him to renounce what he called the 'chaste or objective voice of realism.'[9] The point is made, metafictionally, by the narrator of his 1971 novel *The Book of Daniel*, who notes, while discussing the film version of *The Spy who Came In from the Cold*, that 'life is never this well plotted but the picture is meant to be appreciated for its realism [...] Burton walks around like a man with a realistic load of shit in his pants.'[10] Doctorow would go on to suggest, in his important essay 'False Documents,' that 'there is no fiction or non-fiction as we commonly understand the distinction: there is only narrative,' a point exemplified in his next novel, *Ragtime* (1975), in which historical personages – Harry Houdini, Sigmund Freud, Stanford White – mingle with characters from Doctorow's imagination.[11] Where New Journalism brought the techniques of fiction to the documenting of the 'real,' Doctorow's technique was to bring the 'real' into his novels, and then, through metafictional devices, challenge the ways in which we construct our notion of the 'real.' It was through such metafictional admissions that narrative might, in a sense, be redeemed: 'It is a world born for liars,' he commented, 'and we [fiction writers] are born liars. But we are to be trusted because is the only profession forced to admit that it lies – and the bestows upon us the mantle of honesty.'[12]

Through the 1980s there was also, however, a strand of American writing that was avoiding such admissions and working a towards a 'revitalisation of realism,' in the words of Robert Rebein.[13] Key here was Raymond Carver who best demonstrated 'how to be a serious artist without taking art as his subject matter.'[14] The year before Rebein adumbrated his argument in his book *Hicks, Tribes and Dirty Realists* (2001), the critic Wood, writing in the *New Republic*, had coined the pejorative term 'Hysterical Realism' to describe both the recent work of first-generation postmodernists such as Pynchon and Don DeLillo, and the work of a new breed of writers, like Foster Wallace and Zadie

Smith.[15] The phrasing of Wood's chief charge, that such fiction 'knows a thousand things but does not know a single human being,' seemed a deliberate rebuke to Foster Wallace, who had frequently asserted that fiction is about 'what it is to be a fucking human being.'[16] Whatever value Wood's charge has – and it does have some – it has not stopped Foster Wallace's writing from being seen as the standard-bearer of an emergent 'New Sincerity' in American writing. This writing, which includes the work of Rick Moody, Jennifer Egan, George Saunders, and the later Jonathan Franzen, is generally seen as an attempt to move beyond the irony of postmodernist fiction, and to counter the 'waning of affect' that such fiction effected (at least to the mind of Fredric Jameson).[17] Foster Wallace's short story 'Octet,' from *Brief Interview with Hideous Men* (1999), has been labelled the 'Ur-text of New Sincerity.'[18] 'Octet' is presented as a story – or really a failed story – concerned with achieving empathy and community with its readers; but the extreme metafictionality of the text, the postmodern narratological modes employed, and the liberal extended footnotes which take over the ostensible main text, function to demonstrate just how difficult it is to escape the regime of irony that postmodernism installed. To put it another way, 'Octet' demonstrates the difficulty not so much of being sincere, but of convincing others of one's sincerity. As Smith has suggested, the author seems to be demanding a leap of faith, and whether one can make the leap will likely 'make or break you as a reader of Foster Wallace.'[19] And the story ends by putting its fate in the hands of the reader: 'So decide,' it concludes.[20]

Indeed, while Smith herself had seemingly accepted, in 2000, some of Wood's charges, by 2008 she had become critical of the kind of fiction that he was advocating. Such 'lyrical realism' – Smith points to Joseph O' Neil's *Netherland* (2008), as one example – had made no attempt to grapple with the legacies of modernism or postmodernism and 'blithely continues on its merry road, with not a metaphysical care in the world.'[21] Where Smith saw such realism as shirking metaphysical duties, Theophilus Savvas in his piece in this issue suggests that it may also be unsuitable for grappling with some of the environmental exigencies of our time. In Savvas's reading the posthuman framing of Richard Powers's *The Echo Maker* (2007) offers a more successful engagement with ecological issues than does the humanistic focus on the individual liberal subject found in Jonathan Franzen's *Purity* (2015). For Lee Konstantinou such 'storytelling realism' – Konstantinou points to the work of Clare Messud and Jeffrey Eugenides, as well as Franzen – is to be distinguished from the work of those he dubs 'affective neorealists,' writers who seek to 'jump the gap between the sign and the referent, turning to forms such as the essay, photography, and other archival practices that license a fantasy that one might escape linguistic and conceptual mediation and thereby gain access to the real itself'; chief among these writers are Sheila Heti, Ben Marcus, Ben Lerner, and Teju Cole.[22] The significance of the fact that critics are beginning the task of delineating trends within neorealism is that it comes with the tacit acceptance that the realist turn must now be taken for granted.

Recovery of the Historical

Jameson begins his seminal *Postmodernism; or, the Cultural Logic of Late Capitalism*, with the assertion that the postmodern is 'an attempt to think the present historically in an age that has forgotten how to think historically.[23] In so doing, he both distinguishes postmodernism from modernism and makes central to the distinction the problem of contemporary historical awareness. For Jameson, the cultural environment that is postmodernism has exchanged an interest in the referent represented for an interest in the representation itself. As a result, he contends, 'producers of culture' have available a 'museum' of 'dead styles' that can be imitated, but those imitations will at best achieve only a sort of pastiche that lacks true historical grounding.[24] Seen from Jameson's vantage, even quite historically engaged postmodernist fictions, such as Doctorow's *Ragtime*, Coover's *The Public Burning* (1977), or Kurt Vonnegut's *Slaughterhouse-Five* (1969) can provide 'pseudo-historical depth,' but are otherwise limited in their possibilities to explore contemporary concerns in the context of authentic historical awareness.[25]

While Jameson's remarks have been remarkably influential, others find in them something of a blind spot to the achievements of postmodernist fictions. For Linda Hutcheon, to assert a deficiency of historical sensibility is a misdiagnosis. Hutcheon claims that postmodernism has, in fact, fostered many examples of 'historiographic metafiction,' fictions that are 'intensely self-reflexive [...] yet paradoxically lay claim to historical events and personages.'[26] Such texts, she argues, unite literary practice, historical interest, and the insights of critical theory in such a manner that they display 'theoretical self-awareness of history and fiction as human constructs,' with the consequence that fiction can be a tool for parodic 'rethinking and reworking [...] the forms and contents of the past.'[27] So, while Jean-François Lyotard's proposal that postmodernity displays an 'incredulity toward metanarratives' is, from the perspective of a thinker like Jameson, a hobbling, or even an entire undermining, of the historical import of fiction, Hutcheon reclaims it as the basis for cultural critique.[28] On this view, Barth's commentary on myths of American independence in *LETTERS* (1979), DeLillo's foregrounding of the uncertainty surrounding John F. Kennedy's assassination in *Libra* (1988), or Coover's fanciful mix of Richard Nixon and the Depression-era United States in *Whatever Happened to Gloomy Gus of the Chicago Bears?* (1987) can be read as political critiques whose power derives exactly from their engagement with the contradictions, elisions, and other aporia of historical narration.

While Hutcheon's argument makes space for considering the historico-political import of postmodernist cultural productions, American fiction of the long 1990s (from the Cold-War-close-signaling fall of the Berlin Wall in 1989 to the terrorist attacks of 11 September 2001) increasingly exhibited characteristics incompatible with her definition of historiographic metafiction, while it also avoided regressing to the historical vacuity Jameson asserted. Indeed, fictions of the decade continued to display a concern with the historical past and a metafictive reflexivity, as evident in works like Bharati Mukherjee's *The Holder of the World* (1993), Pynchon's *Mason & Dixon* (1997), Don DeLillo's *Underworld* (1997), and Toni Morrison's *Paradise* (1997). Yet, these and other American novels of the decade displayed a shift with regard to the import of historical consciousness, mixing critiques of the historical past such as those Hutcheon describes with explorations of the possible terms of contemporary community informed by an understanding of that past. Critics soon registered this change in emphasis: in his *After the End of History: American Fiction in the 1990s*, for instance, Samuel Cohen describes the decade's novels as turning away from 'difference, division, and exclusion' and toward something more productive.[29] Likewise, Phillip E. Wegner's *Life between Two Deaths, 1989–2001: U.S. Culture in the Long Nineties* claims many younger authors of fiction and cultural theorists have exchanged an interest in agonistic critique for more productive considerations of 'alternative forms of collective being.'[30] Examples of this tendency can be found, as Michael Walonen argues, in the work of figures such as Colson Whitehead, whose early fictions (notably *John Henry Days*, published in 2001, on the cusp of the post-9/11 world) engage the American past not only as a critique of the 'mythic doxa of history,' but 'as a means of conceptualising historical and political possibilities for their era.'[31]

After 2001, these grapplings with the past are intensified, and in many cases fictions find a way forward, out of postmodernist detachment and toward constructive possibility, via the history most germane to literary texts: literary history itself. In these instances, literary forms are viewed not as mere conventions available for presentation on the terms of pastiche, as Jameson would have it, but as a means to enact affectively powerful and authentic considerations of the present in relation to the reality of the past. One strong example of the effort is William T. Vollmann's *Seven Dreams* series, each volume of which reminds readers that his attempt is not traditional historiography, but a 'Symbolic History,' 'an account of origins and metamorphoses which is often untrue based on the literal facts as we know them, but whose untruths further a deeper sense of truth.'[32] Although the correspondences between the stylistic and generic elements of Vollmann's works and those of his sources – *Argall* (2001) is written in seventeenth-century English, *Fathers and Crows* (1992) employs structural elements of the *Jesuit Relations*, and so forth – may be seen in some senses as akin to the more superficial treatment of such features in postmodernist texts like Barth's *The Sot-Weed Factor* (1960), these components are mingled in Vollmann's novels with autobiographical passages about the research and composition the author undertook in creating the novels. In this manner, the past of the historical novel is brought into relations with the present reality of the field and library research undertaken by the author, establishing a clear connection between his present experience and the past preserved in the archive of texts that shape his own. Similar tactics to this establishment of a connection between the work of the author in the present and the historical material he or she treats are evident in several other notable fictions of the past fifteen years, including Dave Eggers's *What is the What* (2006), which blends biographical information about Valentino Achak Deng with historiographical treatment of Sudanese refugees in the United States, and Michael Chabon's *Moonglow* (2016), which narrates the history of Chabon's own family.

In this issue, Alexander Moran and Christopher K. Coffman examine another way in which literary traditions – especially those codified in generic forms – can open texts toward authentic engagement with the past. Coffman claims that Vollmann finds in literary-historical continuities with the gothic tradition a means to access the unarticulated reality of the broader historical past. In Vollmann's works, Coffman argues, this connection to the past via literary tradition becomes a means to revive historical consciousness and generate community in the present by honouring the ruptures of hemispheric history. Moran posits a wider post-postmodern phenomenon that he terms 'genrefication,' considering how authors such as Whitehead and Jennifer Egan historicise the present by recognising the affective potential contained within generic forms. Although the processes Coffman and Moran describe operate in somewhat different ways, both articles claim a recognition on the part of contemporary authors that literary conventions strengthen fiction's ability to revive historical consciousness in the present. Their arguments could be seen as applying as well to a number of other recent texts that draw extensively on genre fiction and canonical texts of the literary tradition, including Mat Johnson's *Pym*, Bennett Sims's *A Questionable Shape* (2011), Jonathan Lethem's *Motherless Brooklyn* (1999), and Mark Z. Danielewski's *House of Leaves* (2000), among others.

Whether through engagement with earlier literary forms or the delineation of connections between the writing of fiction in the present and the conditions of the historical past, post-postmodern authors have displayed an ongoing interest in – and increasingly achieved a renewal of – historical awareness. In so doing, they have expanded the scope of the contemporary inclination to the recovery of the real, an inclination spurred in part by dissatisfaction with the ironic, postmodern rejection of the possibility of the authentic. To the extent that they have so far succeeded, contemporary authors engaging the deep truth of the past enable readers to recognise the historical conditions of our moment, and to consider terms for community today.

Material Concerns

Genealogies of postmodernist fiction often mention *Tristram Shandy* (1759) as a precursor, and the formal playfulness, presentation of language as constitutive of reality, and generic instability of Laurence Sterne's novel certainly presage similar features in many notable postmodernist texts.[33] Among the other justifications of claims for Sterne's precession are his use of extravagant graphic materials, such as the diagrams of plot structures and marbled and black pages. These visual features, taken alongside the surrounding text, productively bridge the worlds of print narrative and of image and draw attention to the materiality of the book held by the reader in a reflexive fashion. In this regard, Sterne's novel anticipates not only many instances of radically experimental twentieth-century fiction, but also features encountered in more mainstream postmodernist texts, such as the Möbius strip at the start of Barth's *Lost in the Funhouse* (1968), the images and unconventional typography and layout of William Gass's *Willie Masters' Lonesome Wife* (1968), the genre-challenging blend of autobiography and fiction in Hunter S. Thompson's *Fear and Loathing in Las Vegas* (1972), and the assault on the regime of linear print narrative represented by William Burroughs's cut-up trilogy (1961–1964). Additional earlier or contemporary points could be mapped onto this consideration of the heritage of postmodernist manipulations of texts' traditional formal, material, and generic qualities (from illuminated manuscripts and William Blake's prints to children's picture books and the text montages of John Dos Passos's *U.S.A.* [1930–1936]), but such efforts would finally need to accommodate the fact that many earlier experiments with image, typography, layout, and narrative form can seem from the current vantage like only more-or-less prescient ancestors of the interactive and accelerated surround of our hypermediated present.[34]

The ubiquity and effects of digital media initially registered in contemporary American fiction in two ways. One was the consolidation of cyberpunk, a branch of speculative fiction concerned with the social impact of digital technologies in the information age. Not surprisingly, the genre is highly self-aware: the conventions established by William Gibson's foundational *Neuromancer* (1984) were already being subjected to parodic critique by other cyberpunk fictions within a decade, notably in Neal Stephenson's *Snow Crash* (1992). Nevertheless, cyberpunk became an important element of some early assertions that postmodernism had run its course, perhaps most notably those of Avant-Pop. Just as cyberpunk blended the popular genre of science fiction with unconventional narrative elements as a means to think better about emergent digital technologies, so Avant-Pop ignored the popular / high culture divide with an interest in finding a middle ground between mindless consumption of pop culture and ironic subversion of the same. Also like cyberpunk, Avant-Pop was intensely aware of the role of electronic and mass media: Larry McCaffery mentions not only literary texts as examples, but also films, music (the term 'Avant Pop' was taken from a Lester Bowie LP, and rock bands like Stereolab and Sonic Youth get nods), and such television shows as *Max Headroom* and *Twin Peaks*.[35] McCaffery, Mark Amerika, Lance Olsen, Sukenick, and others went on to produce both the theoretical underpinnings and key texts of Avant-Pop. Importantly, the conversation went online early, at the Alt-X website (1993, home of the earliest publications of the *electronic book review*), while acknowledging as well the ongoing relevance of print texts, first in the *Avant-Pop: Fiction for a Daydream Nation* collection published in 1992 by the Fiction Collective Two's imprint Black Ice Books, and then *After Yesterday's Crash: The Avant-Pop Anthology*, issued by Viking's more mainstream Penguin Books in 1995. Intriguingly, Avant-Pop remained entangled with its declared predecessor: the aforementioned anthologies included pieces by postmodernist stalwarts like DeLillo and Coover alongside those of younger authors such as Marcus, Foster Wallace, and Vollmann. Likewise, while Amerika declares in his 'Avant-Pop Manifesto' that 'Postmodernism is dead and we're in the process of finally burying it,' he adds, from its remains Avant-Pop is now born.'[36] In this sense, while cyberpunk, Avant-Pop, and other media-aware fiction of the 1980s and 1990s generally recognised some divergence from early postmodernist writing, they sometimes stumbled in articulating sharp distinctions between the old order and the new – a difficult problem similar to that addressed in each of the articles in this special issue.

The second broad category of notable early engagements with digital technologies by authors of American fiction was driven by an interest in the possibilities new media presented for the composition of narratives. American fiction awoke to opportunities allowed by hypertext upon the release of Michael Joyce's *afternoon, a story* (1987), but, as Astrid Ensslin has argued, the 1990s saw the development of digital technologies that motivated more advanced hyperfictional practice.[37] The work of Joyce and his contemporaries in the late 1980s and very early 1990s took shape in the context of now-archaic platforms for networked communications and the transfer protocols of pre-HTTP web browsing. These early digital fictions were interactive, but, as Ensslin explains, 'use images sparsely and mainly as illustrative or decorative means.'[38] The situation changed somewhat after the mid-1990s, when Internet use became much more widespread due to the ease of access allowed by user-friendly graphic browsers for the World Wide Web (beginning with Mosaic, in 1993) and the development of the commercial Internet (after 1995). Related technological innovations have produced readers of fiction who expect more complexly and seamlessly integrated hypermediated texts (such as Olsen and Tim Guthrie's 2005 novel, *10:01*), ones that offer fictions in which the visual, auditory, and other multi-media features do not merely supplement the written text, but operate alongside it to compose a whole that is 'more than the sum of its constituent parts.'[39] In short, the many possibilities of digital fictions (aka hypermedia, or cybertexts) have been explored over the past three decades, but their material nature, rather than some engagement with any other perceived insufficiencies of postmodernist print fiction, is the primary marker of their distinction from their predecessors.

Where that distinction has more sharply emerged is in print texts produced during roughly the same period. One can approach the nature of the shift by first observing that many postmodernist fictions include images, blend genres, and deploy typographical extravagances as a means of defamiliarization, as Paula Geyh has explained with reference to Kurt Vonnegut's *Breakfast of Champions* (1973).[40] On this view, any material that troubles the process of reading type left-to-right-and-top-to-bottom both renews the reader's experience of the text and reflexively reminds readers that written fiction is typically conceived as a narrative construct embodied in a codex. As a consequence of the latter point, postmodernist metafiction lends itself well to efforts to remind readers of print that they are dealing with a representation of experience embodied in a material form that can serve the ends of unjust authority and control. Hence, a text like Ishmael Reed's *Mumbo Jumbo* (1972), which uses collage of text and image as a means to compose an African American historical counternarrative.

But, for writers since the mid-1990s, the world is already one of digital collage, of electronic textuality that is multimodal, ever-present, and nonlinear. Consequently, texts from the later 1990s, and increasingly since, explore the implications of our new media environment, as implied by the arguments of Kirby's *Digimodernism*. In some cases (like Eggers's *The Circle* [2013] and Franzen's *Purity*), this consideration is one of subject matter. In many others, the engagement with digital media instead, or also, evinces what Peter Boxall describes as 'the strikingly new attention to [...] materiality' in twenty-first century fiction.[41] Aspects of books like the many visual innovations in the novels of Danielewski, the PowerPoint chapter of Egan's *A Visit from the Goon Squad* (2011), the cut-up pages of *Tree of Codes* by Jonathan Safran Foer (2010), the extensive paratexts (glossaries, maps, sketches, timelines, notes, and so forth) of Vollmann's *Seven Dreams*, and the footnotes of Foster Wallace's *Infinite Jest* (1996), stand between traditional print fiction and the realm of digital media, recognising that hypertext and other digital multimedia phenomena are not necessarily hindrances to the representational work of fiction, but something that models and can be incorporated as a means to enact more faithfully that representational work. There is something of anxiety in this impulse, in the sense that one wonders about the demesne of fiction in the new media environment, but a more positive spin, such as that advanced in Daniel Punday's *Writing at the Limit: The Novel in the New Media Ecology*, might be that other media than traditional print offer a 'way of talking about what it means to write and read a print novel'.[42] As the fictions mentioned earlier in this paragraph demonstrate, recent authors grapple in their print fictions with the semiotic power of image and unconventional manipulations of layout and typography, the significance and necessity of which has been sharpened by the rise of digital mediations. In this issue, articles by Ralph Clare and Alison Gibbons demonstrate how the various paratextual materials and typographical experiments of two exemplary recent fictions, J. J. Abrams and Doug Dorst's *S.* (2013) and Olsen's *Theories of Forgetting* (2014), work in a centripetal fashion, encouraging the reader to move beyond the primary narrative, indeed (and contra the intertextuality characteristic of postmodernism) beyond the books, and into cognisance of the ecological and social worlds that lie outside their covers. Although this use of multimodal fiction does turn the reader to the world outside of the virtual, it resists simply condemning the virtual. Instead, these fictions enact a sensitive appraisal of the imbrication of hyper-media and non-digital experience that characterises our digitally mediated world, without abandoning their place in the realm of print fiction.

The Worlding of American Literature

Mukherjee concluded her Gayley Lecture, delivered at the University of California, Berkeley in April 2011, by commenting that 'the academy has not yet developed the grid and the grammar to explore American works that are not quite 'American' in a canonical sense.'[43] Though Mukherjee does not mention postmodernism, many of the writers and critics who have expressed a similar sensibility in the last decade or so suggest that the term has little descriptive value when it comes to the most interesting and exciting of new fiction. There are two ways in which we might conceptualise what is variously called the 'transnational' or 'planetary' turn in American writing. The first is to think about the centripetal forces at play: that is, immigrant writing that is 'changing the contours of a national literature,' as Mukherjee put it in the title of her lecture.[44] The second element results in part from the first: that is, the increased centrifugal force of an American studies that seeks to look beyond the American centre (or perhaps, more accurately, to resist the notion that America is the centre), and to develop strategies for recognising the world *in* the local.

Thinking about this in the context of this special issue, we might begin with the year 1973. Brian McHale and Len Platt, in their introduction to the *Cambridge History of Postmodern Literature*, suggest that the publication of

Pynchon's *Gravity's Rainbow* in 1973, following as it did the use of 'postmodernism' in critical works by Leslie Fiedler, Ihab Hassan, and William Spanos (in 1970, 1971, and 1972, respectively) marks 1973 as the point that postmodernism was 'branded.'[45] In also stressing the significance of a number of world historical events of the year, such as the Arab Oil embargo and the Yom Kippur war, McHale and Platt draw on David Harvey's *The Condition of Postmodernity* which posits 1973 as the year in which the move to the globalised economy is inaugurated. For Harvey, Nixon's decision in 1971 to move away from the gold standard and towards a system of fluctuating exchange rates prepares the ground for the decline of the 'Fordist Regime' – which he dates to 1973 – since by then money was effectively 'de-materialised', as a fully floating system of currency conversion was adopted. With no mechanism to regulate the growth rate of the country's money supply, the US was increasingly drawn into the marketplace of global exchange – a condition which was given greater impetus in the 1980s by the free-market philosophies of President Ronald Reagan, and in the 1990s, by the growth in information technology.[46]

At precisely the same time that the US was entering into a new relationship with the world (at least in Harvey's reading), so too was American studies beginning to move away from the integrationist logic of its myth and symbol school. 1973 was the year that Multi-Ethnic Literature of the United States was founded as a response to the dominance of white male American literature at the Modern Language Association conferences, and the continued circumscription of America, as nation, and idea.[47] American studies had been codified as a discipline in the cultural context of the Cold War – a culture of 'Containment,' and 'an age of conformity', in the words of Irving Howe, writing in the *Partisan Review* in 1954.[48] And the academic projections of American innocence found in the seminal texts of American studies – Henry Nash Smith's *Virgin Land* (1950), R. W. B. Lewis's *The American Adam* (1955), for instance – went hand-in-glove with Cold War questions of assimilability: Who is (an) American? Or what is an American? MELUS, in its mission status, sought to expand 'the definition of American literature through the study and teaching of Latino/a American, Native American, African American, Asian and Pacific American, and ethnically specific Euro-American literary works, their authors, and their cultural contexts.'[49]

Coincidentally, 1973 was also the year at which immigration levels to the US were at their lowest; from that point on they began steadily rising, such that by 1990 the journalist William A. Henry could point out, in a piece for *Time* magazine called 'Beyond the Melting Pot,' that 'someday soon, surely much sooner than most people who filled out their Census forms last week realize, white Americans will become a minority group. Long before that day arrives, the presumption that the 'typical' U.S. citizen is someone who traces his or her descent in a direct line to Europe will be part of the past.'[50] A year later Gish Jen seemed to exemplify the point that Henry was making in her novel *Typical American* (1991).[51] Here, a makeshift family is established by Ralph, a Chinese immigrant, in a narrative which both challenges and resists any notion of the typicality of the title. Jen's text also seemed to set the mood for the nineties; as Aliki Varvogli notes, 'this subversion of the traditional story of immigrant success and acceptance of a new identity is to be found in several other key texts of the decade.'[52]

Such 'subversion' in texts of the 1990s – that interregnum between two deaths, as Wegner put it – was one reason why, by the 2000s, postmodernism seemed no longer to address the critical exigencies of the time. How had it ever been possible to claim that literature had been exhausted? Or that representationalism had come to an end? Even the politicization of postmodernism through poststructuralism seemed flaccid, as Christian Moraru, amongst others, has suggested.[53] These changes precipitated calls for US literature to be placed in the context of its continent (Rachel Adams), to be globally 'remapped' (Paul Giles), and to be seen through 'deep time' (Wai Chee Dimock).[54] It may also be the case, as has been often argued, that the terrorist attacks of September 11, 2001 play a part in this globalising narrative. Slavoj Žižek's oft-cited suggestion that the attacks ought to compel the US to 'risk stepping through the fantasmatic screen separating it from the Outside World, accepting its arrival into the Real World' was echoed by critics such as Richard Gray, who noted the inadequacy of those post-9/11 texts which simply attempted to 'assimilate the unfamiliar to the familiar,' and so domesticate the crisis.[55]

Such a need is also recognised in Moraru's suggestion that what we are seeing is a turn towards a 'Cosmodernism', which is 'replacing postmodernism's conceptual unit, the nation-state, with an ever more networked world.' For Moraru, cosmodern authors are 'increasingly uncomfortable with an approach that, on an important level, reinforces an older worldview that conceptualises and thus furthers 'others' and externalizes alterity *qua* 'theme' and 'form."[56] Moraru declares as 'cosmodern' writers such as Chang-rae Lee, Karen Tei Yamashita, and Jhumpa Lahiri, but significantly also includes less obvious writers, including DeLillo and Safran Foer. Moraru points to *Underworld* as marking a shift from DeLillo's earlier exemplary postmodernist fictions in its engagement with global realities. Giles has also noted that the *world* in the title signifies the novel's 'global reach,' which, by focusing on the 'worlding capacity' of the Internet – 'where everybody is everywhere at once,' as DeLillo has it – induces a sense of 'cosmic communitarianism.'[57] Eggers, of a later generation to DeLillo, but whose earliest writing – most notably his debut, *A Heartbreaking Work of Staggering Genius* (2000) – displayed an obvious debt to postmodernist practice, might also be seen as a writer who has become more attendant to the pressing question of the global through works such as *What is the What* and *Zeitoun* (2009). Bran

Nicol's contribution to this issue picks up on both the matter of the global and the 'typical' in an essay which focuses on Eggers's most recent work. For Nicol, the global is embedded in this writing by virtue of its construction of the US as a 'typical' nation in the globalised twenty-first century world.

A notable consequence of the globalising of American literature and American studies has been the proliferation of, and the greater space afforded to, writing by women. While postmodernist writers certainly wished to use their writing to unsettle the idea of a common national project – which might be understood in terms of the integrationist logic of cold war America noted above – some scholars, such as Nancy Hartsock, remain unconvinced that postmodernism is (or was) a useful tool for feminist politics.[58] In the final article in this issue, Kasia Boddy notes the way in which postmodernism has tended to be seen as marked through male lineage, 'Pynchon begetting DeLillo begetting David Foster Wallace,' and a phallic tendency towards the 'big book,' frequently coded as the Great American Novel. Her overview of this brings to the fore the writing of A. M. Homes, and offers a radical corrective to this male-dominated narrative.

Notes

1. Adam Kelly, 'David Foster Wallace and the New Sincerity in American Fiction', in David Hering (ed.), *Consider David Foster Wallace: Critical Essays* (Austin, TX: Sideshow Media Group Press, 2010), pp. 131–46.
2. Since the special issue of *Twentieth Century Literature* on a similar theme, a number of important new texts and arguments have emerged, and concerns that had seemed pressing then have receded from the critical debate, so that a fresh overview is necessary. Andrew Hoberek (ed.), *Twentieth Century Literature*, special issue: After Postmodernism: Form and History in Contemporary Fiction, 53, no. 3 (Fall 2007).
3. Tom Wolfe, 'The New Journalism,' in Tom Wolfe and E. W. Johnson (eds.), *The New Journalism* (Basingstoke: Picador, 1996 [orig. 1973]), p. 49.
4. Truman Capote, *Music for Chameleons* (Harmondsworth, Middlesex: Penguin, 1993), p. xv.
5. John Barth, 'John Barth: An Interview', *Contemporary Literature*, 6, no. 1 (Winter–Spring, 1965), p. 6.
6. Ronald Sukenick, 'The Death of the Novel', in *The Death of the Novel and Other Stories* (Tallahassee: Fiction Collective 2, 2003), p. 41
7. Robert Coover, 'The Babysitter', in *Pricksongs and Descants* (New York: Grove, 2000 [1969]), pp. 206–39.
8. Ronald Christ, 'Forking Narratives,' *Latin American Literary Review* 7, no. 14 (Spring, 1979), p. 57.
9. E. L. Doctorow, 'False Documents' [1977], in Richard Trenner (ed.), *E. L. Doctorow: Essays and Conversations* (Princeton, NJ: Ontario Review Press, 1983), p. 24.
10. Doctorow, *The Book of Daniel* (London: Penguin, 2006), p. 318.
11. Doctorow, 'False Documents', p. 26.
12. Ibid.

13. Robert Rebein, *Hicks, Tribes and Dirty Realists: American Fiction after Postmodernism* (Lexington, Kentucky: The University Press of Kentucky, 2001), p. 17
14. Ibid., p. 29.
15. James Wood, 'Human, All Too Inhuman', *The New Republic*, July 24, 2000, https://newrepublic.com/article/61361/human-inhuman.
16. Larry McCaffery, 'A Conversation with David Foster Wallace', *The Review of Contemporary Fiction* 13, no. 2 (1993). https://www.dalkeyarchive.com/a-conversation-with-david-foster-wallace-by-larry-mccaffery/.
17. Fredric Jameson, *Postmodernism; Or, The Cultural Logic of Late Capitalism* (Durham: Duke University Press, 1991), p. 10.
18. Iain Williams, '(New) Sincerity in David Foster Wallace's "Octet"', *Critique: Studies in Contemporary Fiction*, 56, no. 3 (2015), p. 300.
19. Zadie Smith, 'Brief Interviews with Hideous Men: The Difficult Gifts of David Foster Wallace,' *Changing My Mind: Occasional Essays* (London: Penguin, 2011), p. 290.
20. David Foster Wallace, 'Octet,' in *Brief Interviews with Hideous Men* (London: Abacus, 2011), p. 136.
21. Smith, 'Two Directions for the Novel', *Changing My Mind*, p. 72.
22. Lee Konstantinou, 'Neorealist Fiction', in Rachel Greenwald Smith (ed.), *American Literature in Transition, 2000–2010* (Cambridge: Cambridge University Press, 2017), p. 111. David Shields' manifesto *Reality Hunger* – mentioned in passing in Konstantinou – documents just a desire for the real, providing a patchwork of quotations – which 'must all be considered as if spoken by a character in a novel (minus the novel' – taken from artists and writers 'who are breaking larger and larger chunks of "reality" into their work.' David Shields, *Reality Hunger: A Manifesto* (London: Penguin, 2011), p. 6, p. 3.
23. Jameson, *Postmodernism*, p. ix.
24. Ibid., pp. 18–19.
25. Ibid., p. 20.
26. Linda Hutcheon, *A Poetics of Postmodernism: History, Theory, Fiction* (New York: Routledge, 1988), p. 5.
27. Ibid.
28. Jean-François Lyotard, *The Postmodern Condition: A Report on Knowledge* (Minneapolis: University of Minnesota Press, 1984), p. xxiv.
29. Samuel Cohen, *After the End of History: American Fiction in the 1990s* (Iowa City: University of Iowa Press, 2009), p. 7.
30. Phillip E. Wegner, *Life between Two Deaths, 1989–2001: U.S. Culture in the Long Nineties* (Durham: Duke University Press, 2009), p. 34.
31. Michael Walonen, '"This Making of Truth is Violence Too, Out of Which Facts Are Formed": Colson Whitehead's Secret History of Post-Reconstruction America in *John Henry Days*', *Literature & History* 23, no. 2 (2014), p. 68.
32. William T. Vollmann, *The Ice-Shirt* (New York: Penguin, 1990), p. 397. Vollmann includes this statement in each of the five volumes of the *Seven Dreams* so far published, of which *The Ice-Shirt* was the first.
33. Brian McHale, *Postmodernist Fiction* (London: Routledge, 1987), p. 223; John Barth, *Further Fridays: Essays, Lectures, and Other Nonfiction, 1984–1994* (Boston: Little, 1995), p. 285; McCaffery, *Postmodern Fiction: A Bio-Bibliographical Guide* (New York: Greenwood, 1986), p. xv.
34. Critics have applied various labels to texts that blend media, including 'ergodic literature' (Espen J. Aarseth, *Cybertext – Perspectives on Ergodic Literature*

[Johns Hopkins University Press, 1997]) and 'multimodal discourse' (Gunther Kress and Theo van Leeuwen, *Multimodal Discourse: The Modes and Media of Contemporary Communication* [Oxford University Press, 2001]). The latter is perhaps the current front-runner.

35. McCaffery, 'The Avant-Pop Phenomenon,' *ANQ* 5.4 (1992): p. 216.
36. Mark Amerika, 'Avant-Pop Manifesto: Thread Baring Itself in Ten Quick Posts', *Alt-X*, http://www.altx.com/manifestos/avant.pop.manifesto.html [Data accessed: 6 June, 2018].
37. Astrid Ensslin, 'Electronic Fictions: Television, the Internet, and the Future of Digital Fiction', in Paula E. Geyh (ed.), *The Cambridge Companion to Postmodern American Fiction* (Cambridge: Cambridge University Press, 2017), pp. 185–6.
38. Ibid., 'Hypertextuality," in Marie-Laure Ryan, Lori Emerson, and Benjamin J. Robertson (eds.), *The Johns Hopkins Guide to Digital Media*, (Baltimore: Johns Hopkins University Press, 2014), p. 262.
39. Ibid.
40. Paula E. Geyh, "Between Word and Image: The Textual and the Visual in Postmodern American Fiction", in Paula E. Geyh (ed.), *The Cambridge Companion to Postmodern American Fiction* (Cambridge: Cambridge University Press, 2017), p. 168.
41. Peter Boxall, *Twenty-First-Century Fiction: A Critical Introduction* (Cambridge: Cambridge University Press, 2013), p. 10.
42. Daniel Punday, *Writing at the Limit: The Novel in the New Media Ecology* (Lincoln: University of Nebraska Press, 2012), p. 2.
43. Bharati Mukherjee, 'Immigrant Writing: Changing the Contours of a National Literature,' *American Literary History* 23, no. 3 (1 September 2011): pp. 680–696, https://doi.org/10.1093/alh/ajr027.
44. Shirley Geok-Lin Lim, 'The Ambivalent American: Asian American Literature on the Cusp', in Shirley Geok-Lin Lim and Amy Ling (eds.), *Reading the Literatures of Asian America* (Philadelphia: Temple University Press, 1992), p. 18.
45. Brian McHale and Len Platt, 'General Introduction', in Brian McHale and Len Platt (eds.), *The Cambridge History of Postmodern Literature* (Cambridge: Cambridge University Press, 2016), p. 7. For McHale and Platt, 1973 is the year in which postmodernism enters its 'major phase.' But, as our analysis here suggests, it might be more accurate to think of it as the high point of postmodernism, and so also the year when its decline commences.
46. The summary of Harvey's work here draws on Paul Giles's in *The Global Remapping of American Literature* (Princeton: Princeton University Press, 2011), p. 13.
47. For the history of MELUS, see Katharine Newman, 'MELUS Invented: The Rest is History,' *MELUS* 16, no. 4 (1989–1990), pp. 99–113.
48. Irving Howe, 'The Age of Conformity,' *Partisan Review* 21 (January-February 1954), https://www.dissentmagazine.org/online_articles/irving-howe-voice-still-heard-this-age-of-conformity.
49. See http://www.melus.org/.
50. William A. Henry, III. 'Beyond the Melting Pot', *Time* 9 April 1990, p. 28.
51. Gish Jen, *Typical American* (Boston: Houghton Mifflin, 1991).
52. Aliki Varvogli, 'Borders and Mixed-Race Fictions', in Stephen J. Burn (ed.), *American Literature in Transition: 1990–2000* (Cambridge: Cambridge University Press, 2017), p. 223.

53. Christian Moraru, 'Postmodernism, cosmodernism, planetarism', in McHale and Platt (eds.), *Cambridge History*, p. 488.
54. Rachel Adams, *Continental Divides: Remapping the Cultures of North America* (Chicago: University of Chicago Press, 2009); Wai Chee Dimock, *Through Other Continents: American Literature Across Deep Time* (Princeton: Princeton University Press, 2008); Paul Giles, *Global Remapping.*
55. Slavoj Žižek, *Welcome to the Desert of the Real* (London: Verso, 2002), p. 49; Richard Gray, *After the Fall: American Literature Since 9/11* (Oxford: Wiley-Blackwell, 2011), p. 30.
56. Moraru, 'Postmodernism, cosmodernism, planetarism,' pp. 488, 489. For a fuller discussion, see Moraru, *Cosmodernism: American Narrative, Late Globalization, and the New Cultural Imaginary* (Ann Arbor: University of Michigan Press, 2010).
57. Paul Giles, 'Globalization,' in Stephen J. Burn (ed.), *American Literature in Transition: 1990–2000* (Cambridge: Cambridge University Press, 2017), p. 239; Don DeLillo, *Underworld* (London: Picador, 1998), p. 808.
58. Nancy Hartsock, 'Postmodernism and Political Change: Issues for Feminist Theory,' *Cultural Critique*, no. 14, The Construction of Gender and Modes of Social Division II (Winter, 1989–90), pp. 15–33.

Disclosure statement

No potential conflict of interest was reported by the author(s).

Vegetarianism in the Anthropocene: Richard Powers and Jonathan Franzen

Theophilus Savvas

ABSTRACT

This article uses the representation of vegetarianism in Richard Powers' *The Echo Maker* (2006) and Jonathan Franzen's *Purity* (2015) as a way to think about broader issues of ecological engagement. It argues that these issues are related to the ways in which each writer approaches questions of subjectivity and form after postmodernism. It concludes that the posthumanist dimension of Powers' novel, achieved through formal experimentation, is a more successful engagement with the questions posed by the age of the Anthropocene than Franzen's continued realism.

A recent issue of the *Times Literary Supplement* features a review of two books which are concerned with cultural representations of meat, and another which considers four books focused on the ethics of eating meat.[1] This suggests that the prominent trend in debating the ethics of eating, highlighted in the wide-readership of books such as Eric Schlosser's *Fast Food Nation* (2001) and Michael Pollan's *The Omnivore's Dilemma* (2007), has taken a specific, and not unexpected, turn. In recent years, the ethics of eating meat has become framed as part of a wider debate on global sustainability and climate change with significant evidence now suggesting that reduction in or elimination of foods derived from animals would provide global economic and health benefits.[2] As such it is hardly surprising that two writers frequently described as 'econovelists' – Richard Powers and Jonathan Franzen – have included the topic in recent novels.[3] Both these writers also feature prominently in the conversation about postpostmodernism, and in this piece I use those ethical debates as a way to focus on matters of subjectivity and form after postmodernism.[4] In the conclusion I frame these matters within the context of New Sincerity and the emergent concept of the Anthropocene to suggest that it is Powers' *The Echo Maker* (2006), rather than Franzen's

Purity (2015), that most successfully addresses the cultural exigencies of the present.

I. *Purity* and human failure

There is a long history of association of female bodies with meat. It is long enough and important enough that one scholar – Carol J. Adams – has written of the need for a 'feminist-vegetarian critical theory' to address the matter of 'the sexual politics of meat'.[5] Adams provides myriad examples of the association, as well as a framework for understanding the metaphor, 'woman-as-meat', which allows her to make a convincing case for the suggestion that carnivorism is an 'integral part of male dominance'; vegetarianism thus demonstrates a 'sign of dis-ease with patriarchal culture', and ought always be 'part of the practice of feminism.'[6] Anabel Laird in Jonathan Franzen's fifth novel, *Purity*, would certainly agree with Adams. When she is introduced to the reader she is wrapped in butcher paper with 'YOUR MEAT' scrawled across it as a protest against the underrepresentation of females on the Faculty of Tyler Art College.[7] She continues her protestation of the linked exploitation of females and animals throughout her time at the college, and, for her final project at Tyler – a film titled 'A River of Meat' – splices together footage of a cow being bolt-gunned in a slaughterhouse with images of the coronation of Miss America in 1966. These are preparatory pieces for the major work of her life: the painstaking construction of a film detailing the inscription of a grid of 232-square-centimeter 'cuts' on her body, each of which she will spend a week acquainting herself with, in a bid to 'reclaim possession of her body, cut by cut, from the world of men and meat.' 'After ten years,' we are told, 'she'd own herself entirely' (402). Anabel's rejection of the patriarchy is reflected in her rejection of her father's fortune, the source of which is his work with McCaskil, one of the biggest corporate meat producers in the country. Literalising the metaphor that Adams highlights becomes both Anabel's life's work, and a way of reworking the conditions of that life.

The presentation of this radical vegetarian-feminist warrants further attention because the way in which Anabel and her beliefs are framed in the novel suggests some of the reasons why she might feel the need to 'reclaim' herself from the world of men in the first place. That emphatic act of rebellion through which the reader is first acquainted with Anabel is undercut by the fact that the narrative trigger for it is the presentation, via a tip-off – and as if on a plate – of Anabel to Tom Aberrant, editor of the school magazine, as a possible subject for a juicy report. Anabel's story, then, is in the hands of a controlling male editor, even before we meet the woman herself. Anabel and Tom begin a relationship that will eventually see them married, but that relationship, and Anabel's art, is nearly always focalised through

Tom, and so seen through the male prism. This perspective undercuts and trivialises Anabel's reasons for her vegetarianism; in so doing it also necessarily undercuts and trivialises her feminist ideals. The abstinence from flesh that Anabel has imposed upon Tom as a precondition of their relationship leaves him 'constantly half nauseated', and the description of Anabel as 'full-chestedly anorexic' conflates the 'symptoms' of her dietary choice with those of an illness usually considered in terms of body-image issues; it also connotes that there is something unnatural about her retention of female attributes (195).[8] Tom, we have been told, is 'not afraid of anyone's opinion of how he looked', suggestively furthering the notion that Anabel's malady is female and vain (177). Vegetarianism, then, is figured as unnatural and unhealthy; it is constructed as a disorder of the female mind, like hysteria, which, as with all mental illnesses, has a concomitant effect on the body. When, after a few years, both the marriage and Anabel's mental health start to fail, Tom feels guilty, commenting, 'I couldn't leave until I'd helped her out of the stuck place I'd allowed her to fall into' (408). Both Anabel's moral position and her agency are undermined by the characters' pronouncement on her, and any attempt by Anabel to work her way out of that perspective – to 'own herself entirely' – seems doomed.

One might be tempted to put this down to characterisation, with Tom's comments constituting the expression of the inevitable frustrations of a relationship. However, the non-chronological structuring of the novel frames how we view the dietary proclivities of Anabel, and seems to work to confirm this perspective on her. The novel opens with a mother lamenting the state of her body – and life – in a telephone conversation with her daughter: 'My body is betraying me again. Sometimes I think my life is nothing but one long process of bodily betrayal' (3). The daughter – Purity 'Pip' Tyler – points out the universal nature of these concerns, but her mother is not pacified: 'This is the terrible thing about bodies. They're so visible, so visible,' she concludes (4). These complaints, combined with her subsequent rejection of Pip's offer to bring her a cake with stevia in it because the sugar substitute has a deleterious effect on her 'mouth chemistry,' means that we are likely to agree with Pip's assessment of her mother: 'problematic,' if not quite 'crazy' (3-4). Reviewers of *Purity* have certainly concurred with this view of the mother: 'not-quite-sane' was the verdict of Colm Toibin in *The New York Times*, an 'oppressively needy hypochondriac', suggested Duncan White in *The Daily Telegraph*, 'a fully-fledged Miss Havisham', wrote Tim Adams in the *Guardian*.[9] Within these first few pages we also learn, but only indirectly, of the unsurprising dietary choice of this 'Hippie single mom': one of those on Pip's shortlist of possible partners for her mother is deemed more suitable than the others because he is 'likewise a vegan' (6).[10] That veganism is coded, then, as an attempt on behalf of a 'problematic' woman to establish control over the only part of her life amenable to it: her body. Corporeal in the original sense of 'to do with the body' rather than the spiritual, the concerns of Pip's mother seem self-absorbed in the extreme. The mother here – 'Penelope Tyler' – is Anabel, who, in her struggle to reclaim her life from patriarchy has disavowed completely her former identity – though the intricate nature of the plotting means that the reader does not find this out until much later in the novel. The effect of this is that when Anabel is introduced in a following section set in the narrative past, the reader has already been primed to read female abstinence as the site where physical and moral vanity coincide; it encourages us to read her feminist-vegetarian ethic as the result of and perhaps a mask for these concerns.[11]

The opening also, of course, proleptically confirms the view that without a controlling male – her father or Tom – Anabel cannot survive. The narrative seems to endorse the view of male predation and hopeless female victimhood set out by its nastiest character, the appropriately named Andreas Wolf, 'internet outlaw' (10). In an email to Pip, Wolf writes:

> Maybe being male is like being born a predator, and maybe the only right thing for the predator to do, if it sympathises with smaller animals and won't accept that it was born to kill them, is to betray its nature and starve to death. But maybe it's like something else – like being born with more money than others. Then the right thing to do becomes a more interesting social question. (66)

After the revelation of Wolf's secret abuse of young, vulnerable women when acting as a church counsellor, his thoughts here can only be interpreted as (hardly coherent) amoralistic solipsism designed to rationalise his own behaviour; it certainly does not help that the narrative itself (rather than simply Wolf) seems to offer up the rather tired trope of dysfunctional childhood and oedipal desires as the cause of (if not necessarily an excuse for) his abusive tendencies. That the much older Wolf successfully seduces Pip – into working for him, into a relationship with him – as part of what emerges as a complicated plot to get revenge on her father, only confirms the novel's message of the vulnerability of women.

It is surely one of the functions, and perhaps the main function – apart from to provoke cynical laughter – of Anabel as a flat character to demonstrate the more rounded, if still vulnerable, character of Pip. Pip, we are told, has learned from her mother 'the importance of leading a morally purposeful life', but she 'shudders' at the word 'purity' (29, 47). In this way, her desire 'to *do* good [deeds]' ought to be contrasted against the rather different (and impossible aim) of *being* good, which, Franzen seems to intimate marks Anabel. Pip is marked as one who will shun the idealism of the most ardent character in the novel – her mother – in favour of doing what she can. *Purity* emerges, then, as a paean to the importance of being realistic, which Anabel is not. Early in the novel, Pip notes her mother's 'unworldliness', and Tom's mother, horrified at his choice of girlfriend, implores him to find a more 'REALISTIC person to make a happy life with' (7, 397; capitals in original); his experience with Anabel, indeed, leaves him with 'a lifelong allergy to unrealistic women' (443). Tom's decision to leave Anabel, and accept a 20-million-pound cheque from her father, marks his return to 'reality' in the novel, as he uses the funds to establish his investigative newsmagazine and thus 'do good' with the impure money. Tom's compromise is one that Anabel – who has run off, pregnant with Pip – would not accept. But, near the end of the novel, and in the narrative present, Anabel (now Penelope) is persuaded by Pip to finally take some of her father's fortune because, in Pip's words, 'it's real' (554). Whether this is intended as a source of hope – the acceptance of an inheritance that will allow for a happier future (for Pip, at least) – or as a more cynical suggestion that, in the end, ideals mean nothing is an open question. But it certainly suggests that Franzen is continuing the trend of *Freedom*, in which he elaborates 'how bogus is the very notion of sustaining a uniform world of coherent values – an ideological stance capable of withstanding all challenges to it,' as Philip Weinstein puts it.[12] Anabel's worldview is characterised, caricatured, perhaps, as just such a bogus view – a struggle for an impossible, and, in the end, destructive 'purity' of body, mind and soul. Given that Tom's acceptance of the money brought with it a renunciation of vegetarianism, one might wonder what will become of Anabel's final acceptance of a reality premised upon money rather than ideals: the implication seems to be that it must also entail a repudiation of her vegetarian-feminist ethic.

If the radical idealism of Anabel is stymied by the urge towards accepting 'reality' within the novel, it is also, I would suggest, constrained by the form of the novel. Some of the consequences of Franzen's devotion to realism have been discussed by Margaret Hunt Gram in her reading of *Freedom* (2010). Hunt notes that the novel cleaves to a belief in the liberal individual subject (partly because of Franzen's Lukácsian conception of realism), and suggests that this prevents it from successfully incorporating within its discourse one of the main themes: overpopulation. Unplottable at the level of the individual, Franzen can only represent this element by having Walter Berglund speechify, producing what Gram labels 'discursive disruptions.'[13] In *Purity*, the effect of this commitment to the individual subject, I would suggest, is that Anabel's vegetarianism can only be conceived as 'an individual moral adventure'; as a result, it becomes little more than a mask for problems of the self, as we have seen.[14] The novel does at one point gesture towards the broader context in which the ethics of eating needs to be placed:

> [...] to drive east on Amarillo Boulevard was to pass, in quick succession, the high-security Clements Unit prison complex, the McCaskill meat-processing facility, and the Pantex nuclear-weapons plant, three massive installations

> more alike than different in their brute utility and sodium-vapor lighting. In the rearview mirror were the evangelical churches, the Tea Party precinct, the Whataburgers. Ahead, the gas and oil wells, the fracking rigs, the overgrazed ranges, the feedlots, the depleted aquifer (173)

But this only makes the dismissal of the vegetarianism (and by proxy the feminism) of Anabel even more problematic. Since the logic of the novel – in the sense not only of how other characters respond to Anabel, but how the structure frames the reader's response to her – suggests Anabel's disconnection from reality, with the corollary implication being that she ought to accept the world of her father and McCaskill, it is difficult to see how there can be any resistance to the rest of this clearly pejorative image of the States. The novel, in other words, accepts this world, as Anabel is persuaded to, and in so doing becomes complicit in it.

II. *The Echo Maker* and non-human possibility

In 'Making the Rounds', Richard Powers writes that,

> physics has increasingly moved away from reducing systems to individual, controlled variables and towards representing by means of massive simulation. To understand rich phenomena in the real world, new sciences build analogous rich evocative models and then explore the systemic effects of small changes within the simulation.[15]

Powers' description of the new physics might also serve as a description of the way in which the novel has traditionally functioned. Certainly in Powers' 2006 novel, *The Echo Maker*, the world figures as just such a simulation. Or at least it does for Mark Schluter, the character around which the novel rotates. *The Echo Maker* opens with the aftermath of a car crash in which Mark has suffered a severe brain trauma, leaving him with Capgras Syndrome, a condition which severs the connection between external reality and emotion. Although Mark sees the world around him accurately, his brain no longer produces the affective response that gives that world meaning. He can recognise Karin, his sister, for instance, but he cannot recognise her *as his sister*; for Mark, this Karin is an imposter, a nearly perfect replica of the real Karin. As the novel proceeds this failure of affective association extends first to Mark's dog, then to his home, and eventually to the whole town. The tightly controlled plot of the novel – a hallmark of Powers, whose fiction manages to dovetail (not always successfully) the highly cerebral and the narrative drive of a bestseller – hinges upon two questions: what happened to Mark on the night of his accident? and will he ever recover his true self and see the world around him for the reality that it is? While Powers dutifully answers the former of these, the latter is held in abeyance, for it represents precisely the kind of question that Powers as a novelist is interested in troubling and undermining.[16]

The Echo Maker also tells the tale of Gerald Weber, a celebrity neuroscientist and popular science writer, whom Karin enlists for a second opinion on Mark's condition. Weber, in contrast to the hospital's doctor, argues that Capgras Syndrome is not simply the result of localised trauma, but rather a manifestation of the system trying to *maintain* normality: 'whatever lesions he has suffered, he's also producing psychodynamic responses to trauma,' Weber suggests.[17] Capgras Syndrome, then, is a product of the brain's homeostatic impulse, and, as Weber suggests in a lecture, is only an exaggeration of the way in which an undamaged brain functions: 'The job of consciousness is to make sure that all of the distributed modules of the brain seem integrated' (459). Mark's mind 'smoothes over' the disconnections since, as Weber puts it, 'Reason invents elaborately unreasonable explanations to explain a deficit in emotion. Logic depends upon feeling' (94). In an attempt to trigger emotional memory in him, medical staff ask Mark about his job at Iowa Beef Processors. Mark's palpable relief – 'thank God', he thinks – that they do not ask him how he feels towards the slaughtered animals is telling (56). It suggests that this was the very question that they should have asked, for it would have provoked the kind of affective response the medical staff were seeking. The implication here is that Mark's job has already required that he suppress an intuitive emotional response to his work. This is, perhaps, not surprising given the nature of that work, but we also learn, via his sister's reminiscence, that he had been exceptionally fond of animals as a child, and that he would 'relate long epics from Animalia, the country humans couldn't get to, populated by heroes, rogues, tricksters, and victims' (27). 'Animals like me,' the eleven-year-old Mark had claimed, 'And they did, without fail. Everything on the farm trusted him', confirms Karin (29). The claim of Mark's eleven-year-old self is not just an expression of the presumed and anthropomorphised affective disposition of animals toward him. It is dual coded, for it is also a statement of his own animality: '*animals, like me*', it also implies. It is precisely this awareness of his own animality, and the human place in the wider non-human world, that Mark has had to repudiate to work at the beef processors. In other words, even before the accident, Mark had to sever the connection between external reality and affective response to that reality.[18] The novel, then, forces the reader to question why such disconnections should be necessary in the late capitalist world.

The novel's setting in the Midwest is instructive for an understanding of this, since it is here, in 'the heart of the heartland' of America, that the dramatic decline in farmland communities, and the rise of agribusiness has been felt most keenly.[19] This agribusiness depends for its success on disconnections, as Michael Pollan notes in his bestselling *The Omnivore's Dilemma* which largely focuses on the Midwest, and which was published in the same year as Powers' novel. In his introduction, Pollan writes that,

> what we eat represents our most profound engagement with the natural world [. . . .] Our eating also constitutes a relationship with dozens of other species – plants, animals, and fungi – with which we have coevolved to the point where our fates are deeply entwined [. . . .] What is most troubling, and sad, about industrial eating is how thoroughly it obscures all these relationships and connections [. . . .] But forgetting, or not knowing in the first place, is what the industrial food chain is all about, the principal reason it is so opaque, for it we could see what lies on the far side of the increasingly high walls of our industrial agriculture, we would surely change the way we eat.[20]

Pollan is correct here, but Powers' novel suggests that the possession of facts alone may not be enough to trigger such a change. When Weber and Karin meet over a pizza to discuss Mark, Karin comments,

> I'm surprised they can sell any cow parts at all, in this part of the country. You should hear what goes on at that plant. Ask Mark. It'll put you off your feed for good. You know, they have to clip the horns to prevent the crazed beasts from goring each other. (178)

Karin's word choice here is notable for the way in which it lays bare the tensions and contradictions in our thinking about non-human animals. In referring to 'cow parts' Karin foregrounds the butchery involved, and affirms linguistically that she is aware of the horrors of the meat industry as she reinstates the referent (the cow) absented by the occlusive term 'beef'. While her use of 'feed' (rather than food) might draw together the human and the non-human – we speak more readily of 'animal feed' than we do of 'human feed' – the phrase 'crazed beasts' serves to 'other' the creatures. Karin's surprise at the fact that the treatment of the creatures in the plant does not prevent their parts being sold as human feed stems from the belief that the treatment might render the 'cow parts' unfit for human consumption; her assertion that knowledge of that treatment ought to put one off eating the parts, then, is not an ethical imperative concerned with animal welfare. Knowledge of the facts does not, in fact, 'hinder her appetite', nor does it prevent her from ordering the meat supreme pizza (178).

On her own terms, then, Karin's decision to eat meat is illogical. But it is no surprise that she does not (at this point) make the dietary change spoken of by Pollan. Mark's accident leaves Karin understandably numb, but the brief descriptions of the life she led before it suggests that she had already accepted a life with minimal feeling:

> Past thirty, she had no more time or pride to risk on ambition. Nothing wrong with honest gruntwork for a secure company that lacked all pretension [. . .] She couldn't explain to her brother or anyone: status and satisfaction meant nothing. Competence was all. At long last, her life had stopped misleading her. (16)

If there is an element of willed submission here, it is also a submission called for by the corporate world in which she lives and works.[21] Upon his arrival in Kearney, Nebraska, Weber thinks that he 'might have been anywhere', noting that 'the usual gamut of franchises – motel, gas, convenience store, and fast food – reassured the accidental pilgrim that he was somewhere just like anywhere. Progress would at last render every place terminally familiar' (97). The anonymity of this place is both produced by and reinforcing of the capitalist structure which dictates our tastes, and which requires a commensurate anonymity from individuals. Karin has accepted the depthless life on offer to her. Since 'logic depends upon feeling', Karin, lacking the *affective* response towards non-human suffering cannot (at this stage in the novel) commit to the *ethical* response to such suffering.[22]

The character in the novel who does have a sense of ethical obligation is Daniel, childhood friend of Mark, ex-boyfriend of Karin, and a 'scarecrow vegan' who lives like an 'anchorite' and works for the local crane refuge (89). Daniel, we are told, 'mourned more than the cranes. He needed humans to rise to their station: conscious and godlike, nature's one shot at knowing and preserving itself. Instead that one aware animal in creation had torched the place' (72). What Daniel mourns here is the human failure to live up to the ethical potentialities and responsibilities conferred upon our species by nature and his way of thinking recalls Michel Serres' belief that there is the need for a kind of 'natural contract' (to replace the 'social contract') through which the human would become the 'steward' of the planet.[23] For Serres this would bring forth a new – and better – kind of humanism. Many reviewers suggested that the undeniably preachy tone of Daniel must mean that he is a conduit for the author's own 'self-righteousness'.[24] This kind of charge has dogged Powers' career, but here, at least, seems wide of the mark. Daniel's cringing at the price of a meal in a restaurant, because 'eight dollars is a lot of money to the Crane refuge', his request for a 'plateful of sliced vegetables [...] raw carrots, cucumbers [...]' and his 'quibbling with them' when they arrive, hardly suggest that the novel 'surrenders' to Daniel's views, or that the character is a proxy for the author.

Rather than seeing the novel as a straightforward plea for this kind of humanistic stewardship, we would do better to understand it as trying to balance such claims with those produced by the more recent posthumanist urge. Powers' earlier work has often been associated with the technological posthumanism derived from the work of critics such as Donna Haraway and N. Katherine Hayles; in *Ecosickness in Contemporary American Fiction*, Heather Houser offers a rather strained reading of the posthuman in *The Echo Maker* along these lines. She suggests that Mark 'mutates into the cinematic version of Frankenstein's monster' when the hospital 'slit[s] his throat and put[s] a bolt in his skull', but then concludes that 'Powers seems to disagree with Haraway over the liberating potential of the "cyborg"'.[25] We might do better though to suggest that the slitting of the throat and the bolt through the head are not in fact a reference to James Whale's *Frankenstein* (in which the bolt goes through the creature's neck), but, rather, a gruesome reminder of the two stages of cattle slaughter: mechanical stunning, and exsanguination. The former constitutes the firing of a bolt through the skull of the creature using a pneumatic device or captive bolt pistol, causing massive damage to the cerebrum and cerebellum, a spike in intracranial pressure, and immediate loss of consciousness. The latter involves bleeding the stunned creature by the insertion of a knife into the thoracic cavity and the severance of the carotid artery and jugular vein. Reading the passage this way allows us to understand that Mark, suffering from 'cerebral edema' and requiring a 'ventricular drain' because 'something had spiked the pressure' inside his skull, has been transformed into a creature undergoing the very same procedure that his own work at the Iowa Beef Processors facilitates; accordingly, Karin feels the need to look 'anywhere but at his animal eyes' (10, 8). This moment in the novel does not, then, develop the idea that 'transgressing boundaries that delimit humanness can be severely disabling rather than enabling and generative', as Houser suggests.[26] Rather, it recalls Mark's childhood acceptance of animality, and provides a salient reminder of the suffering of the non-human which predicates the sense of ourselves as human: those creatures must suffer in an inhuman way so that the demarcation between human and animal can be maintained as a difference in kind, rather than of degree.

This suggests the emergence in Powers of a different kind of posthumanism, then, one which has developed through critical animal studies and which, in the words of Cary Wolfe, demonstrates 'that we – whoever "we" are – are in a profound sense constituted as human subjects within and atop a non human otherness.'[27] Wolfe points out the way in which earlier declarations of posthumanism were premised upon the idea of 'human perfectibility', which not only betrays a lingering humanism, but, in certain versions, represents in fact an 'intensification of humanism'.[28] To be truly posthumanist (rather than merely posthuman) according to Wolfe, we must not only acknowledge our ethical obligation to other species – as Daniel in the novel does – but recognise the way in which our world is framed by the non-human. If Mark's 'becoming animal' constitutes one part of this recognition, the form of the novel provides another. Each chapter of *The Echo Maker* is prefaced by a dreamlike depiction of the sandhill crane migration which for a few weeks of the year dominates the Nebraskan plains around the River Platte. These sections serve to envelop the 'terminally familiar' world being produced by the human under late capitalism in a world of non-human strangeness: 'This year's flight has always been. Something in the birds retraces a route laid down centuries before their parents showed it to them. And each crane recalls the route still to come' (4). As the brevity of the human element (the plot of the novel) is highlighted by the deep time of the crane, a genus which has one of the longest fossil histories of any bird and which precedes the human by about 8 million years, so too is the capacity of the human to structure the world implicitly challenged by the fact these sections are situated outside the main ordering principles of the novel as a form: the chapters. It is fitting, then, that one of the most powerful images of the novel is of a posthuman ecosystem of the future:

> when the surface of the earth is parched and spoiled, when life is pressed down to near-nothing [...] nature and its maps will use the worst that man can throw at it. The outcome of owls will orchestrate the night, millions of years after people work their own end. (443)

III. New sincerity and the demands of the Anthropocene

David Foster Wallace's oft-cited suggestion that fiction ought to be about 'what it means to be a fucking human being' has been taken as heralding a 'new sincerity' in fiction after postmodernism.[29] Although Foster Wallace himself offered innovative (sometimes torturous) ways of trying to achieve his aim, it is significant that the case for sincerity is made most convincingly, according to Adam Kelly, by considering those writers, such as Franzen, who 'uphold the canons of realism'.[30] One of the reasons for this is sincerity's apparent dependence on 'the notion of the liberal subject that also underlies classic nineteenth-century realist fiction', as Kelly notes, and as we see in *Purity*.[31] Amitav Ghosh, in *The Great Derangement: Climate Change and the Unthinkable* (2016), notes this focus on the individual subject in the recent fiction of, what he calls, 'sincerity and authenticity'; he suggests that the consequence is that such fiction can only frame moral questions as matters of individual choice.[32] This is, Ghosh argues, inadequate for thinking about the exigencies of our time, which are primarily ecological, not only because these are issues which need to be addressed 'as a collective', but because any individual would then be subjected to a test of sincerity and consistency which most would fail (who can truly say that they do everything possible to help prevent environmental degradation?).

It is effectively this test that Anabel is made to fail by Franzen, as she gives in to what the novel frames as 'reality' by finally agreeing to take some of her father's money to help Pip. That failure might be better understood in the context of an essay by Franzen published in the *New Yorker* in 2015.[33] There Franzen bemoans the fact that climate change has come to dominate the ecological agenda on the grounds that it has had the effect of marginalising the more immediate goals of conservation. He argues that the abstraction of climate change – the way in which any individual's effort to improve the situation has no discernible effect – works against our intuitive logic: 'the human brain evolved to focus on the present, not the far future' so that climate change 'deeply confuses' it.[34] Thus, Franzen frames the contemporary ecological moment as offering a choice between saving birds in the present or saving humans of the future; he declares himself personally in favour of the former. The sensibility behind this strange, defeatist, and implausible argument (decried by many, including the American Audubon Society) produces a tension in *Purity*, which feels like a novel designed to recuperate the form as one primarily concerned with individual selfhood (in the wake of postmodernism's alleged assault on it) written by someone who does not really like – and has little faith in – the human.[35] Anabel's efforts, then, count for nothing in Franzen's fictional world because they would count for nothing in the world outside the novel.

Franzen notes in the *New Yorker* piece that we 'live in the Anthropocene now'.[36] Defined broadly as the epoch when human activity is considered to be the dominant influence on the ecology of the Earth, the concept, although proposed by scientists, has had most impact in the arts and humanities. For Timothy Clark – as for Ghosh – the Anthropocene represents 'a cultural threshold', which requires us to be more inventive in all aspects of critical thinking because the problems it raises 'resist representation of the kinds of scale on which most thinking, culture, art and politics operate.'[37] Clark sees the Anthropocene as demanding nothing less than a revolution in cultural activity, asking: 'at what point does continuing in activities that were once merely normal or even admirable turn, despite itself, into intellectual evasion?'[38] If it was already possible to intuit something intellectually evasive in Franzen's turn to realism as it was articulated and rationalised in 'Mr Difficult', the writer's notorious piece on William Gaddis, then Gram's demonstration of the way in which the ecological engagement of *Freedom* is stymied by this aesthetic decision only furthers that sense.[39] What *Purity*, and the *New Yorke*r piece reveal, however, is that the ecological views are, or have become, just as conservative, just as defeatist, as Franzen's views on fiction.[40]

Franzen's way of setting off the human against the non-human ignores the axiom articulated by the American environmental thinker John Muir: 'when we try to pick out anything by itself, we find it hitched to everything else in the Universe.' The quotation is used as a subheading in Powers' short story 'The Seventh Event', published a couple of years before *The Echo Maker*.[41] The story represents a fictional reminiscence about a late scholar of ecology called Mia Erdmann by a school acquaintance (a fiction writer named Richard Powers) frustrated by the continued assumption 'that all of life hung upon humanity'.[42] Erdmann – a scientist by vocation, but with wide interests – found this assumption reinforced by the novel as a form. Her own work constituted a plea for 'a literature that tried to recover the obscene majority of existence typically brushed aside by the novel of character revelation'.[43] The story provides a clever way for Powers to express an ideal while also incorporating within the narrative his own intuitive response to the difficulty of that ideal: the authorial surrogate notes, 'Erdmann scared me out of the fiction of the self. But I feel a little fraudulent ignoring that self'.[44] *The Echo Maker* is an attempt to negotiate this difficulty, an attempt to balance the desire for a non-human perspective with the constant pull of one's own species. Its ruminations on consciousness and memory make it a novel concerned with the very notion of what a (human) self is; but the oneiric mingling of the human and non-human perspectives highlights the fact that humans are not the only makers of meaning in the world. In so doing it offers an example of the way in which the novel as a cultural interjection might harness postmodernism's challenge to human subjectivity and representationalism, and turn it towards new and urgent ends.

Notes

1. The reviews are: Julian Baggini, 'More Equal than Others', and Ian Sansom, 'Barthes Snacks', *Times Literary Supplement*, 20 July 2016. See http://www.the-tls.co.uk/articles/public/more-equal-than-others-3/ and http://www.the-tls.co.uk/articles/public/barthes-snacks/ [Date accessed: 2 June 2017].
2. See, for example, 'How a Vegetarian Diet Could Help Save the Planet', *Time*, 21 March 2016. http://time.com/4266874/vegetarian-diet-climate-change/ [Date accessed: 2 June 2017]. For the science behind the article, see 'Analysis and Valuation of the Health and Climate Change Cobenefits of dietary Change', *Proceedings of the National Academy of the Science of United States of America*, 113.15 (2016), http://www.pnas.org/content/113/15/4146 [Date accessed: 2 June 2017].
3. Scott Hermanson uses the term 'econovelist' to describe Richard Powers in 'Just Behind the Billboard: The Instability of *Prisoner's Dilemma*', in Stephen J. Burn and Peter Dempsey (eds.), *Intersections: Essays on Richard Powers* (Champaign and London: Dalkey Archive Press, 2008), pp. 60–74, p. 62; Stephen J. Burn notes the applicability of the term for Franzen in his book *Jonathan Franzen at the End of Postmodernism* (London and New York: Continuum, 2008), p. 22. There is not the space here to think more broadly about representations of vegetarianism in fiction, but in the context it is worthy of note that perhaps the most famous literary vegetarian, P.B. Shelley, offered a prescient argument about the inefficiency of pasturage, writing: 'the quantity of nutritious vegetable matter consumed in fattening the carcase of an ox would afford ten times the sustenance [...] if gathered immediately from the bosom of the earth'. Percy Bysshe Shelley, 'A Vindication of Natural Diet [1812]', in David Lee Clark (ed.), *Shelley's Prose; or The Trumpet of a Prophecy* (London: Fourth Estate, 1988), pp. 81–90, p. 86.
4. One of the other writers in this debate, Jonathan Safran Foer, has written an insightful work of non-fiction on the topic: *Eating Animals* (London: Hamish Hamilton, 2009). Foer's novel *Everything is Illuminated* (2002) includes a vegetarian character, since the protagonist is a fictionalised version of the author, but the reference to vegetarianism is slight and so I have not included discussion of it here.
5. Carol J. Adams, *The Sexual Politics of Meat: A Feminist Vegetarian Critical Theory*, Twentieth Anniversary Edition (New York and London: Bloomsbury, 2010).
6. Ibid., p. 217.

7. Jonathan Franzen, *Purity* (London: Fourth Estate, 2015), p. 342. Subsequent references to the novel will be cited parenthetically in the main body of the essay.
8. It should be noted that it is Tom's subsequent partner, Leila, who describes Anabel as 'full-chestedly anorexic'.
9. Colm Toibin, 'Jonathan Franzen's *Purity*', *New York Times*, 26 August 2015, n.p., https://www.nytimes.com/2015/08/30/books/review/jonathan-franzen-purity-review.html?_r=0; Duncan White, '*Purity* by Jonathan Franzen, review', *The Daily Telegraph*, 14 August 2015, n.p., http://www.telegraph.co.uk/books/what-to-read/purity-by-jonathan-franzen-review/; Tim Adams, '*Purity* by Jonathan Franzen review', *The Guardian*, 6 September 2015, n.p., https://www.theguardian.com/books/2015/sep/06/purity-jonathan-franzen-review-piercingly-brilliant [Date accessed: 26 May 2017].
10. 'Hippie single mom' was the verdict of Benjamin Markovits in *The Independent*. Benjamin Markovits, '*Purity* by Jonathan Franzen', *The Independent*, 6 August 2015, n.p. http://www.independent.co.uk/arts-entertainment/books/reviews/purity-by-jonathan-franzen-book-review-10443291.html [Date accessed: 26 May 2017].
11. This ideological construction of veganism as a form of extremism is of a piece with the single instance of it in *The Corrections*, where 'vegan prophets' are catalogued alongside 'bomb-makers' and others on the anarchist fringe. Jonathan Franzen, *The Corrections* (New York: Picador, 2002), p. 341.
12. Philip Weinstein, *Jonathan Franzen: The Comedy of Rage* (London and New York: Bloomsbury, 2015), p. 151.
13. Margaret Hunt Gram, '*Freedom*'s Limits: Jonathan Franzen, the Realist Novel, and the Problem of Growth', *American Literary History*, 26.2 (Summer 2014), pp. 295–316, p. 296.
14. 'Individual moral adventure' is taken from John Updike's review of Abdelrahman Munif's *Cities of Salt* in the *New Yorker* (17 October 1988), and indicates, apparently, what Updike thinks the pattern of a good realist novel should be; the review is discussed in Amitav Ghosh, *The Great Derangement: Climate Change and the Unthinkable* (Chicago and London: University of Chicago Press, 2016), p. 77.
15. Richard Powers, 'Making the Rounds', in Stephen J. Burn and Peter Dempsey (eds.), *Intersections: Essays on Richard Powers* (Champaign and London: Dalkey Archive Press, 2008), pp. 305–310, p. 309.
16. The novel as a form has often gone further than the 'new physics', as described by Powers, in that it has challenged the distinction between the putative real world and the artificial world; this is most explicitly done in postmodernist fiction.
17. Richard Powers, *The Echo Maker* (London: Vintage, 2007), p. 167. Subsequent references to the novel will be cited parenthetically in the main body of the essay.
18. Mark's job is to repair slaughterhouse machinery.
19. 'In the Heart of the Heartland' is the name of Margaret Atwood's review of the novel. *New York Review of Books*, 21 December 2006. http://www.nybooks.com/articles/2006/12/21/in-the-heart-of-the-heartland/ [Date accessed: 2 June 2017].
20. Michael Pollan, *The Omnivore's Dilemma: The Search for a Perfect Meal in a Fast-Food World* (London: Bloomsbury, 2011), p. 10.
21. Karin works for the 'third largest' computer vendor in the country (16).

22. Karin's surprise that these cow parts can be sold 'in this part of the country' misses the way in which the local is imbricated with the global: food from Iowa Beef Processors is not, of course, sold only around the town of Kearney, the states of Nebraska and Iowa, or the Midwest more generally; rather it is distributed throughout the US. The multinational Tyson Foods, which acquired Iowa Beef Processors in 2001, boasts on its website that it produces 1 in 5 pounds of all the chicken, beef and pork in the US. http://ir.tyson.com/investor-relations/investor-overview/tyson-factbook/ [Date accessed: 2 June 2017]
23. Michel Serres, *The Natural Contract*, trans. E. MacArthur and W. Paulson (Ann Arbor, MI: University of Michigan Press, 1995).
24. 'Self-righteousness' is taken from William Deresiewicz's scathing review of the novel. He writes: 'Instead of letting the story speak, he [Powers] is the only one who speaks. Instead of locating meaning in experience, he locates it in ideas. But novels should test ideas, not surrender to them. The same is true of beliefs. Powers's pious self-righteousness is expressed here through Daniel, the Christ-like environmentalist who lives on couscous and currants, turns his heat off at night and finally flees the all-too-human world. Powers is as ethically coercive as he is intellectually pedantic.' William Deresiewicz, 'Science Fiction', *Nation*, 9 October 2006, pp. 25–28, p. 28.
25. Heather Houser, *Ecosickness in Contemporary American Fiction: Environment and Affect* (New York: Columbia University Press, 2014), p. 111.
26. Ibid., pp. 111–112.
27. Cary Wolfe, *What is Posthumanism?* (Minneapolis: University of Minnesota Press, 2010), pp. xiv–x.
28. Indeed, many critics have struggled to precisely locate, or describe the posthumanism of Powers. For Quentin D. Miller, Powers' subject matter is posthumanist, even though he produces 'relatively traditional humanist novels,' so that his 'posthumanism' constitutes more of an attempt to redefine humanism than surpass it; Matt Silva agrees, suggesting that there is a 'vestigial humanism' in *Galatea 2.2*, while for Christopher Taylor, Powers remains 'a liberal humanist at heart'. Quentin D. Miller, 'Deeper Blues, or the Posthuman Prometheus Cybernetic Renewal and the Late-Twentieth-Century American Novel', *American Literature*, 77.2 (2005), pp. 379–407, p. 383; Matt Silva, 'The "Powers" to "Kraft" Humanist Endings to Posthumanist Novels: *Galatea 2.2* as a Rewriting of *Operation Wandering Soul*', *Critique*, 50.2 (2008–2009), pp. 208–224, p. 220; Christopher Taylor, review of *Generosity* by Richard Powers, *The Guardian*, 2 January 2010, n.p., https://www.theguardian.com/books/2010/jan/02/richard-powers-generosity-fiction-review [Date accessed: 2 June 2017].
29. Larry McCaffery, 'A Conversation with David Foster Wallace', https://www.dalkeyarchive.com/a-conversation-with-david-foster-wallace-by-larry-mccaffery/ [Date accessed: 2 June 2017], n.p. Originally in *The Review of Contemporary Fiction*, Vol. 13 No. 2 (Summer 1993).
30. Adam Kelly, 'Dialectic of Sincerity: Lionel Trilling and David Foster Wallace', *Post45*, 17 October 2014, n.p. http://post45.research.yale.edu/2014/10/dialectic-of-sincerity-lionel-trilling-and-david-foster-wallace/ [Date accessed: 1 June 2017].
31. ibid.
32. Ghosh, *The Great Derangement*, p. 128. Ghosh conflates 'sincerity' and 'authenticity', where for Kelly there is an important distinction between the two, but they are writing about the same kind of fiction.

33. Jonathan Franzen, 'Carbon Capture', *New Yorker*, 6 April 2015, online edition, n.p. https://www.newyorker.com/magazine/2015/04/06/carbon-capture [Date accessed: 20 October 2017].
34. Ibid., para. 18.
35. When cutely suggesting that 'climate change is everyone's fault – in other words, no one's' (para 10), Franzen implies that the moral responsibility of the individual is diminished or eroded by arguing the need for collective action. In so doing, he tacitly endorses a staple of conservative American thinking since the time of McCarthy; the sentence, indeed, echoes almost word for word William F. Buckley's argument against Noam Chomsky's view on the culpability of the American populace in the war in Vietnam: 'if everybody is guilty of everything, then nobody is guilty of anything', Buckley commented in their televised debate on the war. 'Vietnam and the Intellectuals', *Firing Line*, 4.13. 3 April 1969.
36. Franzen, 'Carbon Capture', para. 20.
37. Timothy Clark, *Ecocriticism on the Edge: The Anthropocene as a Cultural Threshold* (London: Bloomsbury, 2015), p. 10.
38. Ibid., p. 195.
39. Jonathan Franzen, 'Mr Difficult', *New Yorker*, 30 September 2002, pp. 100–111.
40. Like *The Echo Maker*, *Freedom* includes an engagement with migratory birds. Gram labels this a 'small foray' into 'formal experimentation', however her description of it as 'a tiny plot' reveals that the aspect is in fact assimilated within the realist framework. Compared to the way in which Powers' novel – which was published four years before *Freedom* – incorporates the non-human at the level of structure, Franzen's attempt seems merely gestural; there is nothing like it in *Purity*. Gram, p. 312.
41. Richard Powers, 'The Seventh Event', *Granta* 90, 7 July 2005, pp. 57–74. The Muir quotation is from *My First Summer in the Sierra* (Edinburgh: Canongate, 2014; reprint edition), p. 114.
42. Ibid., p. 59.
43. Ibid., p. 62.
44. Ibid., p. 60. Wendell Berry has made a similar point, noting that, 'A common complaint nowadays is that humans think the world is "anthropocentric," or human-centered. I understand the complaint; the assumptions of so-called anthropocentrism often result in gross and dangerous insubordination. And yet I don't know how the human species can avoid some version of self-centredness; I don't know how any species can'. Berry's tempered, and sensible conclusion is that, 'We must acknowledge both the centrality and the limits of our self-interest. One can hardly imagine a tougher situation'. Wendell Berry, 'Preserving Wilderness', reprinted in Bill McKibben (ed.), *American Earth: Environmental Writing Since Thoreau* (New York: Library of America, 2008), pp. 515–530, p. 527.

Disclosure statement

No potential conflict of interest was reported by the author.

The genrefication of contemporary American fiction

Alexander Moran

ABSTRACT

In recent years, various critics have noted how contemporary American writers are turning to popular genre forms in their work. However, few have adequately addressed how this turn affects the story of literary history. Through close readings of Jennifer Egan's metafictional gothic novel, The *Keep*, and Colson Whitehead's post-apocalyptic zombie horror novel, *Zone One*, this article argues that this recent trend reflects a longer process I am calling genrefication. I begin by analysing how *The Keep* updates the gothic to speak to contemporary concerns, specifically digital communications technology. Egan's text also thematises how the formal limits of genres enable affective experiences for the reader. It then turns to Whitehead's contrasting depiction of genre, one which complicates Egan's ideas somewhat. Drawing on the work of John Fiske, I contend that *Zone One* shows how popular forms develop in relation to power structures, and how the recent turn to genre can be seen as what Fiske calls a 'micropolitics' of resistance. Through readings of these two texts, I argue that genrefication not only accounts for the recent turn to popular genres but also serves as a productive framework to discuss the gradual encroachment of genre into literary criticism.

Introduction

In one of his final lectures, 'When Was Modernism?', Raymond Williams argued that:

> If we are to break out of the non-historical fixity of *post*-modernism, then we must search out and counterpose an alternative tradition taken from the neglected works left in the wide margin of the century, a tradition which may address itself not to this by now exploitable because quite inhuman rewriting of the past, but for all our sakes, to a modern future in which community may be imagined again.[1]

Whether it is the gothic, detective fiction, superhero comics, or zombie thrillers, many contemporary authors are recovering older, and often ostensibly less 'literary' forms for their fiction. In doing so, they are suggesting that writers and critics should question the non-historical fixity of postmodernism, and excavate an 'alternative tradition' in the manner Williams implores. In American fiction, Michael Chabon, Jennifer Egan, Colson Whitehead, Jonathan Lethem, Junot Díaz, Mark Danielewski, and Justin Cronin are just some of the writers whose work represents this turn. It is also a demonstrably wider phenomenon across Anglophone literature: in Canadian fiction, there are the recent genre works of Margaret Atwood and Hilary St. John Mandel; in British fiction, Kazuo Ishiguro has penned both the science fiction *Never Let Me Go* and the fantasy *The Buried Giant*, and there is also the 'New Weird movement', led by China Miéville, defined by authors recovering a Lovecraftian style.[2] This article reads Jennifer Egan's gothic novel, *The Keep*, and Colson Whitehead's zombie horror novel, *Zone One*, as iterations of a process I am dubbing the genrefication of contemporary fiction.

While Michael Chabon and Jonathan Lethem have perhaps been the most vocal proponents of this phenomenon, Egan and Whitehead's texts are discussed here as they not only embody a turn to genre forms, but these novels also thematise the value of genres within their narratives. The first section of this article outlines the manner in which Egan updates the gothic to refer to contemporary communications technology: she contemporises the gothic and gothicises the contemporary. I then discuss the way *The Keep* illustrates the affective potential of genres. Whitehead's *Zone One* is the focus of the second half of this article as it complicates many of Egan's assertions about genre. I read *Zone One* alongside John Fiske's theories of popular culture, and argue that Whitehead's novel illustrates the manner in which popular cultural products, like genres, are shaped and determined by power structures – specifically, the relationships between the state and its citizens, and the market and artists. This article concludes with suggestions of some of the implications of genrefication for literary criticism.

While the history of literature has in part been defined by the debate between the romance and the novel, since around the turn of the millennium this debate has become more acute as more writers have embraced genre forms.[3] In 1989, Ursula Le Guin briefly coined the term 'genrefication' to suggest that the marginalisation of science fiction 'is a political tactic' by 'The Canoneers of Literature' to deny the artistic merit of genre works.[4] What I suggest almost 30 years later is that genrefication is indeed a political concept, but that rather than denigrating genre works, it brings into focus an alternative tradition of literary history. Genrefication has led many critics to query established critical practices.[5] For instance, in *Contemporary Drift*, Theodore Martin suggests a focus on genre allows us to reconceptualise what we mean by 'the contemporary' and allows for a different means of historicising and contextualising the present in light of generic histories.[6] Genrefication, then, refers not only to a new type of writing but also to the sense that a different type of *reading* is required. What is to come after postmodernism, then, becomes a question of revising what Williams calls 'the selective tradition' of scholarship.[7] This article discusses the ways in which Egan and Whitehead's novels suggest new ways of reading, and how genrefication queries and disrupts numerous aspects of literary criticism.

Jennifer Egan: contemporising the gothic, gothicising the contemporary

Egan often works with genre forms: both *Look at Me* and *A Visit from the Goon Squad* have near future/dystopian science fiction endings, and the short story 'Black Box' – released on *The New Yorker*'s Twitter account – is a science fiction/spy thriller. Her most recent work, *Manhattan Beach*, is simultaneously a crime novel and a work of historical fiction. *The Keep* is in many ways a throwback to the earliest iterations of the gothic; it references Edgar Allan Poe's 'The Fall of the House of Usher' in the first few pages and has clear nods to Robert Walpole, Ann Radcliffe, Wilkie Collins, and other key writers of the genre. David Punter outlines the 'most universal features' of gothic texts are the possibility of ghosts, an aristocracy, a castle setting, and a love plot.[8] *The Keep* fulfils these generic requirements: ghosts are suggested at numerous points, there is a Baroness, it is set in a castle, and there is the love triangle between Howard – who owns the castle – his wife, Ann, and Mick (who is actually Ray, the narrator of much of the novel). What is interesting here are the ways in which Egan reformulates these tropes to make the gothic speak to contemporary concerns.

In an interview with Robert Alford, Egan acknowledged the way she consciously works with genres for specific reasons: 'I know there's a way in which the tools that I'm really using as I write are emphases and extrapolation.'[9] Terms such as 'tools' and 'emphases' betray how Egan's turn to genre is distinct from writers such as Chabon, Lethem, and Whitehead. While their embrace of genre is partly the result of a lifelong love of comics (Chabon and Lethem) or zombie films (Whitehead), Egan's gothic novel is not a product of a love of popular forms. Instead, it is a rather academic approach, something Egan further underscored to Zara Dinnen when she put forth, 'when I write fiction, it is often with a cerebral query in mind that may almost seem more suited to academic exploration than fiction writing'.[10] For Egan, the genres she works with provide formal limits to achieve certain ends. Similar to how she updated serial publishing to digital culture with 'Black Box', in *The Keep*, Egan updates the gothic as a tool to emphasise certain aspects of contemporary life – specifically, to defamiliarise communication technologies.

Sam Sacks has recently complained that he believes the phenomenon I am calling genrefication creates texts that lack 'ambivalence – a quality that rarely squares with entertainment'.[11] However, a defining feature of genrefication is that its practitioners tend to not see entertainment and textual ambivalence as mutually exclusive. *The Keep* has three narrative voices, and this metafictive structure makes ambiguity and hesitation central to every layer of the text. The reader is first introduced to the story of the castle, written from the perspective of Danny, Howard's cousin. Then there is Ray, who is ostensibly writing the novel we are reading for his prison writing class, and his perspective of life in prison is interspersed throughout Danny's narrative. Finally, there is Holly, Ray's writing instructor, whose voice only appears in the final section of the text, and to whom Ray mails the manuscript after his fantastical escape. It is within these multiple, circular layers – a structure that mirrors the 'circular stairwell'[12] of the castle where much of the novel is set – that Egan makes numerous points about the value of genre. Contrary to Sacks's claim, Egan demonstrates how working with genre forms need not be formulaic, as *The Keep* mixes metafiction and the gothic precisely to create ambiguity.[13]

Danny's strand of the plot centres on Howard, the owner of an East European castle he wishes to turn into a gothic hotel. Howard is a means for Egan to emphasise her points about contemporary communications. He expresses his dislike of contemporary technology to Danny, his cousin, who has brought a satellite dish with him to Eastern Europe because he is so invested in staying connected: 'The machines are so small now, and using them is so easy – we're a half step away from telepathy.'[14] Howard insists that it is impossible to clarify absolutely who is speaking and that Danny has an unspoken *faith* that this digital reality is as it seems:

> What's real, Danny? Is reality TV real? Are confessions you read on the Internet real? The words are real, *someone* wrote them, but beyond that the question doesn't even make sense. Who are you talking to on your cell phone? In the end you have no fucking idea'.[15]

Howard argues that these connections are reliant on an assumption that what is being communicated is sincere – without this belief, the entire system falls apart. It is on these grounds that he insists, 'We're living in a supernatural world, Danny. We're surrounded by ghosts.'[16] These scenes echo Alan Kirby's arguments in *Digimodernism* that 'Web 2.0 depends so critically on the apparently real that it gives a name ('trolls') to those who reject it.'[17] Danny has to be absolutely invested in the idea that all his connections are 'apparently real', which, as Kirby argues, means 'Wikipedia, message boards, and social networking sites clearly require, in order to function at all, a level of sincerity in their users (impossible to measure objectively).'[18] Sincerity and trust become values, not because of any moral imperative. Instead, they are necessary for these interactions to function. Egan updates the tropes of the gothic genre, then, to suggest that such communication is based upon an unspoken faith in the sincerity of whom one is speaking with.

As mentioned, this focus on technology is only part of Egan's turn to genre; in *The Keep*, she also thematises the value of genre forms. Arthur Krystal makes the distinction that, in comparison to writers of genre fiction, 'It seems … that Chabon, Egan, and Ishiguro don't so much work in genre as with genre.'[19] None of the authors mentioned work in a specific genre throughout their careers, but in an auteur-like fashion hop from genre to genre. Indeed, in interviews Whitehead has accentuated this auteur analogy, stating 'Growing up watching Kubrick, it seems like a normal thing. You do your dark comedy, you do your war movie, you do your science fiction movie, and it's all accessing different parts of your personality.'[20] In a discussion with Robert Alford, Egan posits why she was drawn to the gothic in the first place, 'the kind of fake medievalism of the gothic … the sort of cheesiness, if you will, of that gothic atmosphere'.[21] The cheesiness Egan describes echoes how gothic critic Gerald Hogle outlines the falseness at the inception of the gothic as a genre, that 'its Gothicism [is] … so pointedly fake and counterfeit from the beginning'.[22] In *The Keep*, Egan works with the gothic to emphasise that while genres may arise from a patently false beginning, such artificial limits can still elicit affect.

When Howard lays out his vision of the castle to Danny he harks back to a mythic image of a gothic past, 'Think about medieval times, Danny, like when this castle was built. People were constantly seeing ghosts, having visions.'[23] Howard believes that:

> We've lost the ability to make things up. We've farmed out that job to the entertainment industry … My *mission* is to bring some of that back. Let people be tourists of their own imaginations. And please don't say *like Disneyland*, because that's the exact opposite of what I'm talking about.[24]

Really, in the context of making a functioning business of a hotel, managing experiences like Disneyland is precisely what he is doing. Howard's management of every aspect of this hotel is, in fact, reminiscent of the games of *Dungeons and Dragons* he played as a child; Howard is once again the dungeon master enabling everyone who comes to the hotel to have a gothic experience that he tightly controls. The alternative, to have a gothic experience without such parameters – like Howard's similar childhood trauma where Danny and his friends left him in underground tunnels, or when they are locked in the keep at the end of the novel – is terrifying. Similarly, to make the gothic reproducible for the reader, this affective experience must be organised within specific limits.

The sections of the novel set in the prison also provide many reflections on the concept of genre. The castle is often discussed in similar terms to the prison, and Ray even slips at one point and refers to the prison as 'the castle'.[25] Ray notes the manner in which time freezes for the prisoners at the moment they enter: 'this place is a word pit – words get stuck in here, caught from when the clock stopped on our old lives'.[26] What this suggests is the manner in which genres register a particular moment in time, and the period at which a person enters the genre – here represented by the prison – reflects the language, subjectivity (the 'parts of the personality' Whitehead cites) and historical context of the writer. As Martin argues, 'Genres explain how aesthetic and cultural categories become recognizable as well as reproducible in a given moment, and they demonstrate how the conventions and expectations that make up those categories are sedimented over time.'[27] Egan's text, therefore, builds upon and intersects in a wider generic history, and the inmates of the prison reflect this idea that genres can be read as a register of cultural shifts and developments.

Moreover, the prison can also be seen as a metaphor for the possibilities of genre forms. Holly points out to the members of her writing class that they never open doors – 'How often do you gentlemen touch a doorknob?'[28] Holly challenges Ray and the other students about their lack of agency, and then extends this idea into a metaphor for what fiction can do: 'My job is to show you a door you can open.'[29] While Ray initially dismisses the speech as 'cheesy',[30] its triteness does not render it meaningless: 'A door in our heads, *come on*. But while she was talking I felt something pop in my chest.'[31] The prison writing class, like the way Egan depicts the gothic genre more broadly, may be seemingly 'cheesy', but Ray is deeply affected: 'since I started that class, everything feels different – brighter, sharper, a little strange, like I'm starting to get sick'.[32] Holly's classes thematise the manner in which learning tropes and techniques can ultimately lead to the opening of doors; indeed, discovering doors is a central trope of the novel, from the metaphorical door Ray opens after his writing class, to the door Danny kicks open to free them from the keep, and the exit Ray manages to find out of the prison. Each instance suggests that genres may seem exhausted, or derivative, but that there are always new doors of affective potential within such generic parameters.

The final section of the novel jumps forward in time, and the perspective switches to Holly, Ray's writing instructor. From here, the narrative becomes even more convoluted: Ray has just revealed himself to be Mick, Howard's friend, and the man who shot Danny. Furthermore, Ray believes the ghost of Danny is dictating the story of the castle to him from his prison window. In addition, this section begins with Holly receiving Ray's novel – seemingly the one we are reading – and then burying it. When the police come to ask her about the now escaped Ray, the inhumed text haunts Holly in a similar manner to Poe's 'The Tell-Tale Heart' – the text we are reading, therefore, becomes a gothic trope within the storyworld of the novel. As well as further complicating this metafictional Möbius strip of the narrative, this section concludes with Holly deciding to visit what is now Howard's hotel. Upon booking, she is promised live medieval music at dinnertime, but other than that the hotel assures her that she will be left alone during her stay.[33] However, such self-exploration is tightly managed by Howard's design. First, she is met at the train station by Jasper, who takes her to the castle,[34] and then she is provided with the very comfortable sounding 'cashmere ... sweatsuit' to wear.[35] Centrally, a welcome note in her room states '*Our premises are secure.* You may go wherever you wish, day or night ... *Our staff is plentiful* and, we hope, unobtrusive.'[36] This is reminiscent of Jane Austen's *Northanger Abbey*, where Catherine Morland is surprised that her beloved gothic novels – which show 'two female hands at the utmost' maintaining castles and abbeys – could be so wrong, as the Tilney Abbey she visits requires practically an army to maintain it.[37] Similarly, in this last section, Egan shows how Howard's dream is to have his visitors explore their imaginations, but only in a specific way. While Austen's point was to show the absurdity of such narratives, in *The Keep* the limits imposed by Howard do not devalue or denigrate Holly's experience in the castle. At the very end of the novel, she stands at the edge of an area Howard has named 'The Imagination Pool', experiences a sense of 'childish excitement',[38] and dives in. Howard's design of the hotel is a neat metaphor for the way Egan's text suggests generic forms can be updated to represent contemporary concerns, and that managed authenticity is a generative means to elicit affect.[39] Like Howard's mastery over the layout of the hotel, Egan's control of the narrative enables the reader to see the ethereal nature of telecommunications, and that the evident artifice of genre does not necessarily devalue the affective experiences that such structures can elicit.

Zone One, genre, and power

Zone One is a post-apocalyptic horror novel that details the attempts of an interim government to rebuild a mirror image of Manhattan in the aftermath of a zombie plague. In depicting such attempts to revive the world that existed before the apocalypse, the novel develops and discusses numerous ideas of how people circulate and reproduce popular culture. Complicating Egan's discussion of genre, *Zone One* outlines how power structures dictate the formation and reproduction of popular forms. John Fiske's writing largely concerns the way popular culture forms and circulates, ideas that are particularly relevant to the ways *Zone One* depicts the relationship between genre forms and power. The survivors in *Zone One* demonstrate numerous instances of what Fiske calls micropolitics; 'The politics of popular culture is micropolitics, for that is where it can play the greater part in the tactics of everyday life.'[40] Fiske argues that 'There is little historical evidence to suggest any form of radical art has produced discernible political or social effectivity.'[41] He posits that 'there is more evidence of the progressive effectivity of popular art on the micro level than there is of radical art on the macro level'.[42] Fiske's emphasis on the ways popular culture can function as micropolitical resistance is particularly relevant when discussing Whitehead's relationship with genre.[43] Whitehead's novel represents not only the utility of genre to depict contemporary concerns in the manner of *The Keep* but also the political potential of working with popular forms such as genres. In exploring this relationship to power, genrefication can be seen to challenge how the story of literary history is told.

Many critics have attempted to trace how genrefication is the result of a steady rise in the cultural standing of genre fiction. Lev Grossman contends that 'We were trained – by the Modernists, who else – to expect a literary revolution to be a revolution of the *avant-garde*: typographically altered, grammatically shattered, rhetorically obscure. Difficult, in a word.'[44] Martin also cites a similar timeline: 'Whereas modernism is well known for its antipathy to genre, and postmodern culture is famously characterized by its pastiche of multiple genres at once … today contemporary literature is marked by noticeably different uses of genre.'[45] This distinction from the *avant-garde* is something that Whitehead's novel brings out; as will be discussed below, *Zone One* embodies a turn to smaller, incremental political interventions. While they do acknowledge the different relationship with genre that contemporary authors demonstrate, Grossman and Martin see literary history develop in an almost fatalistic manner: a linear progression from modernist difficulty, to postmodern genre-play, and now contemporary genrefication. This approach does not quite grasp the way texts such as Egan and Whitehead's disrupt literary periodisation. In Grossman's arguments, modernism becomes a solidified, reified period, an idea of modernism which has been questioned of late. In defining The New Modernist Studies, Rebecca Walkowitz and Douglas Mao outline both a 'vertical' shift – the study of works of the modernist period that are not high modernist and experimental, and also a 'temporal shift', which has led to the expansion of what period modernism refers to.[46] In doing so, they reflect a turn to exploring the 'wide margin of the century' that Williams called for. In defining his concept of 'contemporary drift', Martin does suggest genre represents an 'alternative historicism',[47] but in many ways his arguments do not go far enough: he does not highlight how genrefication also embodies a wider 'drift' and challenges the non-historical fixity of not just postmodernism but also a reified form of modernism that recent scholarship has sought to disrupt. In drawing out the power relations that distort and define the development of popular forms, *Zone One* opens up wider questions about how the literary canon has formed and continues to be reproduced.

In response to Grossman's contestations, Arthur Krystal points out how Raymond Chandler, Dashiell Hammett, David Goodis, H. P. Lovecraft, and Philip K. Dick – all historically seen as 'pulp' writers – have been recently selected by the Library of America.[48] This alludes to another process the term genrefication intends to capture – the *gentri*fication of genre fiction. John Cawelti, possibly the foundational theorist of what he terms 'formula fiction', suggested in 1976 that 'Because of their association with the times of relaxation, entertainment, and escape, this type of story has been largely ignored by literary scholars and historians or left to the mercy of sociologists, psychologists, and analysts of mass culture.'[49] Only a few years later, in 1982, Alastair Fowler complained that 'Our age has a great appetite for studies of writing that is hardly worth studying. Thrillers, detective stories, science fiction, advertisements, pop poetry, pornography . . . .'[50] He argued that we must maintain a concept of literary distinction, 'Shall we in the name of anti-elitism deprive the people of their legitimate inheritance?'[51] While he largely disparages genre fiction in this text, science fiction is singled out as a legitimate area of study.[52] This gradual encroachment of genre into academic study is part of the process of genrefication; the *gentri*fication of genre means there has been a slow acceptance of the vertical expansion of formal possibilities for writers, and for critics.[53] However, while *The Keep* argues for the value of genre forms, what *Zone One* highlights – and Whitehead's texts more broadly argue – is that to gentrify genres erases the history of struggle these popular forms often reflect.

That power relations distort and control the reproduction of history and popular culture is a key theme in two earlier Whitehead novels, *John Henry Days* and *Apex Hides the Hurt. John Henry Days* traces how the legend of John Henry develops from a folk tale about an African American labourer whose final act is to beat a steam drill in a competition – which demonstrates Fiske's point that folk culture is 'a culture of deprivation, oppression or slavery'[54] – and into a piece of popular culture, one that is consumed and reproduced in myriad ways throughout the twentieth century. In *Apex*, an advertising executive is hired to rename a town, and the central idea is that those who pay to reproduce history control its reproduction – as the protagonist muses, 'With historians and grocery clerks, the customer is always right.'[55] The gentrification of genre fiction, then, can work to ignore, or whitewash, the historical struggles and compromises that define many popular forms.[56] The way Whitehead extends this argument about the role of power relations in the formation and reproduction of popular genres in *Zone One* is the focus of the rest of this article.

In the novel's post-apocalyptic world, the protagonist Mark Spitz notes that 'It was impossible to find a gossip magazine or newsweekly that had been published beyond a certain date. There was no more gossip and no more news.'[57] In *The Omega Man* – the movie which lends its name to Mark Spitz's squadron – the freezing of time is represented by the numerous calendars that display the date as March 1975. In *The Keep* time has stopped for the inmates as they have been incarcerated: in *Zone One*, time has seemingly frozen as there is no more gossip, no more popular culture to circulate. Fiske describes how:

> one of the essential functions of cultural forms is that they should give a shape to time, so narrative and music (our two dominant cultural forms) give a pattern and structure to time that enable us to have some sense of control over it, even if the control is only that of being able to handle it conceptually.[58]

Mark Spitz notes that just after the collapse, their lives had become a single 'discrete and eternal moment'.[59] The development of a popular culture breaks up this eternal moment and provides the survivors with some control over how they experience time.

The new government, based in Buffalo, attempts to re-impose law and order, and Mark Spitz begrudgingly accepts that 'it seemed to work, the return of the old laws. In reconstruction, you knew where you stood'.[60] These decrees are a performative act to help inculcate a belief in the future, and a connection to the world before the collapse: 'There had been laws once; to abide by their faint murmuring, despite the interregnum, was to believe in their return.'[61] Buffalo also sends down t-shirts and buttons, and attempts to brand the recovery with catchphrases like 'The American Phoenix' and 'We Make Tomorrow!'[62] Consequently, the interim government attempts to inspire belief in the recovery by circulating a forward-looking commercial culture. However, such slogans are an instance of what Fiske would call – using terms borrowed from Russian linguist Valentin Volosinov – the 'uni-accentual' language of 'imperialising power', as opposed to the 'multi-accentual' vocabulary of popular culture.[63] As the world is rebuilt, *Zone One* provides a particular window on the development of a 'multi-accentual' language of popular culture.

The popular culture that does form in this new world is not defined by these buttons, t-shirts and slogans. In *Weapons of the Weak: Everyday Forms of Peasant Resistance* James C. Scott develops the idea of 'everyday resistance':

> Those with power in the village [of Sedaka, Malaysia] are not, however, in total control of the stage. They may write the basic script for the play but, within its confines, truculent or disaffected actors find sufficient room for manoeuvre to suggest subtly their disdain for the proceedings.[64]

For instance, the name 'Pheenies' that the members of the populace have given themselves is a name divested of its original 'Phoenix from the ashes' meaning. In micropolitical acts of everyday resistance, the survivors develop their own multi-accentual language, expressing subtle disdain with the uni-accentual decrees of the interim government.

Those survivors who are tasked with clearing Manhattan of zombies have a new dialect that reflects their militarised existence, 'The sweepers gobbled and assimilated the military lingo into their systems with gusto. Mingled with the fresh slang, the new vocabulary of the disaster was their last-ditch armor plate.'[65] That their new language is described as protecting them is telling; it points to what Fiske calls – via the work of Michel de Certeau – the art of making do: 'There is no "authentic" folk culture to provide an alternative', because such culture does not truly exist, 'and so popular culture is necessarily the art of making do with what is available'.[66] The new vocabulary of disaster is an embodiment of the art of making do; their language both reflects their militarised existence and the attempt to protect themselves from harsh realities. Fiske asserts that popular culture is formed by the disempowered, and in response to the dominant culture and ideologies of the age; as *Zone One* demonstrates, popular culture is a negotiated product of this context and environment. Popular forms such as genres are therefore reflective of negotiations and resistance with power structures that are the product of the art of making do.

Another example of micropolitical everyday resistance can be seen in a flashback that explores how Spitz was tasked with clearing abandoned cars from highways. Their route is dictated by the favoured 'pet shortcut' of a general,[67] and so the way the world is reproduced and reformed is dictated by political power. Spitz works for a character called Quiet Storm, who is very particular about how the cars are placed, and sometimes orders cars to be driven miles to be placed somewhere specific. Only towards the end of the novel does he find out she had been writing messages with the cars: 'What readership did she address? Gods and aliens, anyone who looks down at the right time, from the right perspective. To Anyone Who Can Read This: Stay Away. Please Help. Remember Me.'[68] The messages that Quiet Storm writes, all while achieving her set task, are an example of a micropolitical act; her messages represent her making do with what she has. Her messages, her art, are therefore formed in negotiation and dissent with the demands of power structures. Extrapolating such a concept to genre, it can be seen how popular genres are also the product of such compromises and negotiations.

If interventions and developments within genre forms are seen as examples of micropolitical acts, this suggests a reorientation away from attempts to see political engagement as exclusively the domain of experimental texts. Josh Lukin has coined the term 'genre-poaching' to describe the slightly earlier phenomenon 'whereby "literary" or "serious" fiction writers appropriate elements from popular genres'.[69] Relatedly, in the context of her polemic that contemporary literary aesthetics often mirror the logics of neoliberalism, Rachel Greenwald Smith persuasively argues that 'to see formal techniques, old, new, estranging, intimate, experimental, conventional, as a mere grab-bag of neutral tactics waiting to be marshalled for the success of the individual work neutralises their radical potential' – it celebrates what Smith calls an aesthetic of compromise.[70] Genre-poaching, if applied to novels such as Whitehead's, would neutralise both the political value of genres in the manner Greenwald Smith outlines, and dehistoricise the historical developments of such popular forms. These relationships with genre are not exclusively evidence of a compromise aesthetic; instead, these micropolitical acts intend to disrupt and intervene in wider debates about literary value, what forms a writer can work with, and also how we read. Genrefication, then, in Whitehead's novel, is depicted as a micropolitical intervention into such concerns; in this sense, Whitehead nuances and complicates Egan's depictions of genre, even cautioning against the way the gentrification of genre can obscure what are the affective roots, origins, and purpose of genre forms. *Zone One* suggests that the means by which these affective events are reproduced are in constant negotiation and dissent with power structures.

Conclusion

Raymond Williams contends that once there is 'a certain persistence of typical factors', a new cultural movement can be defined.[71] The persistence of typical factors evident in contemporary American fiction is also a turn to the typical, to genre forms that have persisted. While appearing to be derivative and generic, different versions of, and reasons for, genrefication, are embodied by each text: *The Keep* updates the gothic to speak to the contemporary and suggests generic forms do not necessarily deny affective potential. *Zone One* complicates such assertions and shows how the reproduction of popular forms is often compromised or distorted by power. What is to come after postmodernism, then, is partly a revision, a vertical reappraisal, of what modernism and postmodernism have come to refer to.

Notes

1. Raymond Williams, 'When Was Modernism?' *New Left Review*, 175.1 (1989), pp. 48–53, p. 52, italics in original.
2. See Kate Marshall's work for a summary of this movement, which she intriguingly connects to the realist and naturalist texts of the late nineteenth century. 'The Old Weird', *Modernism/Modernity*, 23.3 (2016), pp. 631–49.
3. Gillian Beer, *The Romance* (London: Methuen, 1970) is still perhaps the finest explanation of the development of romance fiction into genre fiction.
4. Ursula Le Guin, *The Language of the Night: Essays on Fantasy and Science Fiction* (Minnesota: Women's Press, 1989), p. 3. Le Guin spells it slightly differently, 'genrification'.
5. To name a few: Mark McGurl briefly touches upon what he calls 'meta-genre fiction' in *The Program Era: Postwar Fiction and the Rise of Creative Writing* (Cambridge, MA: Harvard University Press, 2009), p. 217. McGurl's book is the focus of Clare Harlan Orsi's earlier use of the term 'genrefication', whereby she argues literary fiction is a genre: 'Notes Towards a Genrefication

of Literary Fiction', *Mayday Magazine*, 4 (2011). http://maydaymagazine.com/issue4nonfictionorsigenrefication.php [Date accessed: 15 May 2017]. Linda Hutcheon's canonical definitions of postmodern fiction as 'historiographic metafiction' serve as the springboard for Martin Paul Eve's definitions of 'taxonomographic metafiction', which he develops in relation to Thomas Pynchon's later fiction and Sarah Waters' novels: 'New Rhetorics: Disciplinarity and the Movement from Historiography to Taxonomography', in Giuseppe Episcopo (ed.), *Metahistorical Narratives & Scientific Metafictions: A Critical Insight into the Twentieth-Century Poetics* (Naples: Edizioni Cronopio, 2015), pp. 101--22. Andrew Hoberek builds from Gordon Hutner's discussions of middlebrow fiction to outline the ways in which what I am calling genrefication challenges distinctions between the literary and the middlebrow: 'Cormac McCarthy and the Aesthetics of Exhaustion', *American Literary History*, 23.3 (2011), pp. 483–99. In a more recent article, Hoberek argues David Foster Wallace's fiction anticipates the contemporary turn to genre: 'Epilogue: 2001, 2008, and After', in Brian McHale and Len Platt (eds), *The Cambridge History of Postmodern Literature* (New York: Cambridge University Press, 2016), pp. 497–514. Sam Sacks also discusses the recent turn to genre as 'escapist art' in *The New Republic*. Sam Sacks, 'They Could Be Heroes', *The New Republic*, 14 March 2017, pp. 44–9, p. 49, a dismissive definition that this article challenges.

6. Theodore Martin, *Contemporary Drift* (New York: Columbia University Press, 2017), p. 7.
7. Raymond Williams, *The Sociology of Culture* (New York: Schocken Books, 1982), p. 229.
8. David Punter, *The Literature of Terror: A History of Gothic Fictions from 1765 to the Present Day* (New York: Longman, 1996), p. 2.
9. Robert Alford, 'Celebrating the Possibilities of Fiction: A Conversation with Jennifer Egan', *Pop Matters*, 20 February 2012. http://www.popmatters.com/column/154523-celebrating-the-possibilities-of-fiction-a-conversation-with-jennife/ [Date accessed: 15 May 2017].
10. Zara Dinnen, '"This Is All Artificial": An Interview with Jennifer Egan', *Post45*, 5 May 2016. http://post45.research.yale.edu/2016/05/this-is-all-artificial-an-interview-with-jennifer-egan/ [Date accessed: 15 May 2017].
11. Sacks, 'They Could be Heroes', p. 49.
12. Jennifer Egan, *The Keep* (New York: Little Brown, 2006), p. 22.
13. For an exploration of the gothic and metafiction, read: Sherry R. Truffin, 'Creation Anxiety in Gothic Metafiction: The Dark Half and Lunar Park', in Charles L. Crow (ed.), *A Companion to American Gothic* (Malden, MA: Wiley, 2014), pp. 56–67.
14. Egan, *The Keep*, p. 4.
15. Ibid., p. 130.
16. Ibid.
17. Alan Kirby, *Digimodernism: How New Technologies Dismantle the Postmodern and Reconfigure Our Culture* (New York: Continuum, 2009), p. 142. There is no space to discuss it here, but this need to believe the sincerity of whom one is interacting with may be another reason for The New Sincerity that Adam Kelly traces across contemporary fiction and culture.
18. Ibid., p. 142.
19. Arthur Krystal, 'It's Genre! Not that there's Anything Wrong with It!', *The New Yorker*, 24 October 2012. http://www.newyorker.com/books/page-

turner/its-genre-not-that-theres-anything-wrong-with-it [Date accessed: 15 May 2017].

20. Michelle Dean, 'Colson Whitehead: "My Agent Said: Oprah. I Said: Shut the Front Door"', *The Guardian*, 17 August 2016. https://www.theguardian.com/books/2016/aug/17/colson-whitehead-underground-railroad-oprah-book-club [Date accessed: 15 May 2017].
21. Alford, 'Celebrating the Possibilities of Fiction'.
22. Jerrold Hogle, 'Introduction: Modernity and the Proliferation of the Gothic', in Jerrold Hogle (ed.), *The Cambridge Companion to the Modern Gothic* (Cambridge: Cambridge University Press, 2014), pp. 1–19, p. 15.
23. Egan, *The Keep*, p. 44.
24. Ibid., p. 45, italics in original.
25. Ibid., pp. 97–98.
26. Ibid., p. 57.
27. Martin, *Contemporary Drift*, p. 7.
28. Egan, *The Keep*, p. 18.
29. Ibid., p. 18.
30. Ibid., p. 19.
31. Ibid., italics in original.
32. Ibid., p. 57.
33. Ibid., p. 234.
34. Ibid., p. 235.
35. Ibid., p. 236.
36. Ibid., pp. 236–7, italics mine.
37. Jane Austen, *Northanger Abbey* (London and New York: Penguin Books, 2003), p. 174.
38. Egan, *The Keep*, p. 47.
39. Lee Konstantinou makes a similar point about the chapter written in PowerPoint in Egan's *A Visit from the Goon Squad. Cool Characters: Irony and American Fiction* (New York: Harvard University Press, 2016), p. 43.
40. Ibid., p. 46.
41. Fiske, *Understanding Popular Culture* (New York: Routledge, 2010), p. 191.
42. Ibid., p. 191.
43. To see the way popular forms are defined by power relations is analogous to John Frow's Foucauldian-inflected definitions of genre, whereby genres 'actively generate and shape knowledge of the world', and 'generically shaped knowledges are bound up with the exercise of power'. *Genre* (New York: Routledge, 2015), p. 2. To see how genre theory has changed and developed over time, one can compare Heather Dubrow's historicist definitions in *Genre* (New York: Methuen, 1982), with Frow's more recent work.
44. Lev Grossman, 'Good Books Don"t Have to Be Hard', *Wall Street Journal*, 29 August 2009. https://www.wsj.com/articles/SB10001424052970203706604574377163804387216 [Date accessed: 15 May 2017].
45. Martin, *Contemporary Drift*, pp. 8–9. One such example of this kind of research would be Leif Sorensen's discussion of H.P. Lovecraft and modernism: 'A Weird Modernist Archive: Pulp Fiction, Pseudobiblia, H. P. Lovecraft', *Modernism/Modernity*, 17.3 (2010), pp. 501–22.
46. Douglas Mao and Rebecca L. Walkowitz, 'The New Modernist Studies', *PMLA* 123.3 (2008), pp. 737–48, pp. 737––8. For an excellent explanation of how New

Modernist Studies came to be, read Sean Latham and Gayle Rogers, *Modernism: Evolution of an Idea* (New York: Bloomsbury Academic, 2015).

47. Martin, *Contemporary Drift*, p. 21.
48. Arthur Krystal, 'Easy Pleasures: Guilty Pleasures Without Guilt', *The New Yorker*, 28 May 2012. http://www.newyorker.com/magazine/2012/05/28/easy-writers [Date accessed: 15 May 2017].
49. John Cawelti, *Adventure, Mystery, and Romance: Formula Stories as Art and Popular Culture* (Chicago, IL: University of Chicago Press, 1976), p. 1.
50. Alastair Fowler, *Kinds of Literature: An Introduction to the Theory of Genres and Modes* (Cambridge, MA: Harvard University Press, 1982), p. 10.
51. Ibid., p. 10.
52. Ibid., p. 226. See Elana Gomel's discussion of *avant-garde* genre fiction for a summary of how science fiction became central to many critics, specifically Brian McHale, Darko Suvin, and Fredric Jameson. 'Rotting Time: Genre Fiction and the *Avant-Garde*', in J. Bray, A. Gibbons & B. McHale (eds), *The Routledge Companion to Experimental Literature* (London: Routledge, 2012), pp. 393–406.
53. As Martin notes, not all genres have achieved the same caché as of yet. He cites the gendered nature of the genres that have been revived. Martin, *Contemporary Drift*, p. 12.
54. John Fiske, *Power Plays Power Works* (New York: Routledge, 2016), p. 219.
55. Colson Whitehead, *Apex Hides the Hurt* (New York: Doubleday, 2006), pp. 140–1.
56. The term whitewashes here points to the importance of race in this process, and something I do not have the space to properly account for here. *Zone One* is mistakenly discussed as a post-racial text by many critics, but for an account of race and the zombie figure read Jessica Hurley 'History Is What Bites: Zombies, Race, and the Limits of Biopower in Colson Whitehead's *Zone One*', *Extrapolation*, 56.3 (2015), pp. 311–33.
57. Colson Whitehead, *Zone One* (New York: Knopf Doubleday, 2011), p. 11.
58. Fiske, *Understanding Popular Culture*, p. 53.
59. Whitehead, *Zone One*, p. 50.
60. Ibid., p. 89.
61. Ibid., p. 38.
62. Ibid., p. 26.
63. Fiske, *Power Plays Power Works*, p. 31.
64. James C. Scott, *Weapons of the Weak: Everyday Forms of Peasant Resistance* (New Haven, CT: Yale University Press, 1985), p. 26.
65. Whitehead, *Zone One*, pp. 78–9.
66. Fiske, *Understanding Popular Culture*, p. 13.
67. Whitehead, *Zone One*, p. 144.
68. Ibid., p. 233.
69. Josh Lukin, 'Introduction: Genre Poaching in Contemporary Fiction', *Genre*, 42.3–4 (2009), pp. 1–3.
70. Rachel Greenwald Smith, 'Six Propositions on Compromise Aesthetics', *The Account*, 3 (2014). http://theaccountmagazine.com/article/six-propositions-on-compromise-aesthetics [Date accessed: 15 May 2017].
71. Williams, *The Sociology of Culture*, p. 199.

Disclosure statement

No potential conflict of interest was reported by the author.

ORCID

Alexander Moran http://orcid.org/0000-0002-9116-4419

Feverish fictions: William T. Vollmann and American literary history after postmodernism

Christopher K. Coffman

ABSTRACT
The rise of the New Sincerity in contemporary American fiction has largely been read on terms provided by a handful of early proponents. This article contends that more complex formulations of the notion are necessary if it is to remain useful as a descriptor for important qualities of recent texts. Among issues in need of greater attention are the implications of the New Sincerity for historical awareness, a topic I pursue via consideration of William T. Vollmann's grappling with literary history. I argue that Vollmann's works offer more than the pastiche that allegedly defined historical consciousness in postmodernist fiction. His intertextual engagements with Edgar Allan Poe are especially valuable for modelling some of the ways recent fictions bypass postmodernist ahistoricism in favour of connections to a usable past, and, especially, a usable literary tradition. Readings of Vollmann's 'The Grave of Lost Stories' (in several editions) and 'The Cemetery of the World' show how he employs research in the textual archive as a figuration of relations to the past that can serve the ends of renewal and recovery.

David Foster Wallace's 'E Unibus Pluram: Television and U.S. Fiction' (1993) remains a touchstone piece for arguments that one strand of contemporary fiction is marked by a commitment to sincerity, in response to the endemic irony of postmodernist texts. While Wallace and his critics offer valuable insights, viewing his generation as narrowly defined by the terms of 'E Unibus Pluram' risks a dangerously reductive critical apparatus, one that elides the lack of consensus with regard to how the New Sincerity and its implications are best realised aesthetically. Among the less-remarked of these implications is the importance of the New Sincerity for literary history. Fredric Jameson famously articulated the problems of historical awareness in postmodernity: 'Cultural production … can no longer gaze directly on some putative real world.' Instead, 'we are condemned to seek

History by way of our own pop images and simulacra of that history'.[1] The import of these remarks is damning for literary texts. Rather than a living tradition, postmodernism leaves authors with a historical awareness that offers only opportunities for simulations of dead styles via pastiche. William T. Vollmann stands as a striking example of an author who has taken steps to work through the challenges of literary-historical connection Jameson describes. Vollmann's form of the New Sincerity is not entirely one with all others, but his devotion to empathy and the value of fiction in fostering it are a sure point of congruence. Furthermore, his treatment of literary history is remarkable in that among his achievements is the recovery of earlier aesthetic forms and modes as a living tradition. As such, his fictions demonstrate no detachment from the past, but a persistent devotion to revitalising the past as a means to renewing engaged fiction in the present.

In 1990, Larry McCaffery asked Vollmann which contemporary authors he admires. His response is provocative in several ways, not least in that it basically ignores – with the arguable exception of Vladimir Nabokov – all of the major figures of post-1945 American fiction. William S. Burroughs and Thomas Pynchon, who may, given the nature of *You Bright and Risen Angels* (1987), be expected entries on a list provided by Vollmann in 1990, are nowhere to be found. Also absent are the other usual suspects of maximalist, encyclopaedic metafictions, such as John Barth and William Gaddis, and any younger peers Vollmann met early in his career, like Wallace. Perhaps even more intriguing, and more to the point in this article, is that Vollmann's sense of 'contemporary' encompasses at least two centuries. Such an expansive view of the literary moment allows him to assert that, among his contemporaries, 'Hawthorne may be the best.'[2]

The pre-eminence of Nathaniel Hawthorne on Vollmann's list points readers in the direction of nineteenth-century American literature and provokes reflection on Vollmann's conception of an American literary tradition. Given his oft-expressed interest in foreign literatures, a view of Vollmann as participating in a narrowly defined national tradition would be misrepresentative. Yet, his openness to a remarkable number of international influences is part of what makes the question of his relation to his American literary predecessors particularly intriguing. For any critic to describe the growth of a properly American tradition is an ever-more-fraught effort, but those figures F. O. Matthiessen credits with its invention – Ralph Waldo Emerson, Henry David Thoreau, Herman Melville, Hawthorne, and Walt Whitman – still demand accounting. Furthermore, their relevance to Vollmann cannot be overstated: he also mentions Melville in his reply to McCaffery, and Jonathan Franzen has asserted that Melville and Whitman are the most appropriate points of comparison for Vollmann.[3]

In the following pages, I consider connections between Vollmann's fictions and the works of a nineteenth-century author conspicuously absent from

Matthiessen's accounting: Edgar Allan Poe. Like Hawthorne and Melville, Poe is included in Vollmann's list of admired contemporaries, but his case remains something of an exception for critics. He is regarded by many as 'our greatest bad writer', and his works do not sit comfortably in the mapping of American literature offered by Matthiessen and his disciples.[4] What the figure of Poe does embody is a counter-tradition to that represented by Emerson, Thoreau, and Whitman: he can be read alongside Hawthorne and Melville as a figure of Dark Romanticism; the celebration of his work by such authors as Charles Baudelaire and Stéphane Mallarmé suggests that his troubled native reception may be due to the fact that his writing is more suited to foreign than domestic standards; and, he must occupy a prominent position in any commentary on American gothic literature. In short, Poe's place in American literary history is both highly problematic and indisputably important, and his contested reputation is what makes him such an appropriate choice as a case for exploring the sense of literary tradition that emerges from Vollmann's works.

My more specific contention is that Poe and the tendencies of gothic literature offer themselves as a lens through which one can assess Vollmann's deep, if troubled, engagement with America's literary history, an engagement that presents American literature as the offspring of two incompatible impulses: one generative and erotic, the other stifling and self-destructive. The following readings of Vollmann's 'The Grave of Lost Stories' and 'The Cemetery of the World' aim to demonstrate that Vollmann diagnoses both literary achievement and the historical archive as seductive illnesses, very much in keeping with Jacques Derrida's arguments regarding the archive as enacting both conservation and violence. The American literary history Vollmann tacitly affirms is, in this sense, at once damning and redemptive; authors must constantly risk destroying themselves and the genealogies on which claims for an American literary tradition may be built, but they do so with the profit of participation in that very tradition. Consequently, engagements with the literary past are in Vollmann's texts more than an exercise in postmodern pastiche; instead, his fictions indicate the terms on which the present can be conceived as a liminal zone, a moving threshold in which the past continually proffers itself to creative ends that rely upon historical connection.

Vollmann's gothic

Vollmann's combinations of fiction and non-fiction, as well as of fiction's various traditions and modes, have resulted in hybrid texts largely resistant to generic or modal characterisations. Nevertheless, his works display numerous debts to the gothic novel. One could turn, for instance, to the *Seven Dreams*. This series of historical fictions devoted to rethinking the American past includes meditations on grotesque corpses, cannibalism, torture, and ghostly hauntings. Such characteristics serve cumulatively to suggest that to read Vollmann as operating entirely outside of the gothic tradition is rather to miss the point. Françoise Palleau-Papin recognises as much in the introduction to her collection of essays on *The Rifles* (1994), ascribing some of its ancestry to such pieces as Samuel Taylor Coleridge's 'The Rime of the Ancient Mariner' and Poe's *The Narrative of Arthur Gordon Pym of Nantucket*.[5] A similar point is expanded into a revealing reading of the novel by Catherine Lanone, who argues Vollmann employs gothic tropes as a means to explore the gendered, racial, and political terms of imperialism.[6] Her argument is developed with reference to Vollmann's deployment of the gothic both as a genre with origins roughly concurrent with the high-water mark of European colonialism, and as a shaping force on event and character in the often-phantasmagorical narrative that is *The Rifles*. This demonstrates that the gothic is not something Vollmann employs only when the text at hand is governed by the mode's conventions, as in the case of most of the pieces in his collection of ghost tales, *Last Stories and Other Stories* (2014). Instead, his historical and other fictions draw on gothic conventions with some regularity, and to a diversity of ends – among others as a way of exploring ideological hauntings, as a means to approach the ghosts of his personal past, and as material for unsettling the readers' expectations with regard to such literary conventions as genre.

Examples of the latter intention abound in Vollmann's works, and not always in texts that engage the gothic across their entirety. Take, for example, the appearances of abject bodies in Vollmann's prostitute writings. Daniel Lukes has made the point with reference to figures from books like *Whores for Gloria* (1991), *Butterfly Stories* (1993), and *The Royal Family* (2000) that Vollmann's prostitutes pass along their illnesses to their customers, undercutting johns' claims to virile masculinity via a cross-gender sharing of physical deficiencies and decay.[7] Similar claims might be made with reference to many of his other characters, like the Boarding Care Men of 'The Blue Yonder,' of whom Vollmann writes:

> when they fell asleep in the afternoons their flesh did fall into dimness; their chins doubled and tripled, their fingers dangled, and their hair grew down their shoulders with the airiness of hanging ferns. When they woke up again, life continued to fall out of them. They had crooked black mouths. Acid sweat ate holes in their stiff scaling socks. Their bulging bellies bloomed with hernias like immense chestnuts.[8]

Such passages both display Vollmann's debt to the gothic and anticipate the development, as his career proceeds, of increasingly complex considerations of the relations between the living and the dead, and between the literature of the past and that of the present.

Vollmann's Poe

If a lifelong tendency toward gothic horror in Vollmann is undeniable, so too is his acknowledgement – presented early and periodically reasserted – of its traditions in America. *You Bright and Risen Angels* may in some senses best be understood as a cyberpunk extravaganza, but it alludes to several authors whose place in the annals of American gothic fiction is well established. The first page of the novel offers a fantasy about the narrator's revivification of Ambrose Bierce in Mexico,[9] and readers later encounter a tale told by Mr. White about the adventures of one Ichabod Crane, who has been transmogrified into 'a bastard Jewish halfbreed'[10] and 'nigger sax player'.[11] The tale supplements White's corporate imperialism with celebratory claims for racial purity, thereby instituting the grounds for a strident ethnic nationalism and adding another register to the score of his troubling schemes. Poe likewise appears in the book, and while references to him and his works serve less as material for narrative development than do those related to Bierce and Washington Irving, he and his words are a means to offer comment on the main plot from narratively oblique angles: he is quoted in a footnote,[12] gets paired with H.P. Lovecraft as the subject of an academic conference,[13] and lends a passage from 'The Spectacles' as an epigraph.[14] Allusions to Poe and his works populate many of Vollmann's later books as well, but a survey of those moments is perhaps less useful than consideration of a work in which his place is most central: 'The Grave of Lost Stories.'

'The Grave of Lost Stories' first appeared in *Conjunctions* (1989), and also stands as the concluding story of *Thirteen Stories and Thirteen Epitaphs* (1991). It draws on Poe's poems, stories, and other writings, and features Poe as protagonist. The dramatic situation can be sketched quickly: Poe, delirious from strain and, presumably, alcohol, spends his days attempting to complete fictions, thus bringing them to life and saving them from an otherworldly pit of despair known as the Grave of Lost Stories. This Grave, a 'concentrated vortex of corruption',[15] is repeatedly described with all the vague and miasmatic detail one might expect from a gothic tale, as when one reads that 'There was a stifling horror about the place, about which hovered the most vile and pestilential fumes.'[16] The Grave is packed with decomposing skeletons of stories, which Poe imagines as 'composed of variegated vertebrae the hue and sheen of black crystal'.[17]

While some might argue that the historical past is prohibitively foreign to the present, Vollmann counters this position with a vision of the author as part of a continuum, a participant in a tradition rather than a belated footnote or frustrated aspirant to it. As Vollmann's Poe seeks to write the stories into life from out of this Grave, he sometimes hears them 'struggling desperately to breathe'.[18] His literary inspiration, it therefore seems, is a means for their inhalation – but not their inception. The situation is intriguing as a vision of literary origins, not least due to its conception of creation as an act of recovery. The stories precede the author, and while they are neither fully fleshed nor self-sufficient, they do have a life independent of Poe. Near the conclusion of the text, Psyche (who is a posthumous incarnation of Poe's wife, and serves a role akin to that of Virgil to Dante or the Sibyl to Aeneas) tells Poe that he 'should not destroy the paper of the dead Stories because that hurts them', suggesting that his failure to complete one of them is not its end.[19] The untold stories exist, in other words, both before and after the author, and await salvation by some – but no specific – pen. That Poe or anyone else in particular wrote them into existence is finally a matter of relative insignificance; what matters is that the tales get told. This vision of literary creation proposes that creation must call forth that which advertises itself as available even as it remains segregated from the common realm of existence. The writer must in this sense be a psychopomp or necromancer, working magic that negotiates the divide between the accessible and the hidden, and the act of writing is, in turn, not so much a matter of invention as re-inscription.

Furthermore, Vollmann establishes a mutually generative relation between creator and story; this incestuous relation between the author and his tales – which are at once offspring and seductresses – reinforces a sense of close connections between the literary present and the literary past. Stories appear to Vollmann's Poe in the guise of some woman in distress, and they bear the name of figures from one or another work concerned with a doomed (and usually beloved) woman, such as Madeline Usher, Ligeia, Lenore, Ulalume, Morella, or Berenice. In the few passages in which Poe's attention is drawn away from his own increasingly weak creative and physical state – with regard to the latter of which sexual impotence is suggested ('he is not a man in the full sense of the word'[20]) – the dying story-women find their parallel in the dying Mrs. Virginia Poe. Poe's wife was, famously, significantly younger than Poe and his first cousin, and her decline due to tuberculosis runs in tandem in Vollmann's presentation with the miseries endured by Poe's heroines. That he addresses his wife as 'little Sis' reinforces a sense that accusations of both the impropriety of his marriage and the erotic charge and incestuous nature of his compositional process are very much on the mark.

Vollmann's dramatisation of the creative moment is hardly a naïve presentation of an untroubled relation to the past. Set against the seductive, if transgressive, eroticism of Poe's creative act is an increasingly powerful destructive impulse. The wards of the Grave are guarded by a demonic '*Vulpine Presence*' that either frustrates Poe's completion of the tales or condemns their protagonists to suffering and death. The creature interferes with Poe's compositional process, as when he tries to write 'Morella': it 'pursed its black lips and blew upon the paper so that it fluttered like an ocean … and Morella was gasping with asphyxiation'.[21] It follows him, too, away from his writing desk, 'striding alongside him with its arm about his waist'.[22] The demon with which Poe struggles is not only an external haunt, but a definitive part of Poe himself. It comes with him into the room of his dying wife, 'so that when he bent down to kiss her lips it did the same, breathing into her nostrils until she whispered that terrible smell, Eddie and he said ... I I I'.[23] This increasing nearness of Poe and his nemesis ultimately sees the two collapse into one, so that when he looks upon the tomb of Ulalume, he declares 'I *killed* her,' and recalls 'how the suffocation had been consummated'.[24] If the speaker of Poe's 'Ulalume' finds himself unwittingly at the grave of his beloved, Vollmann's Poe finds himself at the grave of his beloved victim. The union of erotic affection and death in one object alludes to Poe's claim in 'The Philosophy of Composition' that the death of a beautiful woman is the most poetic of subjects, but it also foregrounds the degree to which his creative urge is, in Vollmann's presentation, a destructive one. Insofar as his heroines suffer and die, Poe's stories live by virtue of the negation of beauty, and thus one part of what he tries to save is condemned in the interest of poetic power.

While the erotics of Vollmann's text dramatise a problematic but generally productive impulse, they also explore the degree to which interaction with tradition threatens to overwhelm the author. The close of the text extends this conflation of the productive and the destructive, but turns it upon the writer himself. The reader is earlier given hints that the *Vulpine Presence* mutilates the female characters at the centre of Poe's tales and poems when it cannot entirely prevent them from coming to life. When this mutilation happens to Berenice, Poe's response to her disfigurement (she has the vicious teeth of the Demon) is 'would to God you had died!'[25] Hearing this, the creature turns upon him, declaring: 'No, it is *you* who should have died. Write it.'[26] Poe's concession to this demand seems a suicide note, but one signed with the intention of preserving the tale. When, at the story's end, Poe is abandoned by Psyche at the grave of Ulalume, he unlocks the door and rushes in, intending to join the entombed 'with the fiercely radiant joy of self-destruction'.[27] The seductive nature of this motion toward death is made explicit when Vollmann writes that 'the tomb would open for him like a vagina', but that conviction is finally grounded in a misunderstanding, for 'the interior was a wedge-shaped *cul-de-sac* lined with spikes ... an instant later, the wall-jaws closed upon him',[28] The Demon that haunted him wins in the end, destroying the author by means of the promise of union with his art – even while the latter persists in the tomb, awaiting its next communicant (a later one of whom is, of course, Vollmann himself).

The manner in which Vollmann presents Poe's attitudes to the feminine is particularly interesting given that those attitudes drive the economy of artistic invention in so many of Poe's tales. Many critics have explored the ways in which Poe's creative urge relies on destruction of women. Some more recent readings, however, have argued that Poe may nevertheless be regarded as something akin to a proto-feminist. Leland S. Person, for example, views the violent attitudes toward women as only a first step in Poe's creative process. For critics such as Person, the desire for women is a veil for a desire for self-preservation that is, paradoxically, one with self-destruction. When the woman is destroyed, Poe's narrator's obsessive desires turn back upon themselves, causing a dissolution of boundaries between desiring (masculine) subject and desired (feminine) object.[29] This dissolution generates an I that is an Other; it is a destruction of the self that is also a preservation of the self. In dissolving the gender of the subject, the process makes renewed space for the presentation and preservation of the feminine.

Vollmann dramatises this creative process of destruction and rebirth, but he also conflates it – via the pre-existence of Poe's muse-fictions – with a meditation on the relation between the artist and tradition. The call to destruction is not only the clarion for the obliteration or circumvention of earlier authors, but – as Vollmann's presentation of Poe is likewise a presentation of himself in relation to Poe – also the self-immolation of the contemporary author. In this sense, the tradition speaks only when the author offers himself as material that may be overcome by it. When the creation of art derives from such a moment, one in which the present is preserved by being subjected to the rule of destruction, the tradition is extended. In this manner, destruction is the means to what Vollmann offers as a vision of one sort of success: the preservation for future pens of the tradition embodied in the tales.

The Grave of Lost Stories artist's book

Vollmann has, across his career, periodically produced very-limited-edition artist's books under the aegis of his own CoTangent Press. These texts range in scope from broadsides to elaborate book objects, typically include extensive decoration and illustration (and variants within an edition), and sometimes feature unpublished writings. 'The Grave of Lost Stories' was released in a CoTangent edition of two hundred, of which a handful are deluxe copies, produced with the assistance of Ben Pax (1993). That this story in particular warranted a CoTangent production in addition to traditional publication finds, among its justifications, a fact that is particular to Poe. As Priscilla Juvelis has explained, the artist's book emerged in the 1800s, and numbered among its first examples works by Édouard Manet. In conjunction with Stéphane Mallarmé, Manet produced in 1875 a bilingual, illustrated edition of about ninety copies of Poe's 'The Raven.'[30] Vollmann's decision to enshrine the story that most directly employs the figure of Poe thus nods to the international publication history of what is perhaps Poe's most successful poem.

In deluxe copies of *Grave*, the story's play between creation, destruction, and preservation is presented in a material form more provocative than any allowed by the pages of a traditionally printed text. *The Grave of Lost Stories: 1809–1849* is bound in metal and stone; copper covers are joined by steel hinges and overlaid with marble. The object is remarkably heavy, and larger than all but the biggest of trade books. The edges of the interior are lined with cows' teeth set upright, as if the covers of the tome were jaws, suggesting those of the story's *Vulpine Presence.* Within this dental palisade, one finds four hand-painted wood engravings and the (slightly revised) text of the story printed in multiple fonts by Alastair Johnson. In addition to the deluxe edition, Katherine Spielmann mentions a portfolio edition that was particularly elaborate. In this instance, handwritten pages alternate with illustrations made from poisonous pigments, and a grotesque electrical apparatus is attached to the book: 'pickled squid in bulbous cylindrical specimen jars wrapped with wires running to a primitive transistor'.[31] The book object works as the grave itself: the tale rests inside its marble sepulchre, entombed until an audience is willing to listen to its cries for attention. With its juxtaposition of a promise of secret knowledge and off-putting weight and gruesome decoration, it seduces and prohibits entry in equal measure.

The very materiality of the book object explores playful tensions among a handful of intersecting dualities. Again, I submit that this playful exploration can be read not only as a negotiation of certain problems deriving from Poe's works, but of literary history in general. Michael Hemmingson asserts that Vollmann's use of end matter can be profitably read in light of Jacques Derrida's arguments regarding archive fever, and I would extend the point: Derrida's concepts could be applied to much else transpiring in Vollmann's works.[32] In the case of *The Grave of Lost Stories*, Derrida's description of the competing drives that shape and define the work of the archive are particularly germane.

Among Derrida's concerns is the archive's expression of a tension between revelation and concealment, a tension that Vollmann's CoTangent publication of *The Grave of Lost Stories* stages quite dramatically. Although the archive promises revelation of the origin, it relies for its own preservation (the preservation of the archive, not of that which it contains) on its obscuring the true appearance of the original. The revelation of the '*archē* ... in the nude' would be an effacement of the archive, for '*the origin*' could then speak '*by itself*', with no need any longer for the archive.[33] In other words, one part of the archive's authenticity derives from its revelation of its own existence, and of its concomitant advertisement of itself as the home of the truth. The archive's authenticity is thus grounded in secrecy; its heart (its contents) remains difficult to access and navigate. In keeping with this aspect of the archive, the obdurate mass of the marble-and-metal binding of *The Grave of Lost Stories* cannot easily be overlooked. Indeed, the book is difficult even to move – it asserts its presence and suggests to all who touch it a seductive permanency reminiscent of the Grave of Lost Stories from which Poe calls forth his tales. On the other hand, its very massiveness, the teeth lining the interior of the book, and such features as poisonous paints deter access to its contents. The fetishism of book as object here reveals presence, while that which is seemingly promised by the revelation – some truth won from the grave – recedes.

The Grave of Lost Stories embodies the competing drives of preservation and destruction that Derrida declares are another set of terms on which the archive can be understood. The metal binding and marble covers suggest that the book object might be – doubtless indeed is – more durable than the conventional paper and board wrappings used for most texts, including earlier publications of the story. It offers itself as material memory, keeping the contents safe for later consultation, just as sepulchres both prevent harm from coming to the remains of a corpse and stand as memorials, thereby helping to preserve the body and person of the dead. The obverse of this impulse is, again, a destructive one. The archive in this sense enacts the work of forgetting and repression, exercising its authority as an act of exclusion, as Derrida suggests in observing that the archive's power has been from the first 'a place of election where law and singularity intersect in *privilege*', a privilege connected to the power of those hierophants allowed access to the contents of the archive and thus accorded the honour due to legitimised hermeneuticians of the law.[34] Vollmann's development of the CoTangent book is, in this sense, perpetrating violence against his earlier versions of the text. While mass-produced copies are inscribed via reiterable electronic type, the limited edition, hand-crafted successor erases its ancestors. The revisions to the text (however minor) exclude some measure of their predecessor drafts, and the illustrations and material artefact in general deny the value of the literary magazine and the paperback publications of the text. Any prior version, the CoTangent edition implies, is deficient, not worth preserving, and consequently excluded.

A third point of congruence between Vollmann's project and Derrida's argument concerns more directly an existential dilemma manifest as a frustration of historical presence. Seen positively, Derrida proposes, the archive suggests a mutual satisfaction that the present and the future can offer one another.[35] Vollmann's marble book offers itself as a model of responsibility on the part of the present to the future, asserting 'we in the present have decided that this is work we will do for those who inhabit the future; the preservation may involve something of us, but it is for them: we give ourselves to them'. The anticipation is that the future will respond in kind, taking up the offering and returning it to the present in a more complete and satisfactory form, one fleshed out with the perspective of hindsight and a view of the whole of the present that is obscure to those in it. This latter promise of the archive is that of clarity. At the same time, these promises of communion between past and present via the archive are the aetiological foundation for a profound sickness – archive fever. With its other promises come the archive's suggestion that it can allow a return to the origin, to an ideally ordered past moment that contained the potential of which all that has followed is the result. To respond to this suggestion is to become feverish with a desire for the origin, and its power. This '*mal d'archive*' is a 'compulsive, repetitive, and nostalgic' desire to recover the 'place of absolute commencement'.[36] Such a desire not only demands one disavow the present but shows that one has succumbed to the most invidious temptation of the archive, a blind celebration of the archive's hierarchies, technologies of classification, and elision of incompletion and exclusion. In the case of Vollmann's book-object, the entombment of the text reminds readers of this danger, even as it provokes interest via its promise of access to that which – because of the rarity of the book and the cultural valences of its trappings – offers some hermetic power.

The preceding analysis of 'The Grave of Lost Stories,' in its several incarnations, hopefully illustrates the depth of Vollmann's engagement with the gothic, especially when focused on a representative of a national literary tradition. In the case of his handling of Poe, Vollmann's sense of his native artistic inheritance is informed by an interplay of destruction and creation, and obliteration and rebirth, that the earlier author modelled and to which he is, in Vollmann's hands, subjected. In the next section, I argue that even though Vollmann's use of gothic conventions in relation to the problems of the archive are hardly limited to the negotiation of the literary past narrowly defined, artistic creation and the problems of inscription remain for him part of the problem even when the terms on which the past is engaged are expanded.

The gothic Americas of *Last Stories and Other Stories*

While 'The Grave of Lost Stories' represents a strong early example of Vollmann's exploration of the gothic, it only hints at what Vollmann can offer in an entire book dominated by the mode. The tales collected in 2014's *Last Stories and Other Stories* are given over to relations between the living and the dead that are almost always magical. Among the texts the book offers are a handful set in Querétaro, Veracruz, and Buenos Aires. The presence in the collection of stories set in these locales is notable in part because they stand as some of Vollmann's few portrayals of Latin America. Vollmann's readers will have noted that the five published volumes of *Seven Dreams* (1990–2015), although ostensibly a history of North America, have featured almost no action south of Jamestown. His other books – *Imperial* (2009) of course excepted – also remain somewhat closed to Latin America. A number of stories in *The Atlas* (1996), a few from *Thirteen Stories and Thirteen Epitaphs*, a section of *The Book of Dolores* (2013), and a handful of pages of the final volume of *Rising Up and Rising Down* (2003) offer text and images that derive from his experiences in Mexico, Belize, Guatemala, and Colombia, but these are slight presences in his body of work. In this sense, these Latin American stories in *Last Stories and Other Stories* are exceptionally valuable: they provide some of the few means by which Vollmann's readers can judge whether or not compatible his visions of Latin America and its past are compatible with the portrayals of Canada and the United States in the *Seven Dreams* and elsewhere. These Latin American stories are significant for another reason: they follow the lead of 'The Grave of Lost Stories' in employing the gothic as a means to explore the way histories might fall prey to the dangers of the archive. Indeed, seen in this light, these stories may even be regarded as self-chastisement on the part of Vollmann, an acknowledgement that his record of New World experiences and literatures has often written out Latin American experience in its accounting of America's cultural past and present.[37]

That the gothic is especially suited to evocation of that which has been excluded from the historical archive, of what has been a prohibited presence in written histories, has been proposed by a number of critics, including Teresa A. Goddu. Goddu asserts that the gothic can destabilise conventional notions of the literary canon and of the nation itself.[38] When she turns to the historical past more generally, she observes that potential critiques of the American past are sometimes undercut by denials of American history in general, a move that frustrates the possibility of historical critique by disclaiming entirely its intended object. For Goddu, the gothic has the power to interrupt such closed circuits by virtue of its preoccupation with anxiety, violence, fear, confusion, and guilt – the very sorts of things American histories typically repress.[39] If, as she claims, this is true for the history of the United States, how much more of the case must it be when that national history is placed in its hemispheric and transoceanic contexts? My contention in the following reading of 'The Cemetery of the World' is that Vollmann extends his use of the American gothic tradition to explore the heritage of New World places beyond the United States. In so doing, he foregrounds the powers of the gothic mode that Goddu argues make it so important to consideration of American histories: its ability to draw forth from among the gaps in received history the violence that helps maintain the archive and the historical narratives built on the basis of its authority. This engagement demonstrates, too, his revival of an earlier mode as more than pastiche, and rather a vital means to present a living tradition.

Vollmann's Mexico: 'The Cemetery of the World'

In some senses, 'The Cemetery of the World' is not so obviously concerned with American literary predecessors as is 'The Grave of Lost Stories.' Yet, it is very much a return to the earlier story's preoccupations with the relation of the writer to the past, the simultaneously erotic and self-destructive nature of American writing, and the problems of the archive. Indeed, the exploration in 'The Cemetery of the World' of the power, promise, and danger of the archive is possibly even more suited to a reading in terms of Derrida's discussion of the subject. Perhaps most importantly, 'The Cemetery of the World' demonstrates that appropriate relations to the past can serve the ends of artistic renewal and that reconnection to historical sources is not only possible, but absolutely essential for creation.

The tale is set in Veracruz, and the opening explains that the city was long known as 'the cemetery of the world' because of its many plagues. As one might expect in a gothic tale, Vollmann offers numerous unsettling settings and events, from amputation and decaying buildings to visits to a *bruja* and the presence of a supernatural woman and child who make meals of her lovers. In describing one of the latter, Vollmann writes, with a nod to the monsters and mutilations of the gothic, that he 'lay glossy and swollen like a roasted chicken, ants all over him, a great leaf on his face'.[40] His appearance echoes the description of the city's plague victims, who 'failed almost infallibly, first swelling until their rings cut deep into their fingers and their faces bulged with pus, so that at the moment of decease they often wore the fleshy-lipped grimace of an Olmec head'.[41] The deployment of such relatively superficial characteristics of the gothic tale are hardly in themselves the point, as is increasingly evident when the postcolonial critique they serve emerges. The grotesque deaths contained 'within' the city's 'unsanitary walls', the narrator asserts, are perhaps the result of 'a curse' that 'exhaled itself undyingly from the bloody soil' because Veracruz was 'founded in 1519 by Cortés himself' on the site of a town destroyed by the conquistadors.[42]

The walls of the city thus offer themselves as something like the walls of an enormous tomb – it is a product of colonial destruction, and that destruction has been revisited on later populations of the city in the form of plagues – but I would suggest that these walls are akin as well to the space of an archive. As Derrida explains, the archive is established by both a power of preservation and a power of exclusion. To the extent that Veracruz persists, it is a monument to Spanish colonial efforts. The founding of colonial Mexico is everywhere in its streets, from the Spanish spoken there to the buildings amongst which its population moves. At the same time, the presence of the colonial city is an elision of part of the pre-Contact world, an erasure of the town of Quiahuyiztlaín and its population.

Furthermore, this archival aspect of the place is reinforced by the work of the story's protagonist, Ricardo Ramírez, who is identified as 'A cocky sailor of archives.'[43] Ricardo comes to Veracruz to investigate local records for material relevant to his dissertation on folk legends. He is heartbroken, having recently been abandoned by one Adela, and this emotional state has produced two results: he has thrown himself into his academic work, and he has succumbed to a general hatred for women. His erotic desire for women, in other words, has been transferred to the archive, and what he finds in the documentary history of the place is a parallel to the decay that afflicts the bodies of Veracruz's citizens. The records are 'dwindling like melting ice-shards, verso words showing through, blots spreading and darkening'; they are so damaged by worms that Vollmann repeatedly compares them to wedding lace.[44] The attention given throughout the text to the state of the records Ricardo consults works like the obstinate materiality of *The Grave of Lost Stories*, returning readers to awareness that records have been preserved, that the archive does in fact exist and extends an invitation to encounter the truth. The comparisons of the documents to wedding lace reinforce the invitation's erotic appeal, much like Poe's attraction to his dying heroines in 'The Grave of Lost Stories.' At the same time, the later text's preoccupation with the decay of the records implies that the curse of Veracruz's bloodstained ground has been visited upon the documentary archive as well as the figurative archive of the town itself. Consequently, Vollmann's portrayal of the documents highlights not the archive's positive promise, but the destructive powers of exclusion and omission by virtue of which it exists.

Furthering this sense that the archive is both seductress and grave, and in what seems an overt nod to Derrida, Ricardo succumbs to a fever after coming to Veracruz and immersing himself in the archive, and the illness develops in parallel with his research. The particular objects of his quest are 'the "autonomous" and "universal" elements of Mexican legends', a goal that drives him to seek the Ur-tale from which the Mexican imagination has grown.[45] In abandoning 'his own half-lived life' in preference for hints of this cultural origin, he throws himself into the hands of the plague of Veracruz, and of archive fever.[46] Furthermore, he welcomes the archive's shortcomings, as the gaps in the record allow 'our hero' to 'interpolate whatever he liked'.[47] These interpolations are increasingly shaped by Ricardo's emotional distress, identifying parallels in the Mexican past for the romantic betrayal he suffered at the hands of Adela. Consequently, he becomes obsessed with gathering information about La Malinche, whose history he regards as 'the nation's founding legend'.[48] In Vollmann's presentation, the ghost of Malinche is conflated with La Llorona, and in Ricardo's feverishly misogynistic eyes, the synthesis of these legends provides a suitable figure not only of Mexico's, but also of his personal, past.[49]

Ricardo's preoccupation with Malinche as a figure of national origins, frustrated romantic life, and general obsession with the decaying past of cursed Veracruz culminate in an encounter with an embodiment of all of these aspects of the tale. His feverish search for information about La Llorona leads him to explore some abandoned buildings, where he encounters this ghost of La Malinche in 'the most evil house ... like a castle. Over there on

Hidalgo and Callejón California'.[50] At this moment, and for the first time since his loss of Adela, he experiences a 'sudden lust'.[51] La Llorona is unquestionably a dangerous spirit, a figure of the malicious destruction that typifies the curse that afflicts Veracruz. Nevertheless, she is for Ricardo an object of desire, and, while she normally destroys those she encounters, La Llorona becomes Ricardo's lover, and they have a child.

With the discovery of La Llorona as a living presence from the past, an alternative at which the archive hints but denies in its very presence, Vollmann's story shifts from a record of decay to one that considers how opening oneself to the dangerous ambiguities of the past can lead to renewal and creation. The birth of the child, in particular, emblematises the production of new (if rather unusual) life from out of the personification of the troubled past of Mexico and the elisions of its history. Unlike the detestable La Malinche of whom Ricardo learns in the archive, La Llorona, 'being immortal, was still fresher than the fringed arches of banana leaves', and she eventually goes so far as to leave him in order to avoid having to destroy him.[52] At their final meeting, she gifts him with a leaf that, when made into tea, will allow 'life' to 'go differently for him' after their relationship.[53] And, it does: 'he suddenly loved women – all of them. Not long after that, he completed his dissertation, for which he received highest honours, and a publishing contract with a feminist press'.[54] Furthermore, he enters into a happy marriage and becomes the 'artistic director of the provincial folklore troupe', which stages plays and musical presentations.[55] One notes that these achievements each bring him into more positive relations with the feminine, with his vocation of folklore, and with his own creative powers. In short, in coming to erotic terms with the founding mother of Mexico, Ricardo renews himself.

Unlike Poe in 'The Grave of Lost Stories,' who is finally destroyed by his erotic attraction to the necrotic, Ricardo negotiates his self-destructive attraction to his dangerous lover with great success. His tale ends with a description of his theatrical masterpiece, a 'wordless performance entitled "Salvation"'.[56] In this play, a number of men walk through a maze while being stalked by death. When only one man remains, and death is almost upon him, 'out came a lovely death's-head woman .... The young man flew delightedly into her arms, and she enfolded him just in time to spare him from her rival.'[57] The production brings fame to Ricardo and allows the tale to return to the question of artistic production. In trading his fascination with the archive, which is self-destructive because it so thoroughly honours the equivocal terms of that technology, for participation in a folk tradition that honours that which the archive and related histories omit, Ricardo honours the excluded and the abject. He thereby models how history can be transformed from a tool of destruction to a means for production.

The gothic tales 'The Grave of Lost Stories' and 'The Cemetery of the World' demonstrate Vollmann's engagement with a mode that he has explored most deeply on terms that take shape in relation to Poe. Insofar as this is the case, these stories present a view of the past that suggests some of the ways Vollmann negotiates his national literary history. In both cases, the attachment to that which can persist only on the thanatic terms of the archive – the dead past that remains a tool of hegemonic power and which the archive obscures – is revealed as counterproductive. On the other hand, an engagement driven by an erotic impulse of discovery and creation brings to life, literally in these magic-filled stories, new work grounded in New World traditions, whether those of the American gothic, pulled gasping for air from out of the Grave of Lost Stories, or the darker side of Mexican folklore, dug out of the bloody earth of postcolonial Veracruz.

The more recent story, in particular, is notable for the degree to which it emphasises the need for local response to global crises. The recovery of La Llorona not only redeems the reputation of La Malinche, it also saves the man who recovers her. In this way, the tale suggests that archive fever – including that version of it manifest as a preoccupation with the origins of any particular national literary tradition – can only be overcome by focusing on an effort to meet the tradition's promise of clarity with regard to the past via devotion to historical connection in the present. Like the *Seven Dreams*, which trades slavish adherence to the facts of the historical record for a symbolic history truer than that offered by the archive, Vollmann's treatment of the literary tradition sees past texts as suggestive in both their content and in their silences, and he puts both to work in service of celebrating and clarifying the past. In Vollmann's stories, this transformation of America's national literary tradition becomes the grounds for participation in it by this most global of contemporary American authors, and models one means by which the authors of the New Sincerity can develop their response to postmodernism.

Notes

1. Fredric Jameson, *Postmodernism, or, the Cultural Logic of Late Capitalism* (Durham, NC: Duke University Press, 1991), p. 25.
2. William T. Vollmann, in Larry McCaffery and Michael Hemmingson (eds), *Expelled from Eden: A William T. Vollmann Reader* (New York: Thunder's Mouth, 2004), p. 36.
3. Jonathan Franzen, 'A Friendship', in Christopher K. Coffman and Daniel Lukes (eds), *William T. Vollmann: A Critical Companion* (Newark: University of Delaware Press, 2015), p. 282.
4. E. L. Doctorow, *Reporting the Universe: The William E. Massey Sr. Lectures in the History of American Civilization* (Cambridge: Harvard University Press, 2004), p. 9.

5. Françoise Palleau-Papin, 'Introduction: Un Balzac californien', in Françoise Palleau-Papin (ed.), *William T. Vollmann: Le roman historique en question, Une étude de The Rifles* (Paris: Presses Sorbonne Nouvelle, 2011), p. 15.
6. Catherine Lanone, 'Sources primaires et récriture postmoderne', in Françoise Palleau-Papin (ed.), *William T. Vollmann: Le roman historique en question, Une étude de The Rifles* (Paris: Presses Sorbonne Nouvelle, 2011), pp. 35–45.
7. Daniel Lukes, '"Strange Hungers": William T. Vollmann's Literary Performances of Abject Masculinity', in Christopher K. Coffman and Daniel Lukes (eds), *William T. Vollmann: A Critical Companion* (Newark: University of Delaware Press, 2015), pp. 265–6.
8. Vollmann, *The Rainbow Stories* (New York: Penguin, 1991), p. 399.
9. Vollmann, *You Bright and Risen Angels: A Cartoon* (New York: Penguin, 1987), p. 3.
10. Ibid., pp. 95–6.
11. Ibid., pp. 96–7.
12. Ibid., p. 288.
13. Ibid., p. 421.
14. Ibid., p. 446.
15. Vollmann, *Thirteen Stories and Thirteen Epitaphs* (New York: Grove, 1994), p. 296.
16. Ibid., pp. 295–6.
17. Ibid., p. 297.
18. Ibid.
19. Ibid., p. 308.
20. Ibid., p. 301.
21. Ibid., p. 304.
22. Ibid., p. 302.
23. Ibid.
24. Ibid., p. 310.
25. Ibid., p. 303.
26. Ibid.
27. Ibid., p. 311.
28. Ibid.
29. Leland S. Person, 'Poe's Poetics of Desire: "Th' Expanding Eye to the Loved Object"', *Poe Studies* 34.1–2 (2001), p. 5.
30. Priscilla Juvelis, 'William T. Vollmann: Artist's Books', in Christopher K. Coffman and Daniel Lukes (eds), *William T. Vollmann: A Critical Companion* (Newark: University of Delaware Press, 2015), p. 288.
31. Katherine Spielmann, 'The Book as Apparatus: William T. Vollmann's Special Editions', *The Review of Contemporary Fiction* 13.2 (1993), p. 65.
32. Michael Hemmingson, 'Beyond the Book: William T. Vollmann's End Matter (Appendices, Glossaries, and Extra Texts)', in Christopher K. Coffman and Daniel Lukes (eds), *William T. Vollmann: A Critical Companion* (Newark: University of Delaware Press, 2015), p. 333.
33. Jacques Derrida, *Archive Fever: A Freudian Impression* (Chicago, IL: The University of Chicago Press, 1996), p. 92.
34. Ibid., pp. 2–3.
35. Ibid., p. 36.
36. Ibid., p. 91.

37. A point for future investigation will be the degree to and manner in which Vollmann's career grapples with the Boltonian thesis that Latin America should be studied on roughly the same terms as the United States and Canada. As I suggest in the main text, much of Vollmann's work so far has partitioned the Americas, but there are many signs that this is changing. Antonio Barrenechea's *America Unbound: Encyclopedic Literature and Hemispheric Studies* (Albuquerque: University of New Mexico Press, 2016) offers an insightful explanation of the debates surrounding and implications of Bolton's work.
38. Teresa A. Goddu, *Gothic America: Narrative, History, and Nation* (New York: Columbia University Press, 1997), p. 8.
39. Ibid., p. 9.
40. Vollmann, *Last Stories and Other Stories* (New York: Viking, 2014), p. 316.
41. Ibid., p. 296.
42. Ibid.
43. Ibid., p. 301.
44. Ibid.
45. Ibid.
46. Ibid., p. 302.
47. Ibid., p. 301.
48. Ibid., p. 302. La Malinche was an indigenous woman who served as translator for Cortés. She also became his mistress and bore him a child. While there have been attempts to redeem the historical Malinche, the traditional attitude is that she was a traitor to her culture, guilty of miscegenation and of abetting the success of the conquistadors. Octavio Paz explains in *El laberinto de la soledad* that Malinche is a representation of 'las indias, fascinadas, violadas, o seducidas por los españoles' ['the female Indians fascinated, violated, or seduced by the Spaniards']; consequently, she is a figure of the Mexico that emerged from the conquest and, to the extent that it is shaped by outside influences, of Mexico today ([New York: Penguin, 1997], p. 82.).
49. Folktales about La Llorona relate that she drowned her children while in a confused state, and consequently she walks through the night – usually near rivers – wailing as she searches for them (Anna M. Sandoval, '*Unir los Lazos*: Braiding Chicana and *Mexicana* Subjectivities', in Arturo J. Aldama and Naomi H. Quiñonez (eds), *Decolonial Voices: Chicana and Chicano Cultural Studies in the 21st Century* [Bloomington: Indiana University Press, 2002], p. 217).
50. Vollmann, *Last Stories and Other Stories*, p. 309.
51. Ibid., p. 312.
52. Ibid., p. 314.
53. Ibid., p. 320.
54. Ibid., p. 322.
55. Ibid.
56. Ibid., p. 323.
57. Ibid., p. 324.

Disclosure statement

No potential conflict of interest was reported by the author.

Metaffective fiction: structuring feeling in post-postmodern American literature

Ralph Clare

ABSTRACT

This essay will suggest that post-postmodern literature does not simply 'return to affect' but that it simultaneously reflects upon the limitations and construction of affect in ways that recall postmodernism's penchant for metafiction and self-conscious textuality. Such writing might fittingly be called 'metaffective fiction.' After a brief summary of Affect Theory as it pertains to contemporary literature, this essay offers as its case study a reading of J.J. Abrams and Doug Dorst's post-postmodern *S.* against Nabokov's classic postmodern text *Pale Fire*. My contention is that if metafiction breaks the frame of narrative in order to call attention to its fictive status, metaffective fiction breaks that frame so as to interrogate self-consciously the construction of emotion and affect. Where metafiction underscores the ways in which reality is framed and constructed through narrative, metaffective fiction highlights how emotion and affect themselves are realised and 'framed' or codified. And while metaffective fiction realises that fictionalised emotions aren't real emotions and that affect can never be fully accessible in language, it still both expresses emotion and realises the insufficiencies of that expression. These metaffective fictions attempt to do so as a way of renewing the potential of affect in a neoliberal age that is increasingly commodifying affective labour, leisure, and our everyday emotional lives.

In distinguishing post-postmodern American literature from its postmodern predecessor, several critics have characterised post-postmodernist fiction as one or another kind of a 'return to the real' and focused on the representations of fleshed out characters, emotion, feeling, and affect as key features of such literature.[1] In so doing, this criticism closely follows the avowal of David Foster Wallace and other contemporary authors to commit to creating a literature that values human connection, empathy, emotion, belief, and other-directedness as correctives to the perceived narcissism, cynicism, solipsism, media saturation, and debilitating forms of cultural irony of the postmodern world and what was seen as an aesthetically bankrupt and co-opted postmodern literature.[2] As Robert McLaughlin puts it in an essay heralding Wallace and Jonathan Franzen as representative of this new generation of writers, these authors see literature as 'valuable' for 'finding ways to be human in [the world], and of truly connecting with others.'[3]

Rachel Greenwald Smith's *Affect and American Literature in the Age of Neoliberalism*, however, has challenged these fairly optimistic critical takes on post-postmodern literature's 'return to the real' via its emotional and affective registers. Greenwald Smith argues against what she calls 'the *affective hypothesis*, or the belief that literature is at its most meaningful when it represents and transmits the emotional specificity of personal experience,'[4] chiefly because in the neoliberal era a new subjectivity has been formed – an entrepreneurial subject that is always managing individual or 'private emotions' like commodities and reducing human connections to so much networking. In short, Greenwald Smith claims that novels employing formal innovation to make emotional connections merely conform to the demands of a neoliberal market, while works that stoke

> [i]mpersonal feelings do not conform to a market model, because they [the feelings] are not easily codifiable or recognizable; they do not allow for strategic emotional associations to be made between readers and characters; [and] they emphasise the unpredictability of affective connections.[5]

Ultimately, these 'impersonal works [...] question the expectations that underpin the model of the neoliberal entrepreneurial subject.'[6]

What makes Greenwald Smith's trenchant analysis of feeling and literary form so convincing is its grounding in affect theory, which differentiates between emotion and affect, in contrast to the aforementioned studies of post-postmodern literature that tend to conflate emotion with affect and/or accept the return to the 'real' or 'human' fairly uncritically.[7] As Masssumi explains, emotion and affect 'follow different logics and pertain to different orders.'[8] Emotion, or what is often called affect,

> is a subjective content, the sociolinguistic fixing of the quality of [...] experience which is from that point onward defined as personal. Emotion is qualified intensity, the conventional, consensual point of insertion of intensity into semantically and semiotically formed progressions, into narrativizable action-reaction circuits, into function and meaning. It is intensity owned and recognized.[9]

Emotion, then, is a feeling that becomes consciously recognised or named by a subject and hence becomes 'qualified' or 'semiotically' codified and understood.[10]

Affect, however, is the very preconscious capacity of bodies to affect and be affected in the first place. Affect involves, as Michael Hardt writes, 'both our power to affect the world around us and our power to be affected by it, along with the relationships between these two powers.'[11] In this formulation, affect is intensity, vitality, and it 'arises in the midst of *in-between-ness*' and

> is found in those intensities that pass body to body (human, nonhuman, part-body, and otherwise), in those resonances that circulate about, between, and sometimes stick to bodies and worlds, *and* in the very passages or variations between these intensities and resonances themselves.[12]

One thinks immediately of the affective charge of a crowd at a concert or sporting event as constituting a transmittable 'atmosphere' that affects and is affected by everyone gathered there, yet which no single individual actually 'owns,' even though one's perception and cognition subjectivise emotional states related to the experience. Affect is thus 'outside' the subject, only to be 'registered' when consciousness, by necessity, captures, organises, and codifies what we later call experience from the chaotic welter of the world, much like a cookie cutter presses familiar shapes and bite-sized morsels out of a mass of dough. As Massumi writes, '[w]ill and consciousness are *subtractive*. They are *limitative, derived functions* that reduce complexity too rich to be functionally expressed.'[13] Yet affect, despite its being a kind of invisible pre-conscious force or bodily capacity, has decidedly material and bodily registers as well, as evidenced in the body's autonomic responses, such as a pupil dilating, a shiver, or a sudden reflex, in which the body acts on its own or 'before' consciousness recognises the need to do so.[14] To return to the example of the crowd, it is the rush, excitement, or anxiety that one might find oneself *already bodily transformed by* or *getting carried away by* (the cheer, tapping foot, rapt stare) that speaks to affect's material dimensions. Affect thus always involves the interaction between mind and body, though it scrambles any hierarchical mind/body binary or simple cause/effect logic connected to such a duality. Affect is, in a way, feeling felt both mentally and physically.

This provocative view of affect is at odds with the aforementioned scholarship on post-postmodernism that is, to varying degrees, sympathetic to or supportive of the 'affective hypothesis,' and, at the very least, does not problematise the distinction between emotion and affect. In response, I would like to stake out a middle ground between these two positions, one that does not necessarily brush off post-postmodern literature's move to immediacy and emotional grounding as mere neoliberal capitulation, as per Greenwald Smith, yet in turn complicates the 'return to affect' and its attendant reconstructed humanism, as per Mary Holland and others. I would like to suggest that post-postmodern literature does not simply 'return to affect' but that it simultaneously reflects upon the limitations and construction of affect in ways that recall postmodernism's penchant for metafiction and self-conscious textuality. Such writing might fittingly be called 'metaffective fiction.' To recall Patricia Waugh's famous definition, '[*m*]*etafiction* is [...] fictional writing which self-consciously and systematically calls *attention* to its status as an artefact in order to pose questions about the relationship between fiction and reality.'[15] In kind, what I am calling metaffective fiction is that fiction that self-consciously calls attention to the ways in which emotion and affect are represented in order to interrogate the relationship between them. This can happen in myriad ways. Metaffective fiction may radically break the narrative frame in order to highlight the construction, framing, or codification of emotion and character; it may insist on self-consciously establishing a particular affective relationship with a reader and text that both makes and breaks bonds, compels and repels identification; it may intensify emotional states to the point of over-saturation or excess that bleeds 'out' of characters and narrative frames to become the very tone or atmosphere of a text; it may foreground the materiality of texts as distinctive 'embodied' reads through its formal play; and metaffective fiction might gesture toward affect as that which escapes language and signification altogether in the face of the ineffable or what cannot be adequately represented in language or emotional terms – the so-called unproblematic 'return to the real.' Therefore, the 'meta' of metaffective fiction does not just refer to an awareness of textuality itself but to an awareness of affect that may be said to resonate with affect theory's distinction between emotion and affect in addition to its conception of affect's materiality and potentiality.

What I hope to show is that metaffective fiction is literature that, although it may indeed indulge in realist characters and sentiment, is nevertheless able to tap into or register affect and affective states that go beyond the seemingly 'shallow' representation of emotions – indeed this is what the most successful examples of this literature accomplish. To establish immediacy, sincerity, and closeness between a text and reader, for instance, only to break or discourage those connections a few pages or chapters later not only underscores the fragility and constructed nature of such bonds but can appear an even more cruel, cold, and impersonal practice than establishing a medium-cool tone from a story's outset. Thus, even texts with emotionally identifiable subjects can instigate 'impersonal feelings' or affective charges that might then circulate outside of neoliberal market dictates; for metaffective fictions seek, though not always successfully, to renew the potential of affect in a neoliberal age that is increasingly commodifiying affective labour, leisure, and our everyday emotional lives. Metaffective fictions comprise a literature that has arisen within and in response to neoliberalism and its affective economics. Metaffective fiction, therefore, does not involve emotion recollected in tranquillity, but affect reconstructed in adversity.

Moreover, the influential work on immaterial or affective labour by Michael Hardt and Antonio Negri offers a theory of neoliberalism's affective economics that leaves open the possibility of rejecting and transforming neoliberal subjectivity.[16] For Hardt and Negri, affective labour – examples include cognitive labour (computer programming), service work (restaurant work or health care), or household labour (domestic work) – has become the hegemonic mode of capitalist production.[17] Affective labour has not replaced material labour or quantitatively eclipsed it, but it gestures to a new capitalist dynamic that aims, through the bio-production of affects (mental and bodily things), to create life itself: 'the production of ideas, images, knowledge, communication, cooperation, and affective relations, tends to create not the means of social life but *social life itself*.'[18] Biopower constitutes neoliberalism's way of managing bioproduction, but affective labour has the very same qualities of emergence, potentiality, and autonomy as does affect understood in the Deleuzian/Spinozist vein detailed above. Despite biopower's attempt at containment, Hardt and Negri assert, '[b]iopolitical labour power is becoming more and more autonomous,'[19] and '[b]iopolitical products [...] tend to *exceed* all quantitative measurement and take *common* forms, which are easily shared and difficult to corral as private property.'[20] Thus, in a neoliberal economy that harnesses affective labour, a surplus of affect always escapes recapture by the processes of production that generate it to begin with, for affect is always autonomous.

The same is true of literature and affect. Pieter Vermeulen reminds us that '[l]iterary works are defined by a restless interplay between emotional codifications and affects that inevitably escape them; even if they attempt to control unruly affect and contain it as individual emotion, affect always exceeds these efforts' (9). Since all reading is, of course, bioproductive in a sense – from the tactile sensation of holding a book or device to the cognitive and emotional aspect of the act of reading – one might be tempted to formulate a biopolitics of reading. As Deleuze and Guattari, write, any successful philosophy, art, or literature, 'produce[s] affects that surpass ordinary affections and perceptions' (65), thus forming an independent, autonomous '*bloc of sensations, that is to say, a compound of percepts and affects*.'[21] A biopolitics of post-postmodern fiction, then, might argue that by sharing and spreading affect intersubjectively or by establishing affect as something transmittable between reader, writer, and text, metaffective fiction provokes new literary forms, new potential affects and affective relationships, and perhaps even new subjectivities. Moreover, what makes metaffective fiction unique in contrast to the literature of any period that can be said to be affective, is that metaffective fiction must self-consciously, through a variety of hardcore and softcore metafictional techniques, negotiate the very problem and production of affect in a neoliberal era where it is easily captured and commodified.

Indeed, there are interesting parallels between affective labour and the 'labour' of reading metaffective fiction. Affective labour is, Hardt and Negri write, 'of the head and the heart' and '[o]ne distinctive feature of the work of head and heart [...] is that paradoxically the *object* of production is a really a *subject*, defined, for example, by a social relationship or a form of life.'[22] Because metaffective fiction at times asks its reader to 'do work' when encountering a text's formal breaks, interruptions, recursions, or meta-moments, we might see this invitation to 'work through' the text not as an emotional investment opportunity or chance to learn about strategic identification and networking by identifying with realistic-seeming characters but as a call to engage in an *affective labour of reading* or a form of *meta-affective reading*. For the aesthetic techniques of metafiction help to create ruptures, reflexivity, and distance – the very 'in-between' spaces where affect thrives and pulses. As Patricia Ticineto Clough writes, summarising Massumi, affect is always 'potential and emergent' and its temporality should be understood 'in terms of thresholds, bifurcation, and emergence.'[23] The encounters that can take place in these textual thresholds and spaces where affect is percolating can be spaces where shared and communal affects are produced and distributed, creating an affective virtual commons of a sort, a virtual reading community that may later be actualised in a number of possible ways.

Despite the 'return' to the real, to character, emotion, or affect, these metaffective fictions are aware of the ways in which they construct emotion and affect in an age typified both by cynical disaffection and giddy Millennial optimism. A study of metaffective fiction, then, ought to be concerned with the ways in which emotions, feelings, and affects circulate in, through, and outside of post-postmodern texts (even personal ones) that are produced, distributed, and consumed in a neoliberal affective economy.

For the remainder of this essay, then, I would like to consider how one radically metafictional post-postmodern text creates an affective relationship and sense of immediacy between reader and text through its tone and formal devices, yet simultaneously calls awareness to affect's textual and material (re)productions. My abbreviated case study will be to set J.J. Abrams and Doug Dorst's post-postmodern *S.* alongside Vladimir Nabokov's classic postmodern novel *Pale Fire* (1962), since both of these texts are metafictions from different eras that indulge in linguistic play and puzzles and are concerned, in both form and content, with a reader's relationship to a text. What I hope to show is that *S.* as a metaffective fiction employs emotional and affective aesthetics 'personally' in ways antithetical to the 'impersonal' and metafictional *Pale Fire* that nevertheless provoke affect's potentiality and power. For this reason, *S.* provides a very different sort of affective charge – one fitting for the neoliberal era – than *Pale Fire*, which nonetheless has the ability to produce affects as does a work of literature from any period. *S.*, therefore, emerges not merely as another metafiction generating affects but as a truly *meta*ffective fiction that is responding to the emotional and affective challenges and capacities of its contemporary moment. In short, *S.* is a metaffective fiction, whereas *Pale Fire* is a metafiction.

Pale Fire and metafictional economies of affect

Nabokov's *Pale Fire* is a curious, metafictional novel that challenges the novel's very generic form by mimicking a scholarly edition of a poem. As such, the novel is composed of four parts: first, a foreword by editor Charles Kinbote; second, 'Pale Fire,' a 999 line poem purportedly written by John Shade; third, Kinbote's novella length 'commentary' on the poem, which tells what appears to be a completely unrelated and bizarre story about the adventures of an exiled King of Zembla, Charles Xavier (who seems to be a thinly disguised Kinbote), as well as about Kinbote himself (also a Zemblan ex-pat) and his struggles to adapt to life in America; lastly, is a seemingly scholarly index. The obvious challenge to the reader is to put these parts into some sort of order to make sense of it all. In typical Nabokovian fashion, *Pale Fire* displays a variety of puns, allusions, and linguistic clues (some productive, others dead ends) sprinkled throughout its pages that offer up tempting thematic connections between the novel's disparate parts.[24] The variety of possible solutions that critics have considered over the years – that Kinbote invented Shade; that Shade invented Kinbote; that Kinbote is mad (and may actually be someone named Botkin) and is critically hijacking the poem; that Kinbote/Botkin is or is not the true King of Zembla, is greatly suffering and hoping Shade's art might redeem his life[25] – speaks to the baffling nature of the book. Even premier Nabokov scholar Brian Boyd's elaborate and stunning book-length solution to the novel, while it may be said to 'solve' the novel's central riddle, still does not clear up many delightful textual ambiguities, which is a testament to the novel's interpretive richness.[26]

Pale Fire thus foregrounds postmodern concerns with textuality and authority, such as the relationships between text and context, author and critic, and author and reader. But it might be said to do so in a purely formalist fashion with limited linguistic ends. Ultimately, the novel is inwardly turned, due to Kinbote's obsession, solipsism, and mental illness as well as the novel's linguistic game playing itself. For although these games are sometimes purposefully cyclical, closed linguistic systems – innocent games such as 'word golf' (in which a player seeks the least number moves between two words by changing one letter per move) and Kinbote's amusing circuitous, wild goose chase citations in the index – even the 'open' games that partake in what the poet Shade calls 'combinational delight,'[27] such as the multilingual play, hidden codes, and numerous intertextual allusions, become like so many brain teasers that the reader is invited to try to solve, but which makes her ever aware of the absent presence of the puzzle master, Nabokov himself. When asked why he wrote *Lolita*, Nabokov answered,

> [w]hy did I write any of my books, after all? For the sake of pleasure, for the sake of difficulty. I have no social purpose, no moral message; I've no general ideas to exploit, I just like composing riddles with elegant solutions.[28]

While it is true that Nabokov's formalism is not strictly linguistically solipsistic – Shade's art (much like Nabokov's), as his poem puts it, is based not on 'text but texture' (PF l. 808) and aspires not toward 'flimsy nonsense, but a web of sense' (PF l. 810) – it nevertheless forces one to seek, 'Some kind of link-and-bobolink, some kind/Of correlated pattern in the game' (PF ll. 812-13).

Nabokov's intricate game is carefully designed after Nature, the artist of the universe. If Nature is the unseen uber-artist who makes a sublime and deceptively ordered web of the world, the genius artist such as Nabokov replicates this elegant complexity textually in linguistic patterning via his own finely spun web of words. The author figure thus functions allegorically, as in much metafiction, as a kind of god or creator of the fictional world. Indeed, Nabokov calls himself an 'anthropomorphic deity' in the preface to *Bend Sinister*[29] and often left linguistic clues of his role as creator in his novels, from the use of personal fatidic dates to anagrams of his name at key textual moments that serve as kinds of 'divine signs' or 'seals' of his unseen presence, similar to how patterns in nature suggest some deeper, unknowable principle of design.[30]

This author-deity, the stereotypical Mandarin Nabokov, also casts a foreboding shadow over his pages at times, since 'the Glory of god is to hide a thing, and the glory of man is to find it.'[31] To be sure, we are invited to play the textual game, to have a seat and work out the novel's 'chess problem' that Nabokov so loved composing in both the game itself and his writing, but there is always the sense that we might miss a clue or the overall point, and there remains something slightly adversarial or condescending about the relationship. That Nabokov enjoyed lightly taunting and goading even his most acute readers may be read, on the one hand, as a simple mischievousness and impish delight in winning a devious if harmless game; on the other, it suggests a fundamental imbalance between the composer of the chess problem and its solver or between what Nabokov once called 'the satisfied writer and the grateful reader.'[32] At worst, it is evidence of a solipsistic puzzle master who could not care less about his reader, since '[h]is best audience is the person he sees in his shaving mirror every morning'[33] and '[i]n the long run […] it is only the author's private satisfaction that counts,' [34] a satisfaction that grows the more the reader remains puzzled. [35]

Affects are stimulated and transferred in Nabokov's texts mainly through the translation of Nabokov's 'private language'[36] of memory into sensuous images and details that are then conveyed to the reader through a literary synesthetic method in which mirrored images and suggestive wordplay create enough slippage in meaning to thereby cross modes of feeling, knowing, and sensing in ways that create and multiply new affects instead of capturing and recoding them in familiar ways. Yet this transaction often appears to be a closed-circuit transmission of a privately experienced pleasure of sensation – or affect – to the individual reader who, the more sophisticated she is, the better the payoff. There is always a kind of affective blockage by, or rerouting to or through, the authorial figure. Here is Nabokov as pure aesthete, the one who prized the individual's ability to note and recall the singular detail and was not concerned with the social, the political, or with notions of community in any larger sense. If the reader does not 'feel' like playing the game, however, and the circuit shorts, Nabokov's enjoyment is not abated. Thus, while Nabokov's novels could well be said to generate more affects than most, the reader's affective relationship to the text and its authorial figure can be a fraught one, even for his admirers.

Of course, this is not to say that Nabokov did not have a grander aim to his work, one that probed the constitution of the world, the universe, and reality itself.[37] It could be argued that affect is radically stimulated in much of Nabokov's work in a much less 'private' manner (and particularly by *Pale Fire*) because it poses nature and the nonhuman (even if the nonhuman element is a recognisable anthropomorphised afterlife/metaphysics) as the hidden order(er) behind the chaos of human reality – especially if one is lucky enough to 'solve' the text and arrive at this conclusion. Both Greenwald Smith and Vermeulen, for example, trace the potential of affect to nonhuman networks where affect may be seen to circulate outside of human subjectivity and/or trouble the very notion of the human.[38] Considering Nabokov's scientific and naturalist bent, as well as his metaphysical probing of consciousness within and without Time, his work would appear ripe for a unique exploration of affect and the nonhuman in a Deluezian/Bergsonian vein.[39]

It is not, therefore, that *Pale Fire* does not produce affects or have affective dimensions, for it most certainly does, but that its meta or self-aware qualities do not pertain to a consideration of emotion or affect itself. Yet what makes metaffective fiction unique is not simply that it creates and contains affects, but also its acceptance of the limits of emotional codification, its willingness to explore the ways in which communities are composed by transpersonal affective bonds, and its awareness of affect's importance and potentiality as well as its excessiveness and elusiveness. All of this is evidence of a specific kind of literary engagement with affect, one not witnessed in quite the same way in earlier periods and other literary genres and traditions.

S. as metaffective fiction

The attempt to solve a puzzling text is also ostensibly what Abrams and Dorst's *S.* is about, but with very different ends than those of *Pale Fire* and with oodles of tonal sentiment and sentimentality where Nabokov's novel is, notwithstanding Kinbote's bathos and Shade's pathos, coolly and pleasantly detached. *S.* can also be seen as a kind of bioproductive fiction in that it labours to affect 'the head and the heart' and to create new forms of literature and life. In *S.* we follow the story of a budding romance between a *non grata* grad student, Eric Husch, and undergraduate, Jen Heyward, who meet via notes in the margins of a book – which turn out to be the very marginal notes we are reading, reproduced in the pages of the novel. Jen, having found Eric's misplaced copy of V.M. Straka's *Ship of Theseus* in the university library where she works, returns it with a comment written in the margins. So begins a conversation between the two about the meaning of Straka's existential mystery novel, who the mysterious author really was (he may have been a spy, a revolutionary, a *nom de plume* for a collaboration of authors, etc.), and who the book's confounding editor F.X. Caldeira is. Similar to *Pale Fire*, this investigation entails finding and breaking secret codes in the editor's footnotes, as well as detecting and unscrambling hidden messages in Straka's novel (*S.* even includes a decoder wheel). By the novel's end, the contours of a vast conspiracy begin to take shape surrounding Straka's legacy that may have great historical and political relevance.

All of this is presented to the reader in spectacular form. One purchases a copy of *S.* in a slipcase bearing the novel's title, but the book inside carries the embossed title *Ship of Theseus* by V.M. Straka, and is a perfect simulacrum of a 1950s library book – complete with the scent of an old book and library markings, Dewey decimal and all. Inside the book we find the editor F.X. Caldeira's foreword, followed by Straka's unfinished novel that Caldeira annotates, and a final chapter written by Caldeira to complete Straka's novel. More important is the marginalia itself, which includes Eric's early notes handwritten in pencil, the first conversation between Eric and Jen that runs at times non-linearly the length of the book in ink pen, and several other of the couple's semi-non-linear conversations from different times that appear in differently coloured inks. Also tucked inside the book are loose postcards, letters, photographs, and various ephemera. It is as if the reader has found the very book that Eric and Jen have been writing messages back and forth in.

The book as object, then, is the first way that *S.* reveals its affective biopolitical dimension, which Nabokov's novel does not have. Certainly, there are a number of high postmodern texts that call attention to the book as object does *Pale Fire*. Early examples include William Gass's *Willie Masters' Lonesome Wife*, Kurt Vonnegut's *Breakfast of Champions*, and Raymond Federman's *Double or Nothing*, each of which demonstrates typographical and/or pictorial play. Perhaps the most experimental are Julio Cortazar's *Hopscotch* and B.S. Johnson's book in a box, *The Unfortunates*, both texts that allow the reader to make her way, fragment by fragment, through the text in her own fashion (though at the behest of a frame/introduction). These novels remind us that the literary artefact is an object, that novels and words are autonomous things in the world, and that what we consider to be reality is largely a linguistic and textual construct.

S., in contrast, is an even more radical read in that it overtly stresses the embodied, physical act of reading itself over the (re)turn to text, much like Mark Z. Danielewski's *The House of Leaves*. For *S.* does not just compel the reader to flip back and forth through its pages, it also alerts the reader to the traces of the novel's prior readers' (characters') readings in the personally handwritten notes. The novel thus foregrounds its own status not merely as a physical object but as an object circulating between any number of readers, and it extends this idea metafictionally to the reader herself who picks up the novel. The novel, in a sense, attains a kind of subjectivity and agency here, as opposed to the apparent objective and static autonomy of the traditional literary artefact. Moreover, *S.* physically enacts the very ship of Theseus paradox that Straka's novel of the same name considers philosophically in terms of identity: that a thing (subject or object; S. himself or Theseus' ship) can completely change yet somehow remain the 'same.' *S.* itself, stuffed full of ephemera that falls out when you open it and 'defaced' by marginalia, is a book that is the same yet not the same as when it first rolled off the presses.[40] This book, then, is an object that *matters* (as if 'to matter' were a verb as well): it generates affects, indeed, but it also calls attention to how a nonhuman object can provoke and transmit affects that transpersonally circulate between readers outside of the text.

As such, *S.*'s marginalia becomes the novel's true story – decentring Straka's novel while commenting upon it – and suggests the way in which readers-as-subjects and their extra-textual relationships (reading communities of any size) are formed and matter. *S.* is in many ways a literary rendering of reader-response theory that speaks to the difficulty of the high postmodern text by allegorising the reader's encounter with a sometimes adversarial text that produces affects that dazzle and/or puzzle the reader. It is as if the interpretive problematic of *Pale Fire* is raised to a second meta-level in *S.*, in which the reader's struggle with the puzzle-text is now the real or more important story, underscoring the visceral pleasure of reading and, most importantly, the affective relationship between reader and text and between readers themselves. As a metaffective fiction *S.* therefore updates the postmodern Barthesian notion that, as an early Eric note puts it, 'Storytelling transforms writer/speaker and reader/listener,'[41] in a properly bioproductive fashion by expanding this binary relationship via affect (the 'in-betweeness' of which challenges such binaries) into a larger, potentially more communal one. This entails not simply changing something that already exists but producing something entirely new – new forms of reading (such as compelled by *S.* itself) and new forms of community (Eric and Jen's antiquated version of 'texting').

The embodied act of reading, moreover, is a reminder of the extra-textual, of the material world. This move away from the strictly textual and to what cannot be represented – affect, life itself – except in (literary) forms pertains to the characters as well. For although it may be emotionally sentimental at times, *S.* resists recreating humanist characters that may easily reinforce neoliberal subjectivity. *S.* takes seriously the postmodern view of the linguistic construction of the self and its existence in the trace, what Straka's novel calls the self 'rewritten from a lost first draft' (S., p. 126), yet it also insists on the physical embodiment of self and its extra-textual existence as well. It appeals, bioproductively, to 'the head and the heart.' For we do not encounter Eric and Jen as typical characters 'represented to us' or 'fleshed out' via physical descriptions and actions. Indeed, there is no actual narrator of the novel. The characters are only their words in the margins – even to each other for most of the novel – which gives rise to a meta-aware performative aspect to their relationship, which relies on textuality and materiality. Early on, the budding scholar Eric sees textuality as the primary reality. He states that 'books, docs, artifacts … that's where I think the answers are,' whereas Jens reminds him of the world outside of the text: 'Don't forget PEOPLE, Eric. People have answers' (S., p. 14). Eric is also angered that the university has deleted his personal records, and fears that he 'existed only administratively.' But Jen's reply, that this erasure is, 'Part of your history – not part of you,' gestures again to an extra-textual and linguistic reality of being (S., p. 43).

While Eric's postmodern notions of textuality and the self can at times be problematic, so can Jen's naïve belief that the material world is what is truly real. Since the two meet textually in 'the margin world' (S., p. 47), Jen confesses her fear to Eric that 'I don't really know you at all,' to which Eric responds, 'You know me a little, right? There was a time when people relied on letters to get to know each other' (S., p. 51). And later when Jen tells him, '[y]ou don't know anything about me … ,' Eric replies, 'I know the you who's in the margins' (S., p. 83). Eric's comment recalls the deconstructive critique of a metaphysics of presence by pointing out the ways in which 'letters,' in the linguistic sense, have long constructed the self and its (non)existence in the trace. In a sense, we can only ever know the self in the margins of language, but for Eric this eventually becomes not something about which to despair but something in which to have faith. Thus, Jen's later fear before the two finally meet that 'You'd better be real' (S., p. 191), takes on the more figurative meaning that one should 'be real' through the stories that one tells about oneself – since the two eventually recognise how memory and storytelling can be deceptive to self and other but that it is still necessary to tell stories in order to make sense of the world. In the end, the two learn about the necessity and limits of language in the marginal language game that they play, and realise that the stories they tell each other must be sincere and thus require personal faith in, or belief that, the person to whom they are speaking will reciprocate in kind. If the emotionally feel-good post-postmodern novel can unwittingly produce entrepreneurial neoliberal subjectivity, then it also retains the ability to produce new ethical subjectivities that escape this form – ones that are based upon trust and openness.

The gesture as to what lies outside of representation also extends to the characters' feelings and emotions in a way that calls attention to affect as an autonomous, preconscious force. *S.*'s insistence on a reader's nebulous 'feeling' or intuition as forming an affective and productive reading of the text is clearly at odds with *Pale Fire*, in which such a reading (Kinbote's own) is considered to be madness or a wilful misreading. In *S.* Eric and Jen sometimes follow an instinctual 'feeling' in their reading of Straka, as often as they respond to a 'feeling' that the text generates in them. Early on Eric tells Jen that she needs more than a 'feeling' to support her reading (S., p. xiv) and warns her, 'Careful re: linking everything in a book to the author personally. Sometimes fiction's just fiction' (S., p. 17). But Eric learns that the logic and restrictive textual economy of the affective and intentional fallacies, both of which *S.* challenges, has its limits and that an open transaction or circulation of affect between text and reader can challenge them. This culminates in Jen's answer to one of Eric's first reader's notes that, 'Pain is necessarily a private experience,' to which she replies, 'Not if you have the right person with you' (S., p. 182). Jen's empathic comment here is reminiscent of Wittgenstein's dismissal of a 'private language' in his late work and his argument that language is a kind of game that takes place in a physical form of life, not in a solipsistic vacuum: for meaning can only occur in a shared intersubjective space.

In kind, *S.* points to language's failure to codify affect through sense or sensibility by demonstrating the way in which feelings, as both bodily and mental affects, actually 'make' or 'construct' meaning in non-logical ways that should be respected. By the novel's end, Eric and Jen conduct an ethical reading of the mysterious Straka and his one-time lover-turned-editor Caldeira that attends to the affective textual and extra-textual dimensions of identity and knowledge as they resist judging of Straka and accept certitude only in the ambiguity of feeling. This acceptance marks a departure from the paranoid postmodern text – say, as in the search for V. or the elusive Tristero in Thomas Pynchon's *V.* and *The Crying of Lot 49*, respectively, which the search for 'S' echoes – as the paranoia of conspiracy subsides when Eric and Jen embrace the limits of knowledge and opt out of the chase.[42] In this context, Jen's final note tells Eric to 'put the book down. Come in here and stay,' to which he replies putting the novel's last word under erasure, serves not as a playful postmodern game but as a reminder what language cannot represent. In the end, what remains open to the couple thanks to their appreciation of affect and extra-textual materiality is potentially new forms of feeling and being (together) that escape hegemonic, or even postmodern counter-hegemonic, discourse.

As an example of metaffective fiction, then, *S.* deals in emotion and sentiment in a way that both invites and frustrates readerly identification with the characters by self-consciously calling attention to the textual and extra-textual material capacities of affect and its potentiality as an autonomous, transmittable, and communal force. The marginal notes, inscribed in each character's unique handwriting, sometimes underlined, written in bold, or punctuated with exclamation marks that typify emotional cadence, points to a kind of bio-productive fiction that testifies to the importance of affect generated off, and in part by, the page. That there is a world that exists off the page, so to speak, one that lies outside official records, suggests the potential of affect to escape or to challenge even a neoliberal affective economy that attempts to capture it and put it to work through the production of neoliberal subjects and high-tech products. After all, Eric has stolen his copy of Straka's novel, pulled it out of official, institutional circulation, where it has become a covert, pilfered object that generates surplus affects outside of any specific system. The cliché that books can change the world is thus actualised by the novel's metaffective, formally self-conscious production and transmission of transpersonal affects that emerge as pure potentiality as we trace the live circuit from word to world and back again.

Notes

1. See Stephen Burn's *Jonathan Franzen at the End of Postmodernism* (New York: Continuum, 2008); Robert McLaughlin's, 'Post-Postmodernism', in Joe Bray, Alison Gibbons, and Brian McHale (eds.), *The Routledge Companion to Experimental Literature* (New York: Routledge, 2012), pp. 212–23; and Mary Holland's *Succeeding Postmodernism* (New York: Bloomsbury Academic, 2013), which argues that contemporary literature marks 'a return to affect' because it bends antihumanist postmodern and poststructural theories toward the 'humanist ends of generating empathy, communal bonds, ethical and political questions, and, most basically, communicable meaning' (pp. 8, 17). In another vein, see Adam Kelly's, 'David Foster Wallace and the New Sincerity in American Fiction', in David Herring (ed.), *Consider David Foster Wallace: Critical Essays* (Los Angeles, CA: SSMG Press, 2010), pp. 131–46; and Lee Konstantinou's *Cool Characters: Irony and American Fiction* (Cambridge, MA: Harvard, 2016). What each of these critical views shares, either pointedly or more broadly, is an interest in the particular emotional and affective dimensions of post-postmodernist literature, whether because of its return to more fully realised or 'human' characters that validate the individual (Burn and McLaughlin), its potentially reconstructive empathic humanism (Holland), its desire for sincere and open dialogic communication with the reader (Kelly), or its 'post-ironic' ethos of belief and re-enchantment with the world (Konstantinou). See David Cowart's *The Tribe of Pyn: Literary Generations in The Postmodern Period* (Ann Arbor: University of Michigan, 2015) for an enlightening look at the complex influence of postmodern writers upon their successors that challenges a simple top down model of influence. Cowart's conclusion, for instance, even considers the younger generation's influence upon the older, as well the continuing function of irony in contemporary fiction and culture, and stresses the continuities between generations rather than

positing any clear break – or even the end of postmodernism (192–200). For a consideration of first generation postmodernists' responses to their supposed 'end', see my essay 'The End of Postmodernism', in Stephen J. Burn (ed.), *American Literature in Transition: 1990–2000* (New York: Cambridge UP, 2017), pp. 91–104.

2. For early post-postmodern 'manifestos,' see David Foster Wallace's, 'E Unibus Pluram: Television and U.S. Fiction', in *A Supposedly Fun Thing I'll Never Do Again* (Boston, MA: Little, Brown, 1997), pp. 21–82 and 'An Interview with David Foster Wallace', *Review of Contemporary Fiction*, 13.2 (1993), pp. 127–50; Jonathan Franzen's, 'I'll Be Doing More of the Same', *Review of Contemporary Fiction*, 16.1 (1996), pp. 34–8 and 'Why Bother?', in *How to Be Alone* (New York: Farrar, Straus & Giroux, 2002), pp. 55–97; and William T. Vollmann's, 'American Writing Today: Diagnosis of the Disease', *Conjunctions*, 15 (1990), pp. 355–58. For a later but related take, see Zadie Smith's 'Two Paths for the Novel', *The New York Review of Books* (November, 2008). http://www.nybooks.com/articles/2008/11/20/two-paths-for-the-novel/ [Date accessed: 15 November 2016].
3. Robert McLaughlin, 'Post-Postmodern Discontent: Contemporary Fiction and the Social', *symplokē*, 12 (2004), pp. 53–68 (p. 67).
4. Rachel Greenwald Smith, *Affect and American Literature in the Age of Neoliberalism* (New York: Cambridge, 2015), p. 1.
5. Ibid., p. 2.
6. Ibid., p. 59.
7. Pieter Vermeulen's, *Contemporary Literature and the End of the Novel* (Basingstoke: Palgrave-Macmillan, 2015) also employs a theoretically informed view of affect to argue that American and British contemporary 'fictions dramatise the end of the novel in order to reimagine the politics and ethics of form in the twenty-first century' (p. 2).
8. Brian Massumi, *Parables for the Virtual: Movement, Affect, Sensation* (Durham, NC: Duke, 2002), p. 27.
9. Ibid., p. 28.
10. Deleuzian/Spinozist takes on affect are well represented in Massumi and the collections mentioned below. These collections also contain essays drawing upon Sylvan Tompkins' work on affect. For more work in Tompkins' vein, see Eve Kosofsky Sedgewick's *Touching Feeling: Affect, Pedagogy, Performativity* (Durham, NC: Duke, 2003). See Lauren Berlant's *Cruel Optimism* (Durham, NC: Duke, 2001) and other works for a take on negative affects and public feelings. For a work that blends affect and emotion into an analysis of 'feeling' see Sianne N'Gai's *Ugly Feelings* (Cambridge, MA: Harvard, 2005).
11. Michael Hardt, 'Foreword: What Affects are Good For', in Patricia Ticineto Clough (ed.), *The Affective Turn: Theorizing the Social* (Durham, NC: Duke, 2007), pp. ix–xii (p. ix).
12. Melissa Gregg and Gregory J. Seigworth, 'Introduction', in Melissa Gregg and Gregory J. Seigworth (eds.), *The Affect Theory Reader* (Durham, NC: Duke, 2010), pp. 1–25 (p. 1).
13. Massumi, *Parables for the Virtual*, p. 29.
14. Ibid., pp. 28–9.
15. Patricia Waugh, *Metafiction: The Theory and Practice of Self-Conscious Fiction* (New York: Routledge, 1984), p. 2.

16. See also Maurizio Lazzarato's, 'Immaterial Labor', in Paolo Virno and Michael Hardt (eds.), *Radical Thought in Italy: A Potential Politics* (Minneapolis: University of Minnesota Press, 1996), pp. 133–46.
17. Michael Hardt and Antonio Negri, *Multitude: War and Democracy in the Age of Empire* (New York: Penguin, 2004), pp. 103–15.
18. Ibid., p. 146.
19. Michael Hardt and Antonio Negri, *Commonwealth* (Cambridge, MA: Harvard UP, 2009), p. 142.
20. Ibid., pp. 135–6.
21. Gilles Deleuze and Félix Guattari, *What is Philosophy?* trans. Hugh Tomlinson and Graham Burchell (New York: Columbia UP, 1996), pp. 65, 165.
22. Hardt and Negri, *Commonwealth*, pp. 132, 133.
23. Patricia Ticineto Clough, 'The Affective Turn: Political Economy, Biomedia, and Bodies', *The Affect Theory Reader*, pp. 206–25 (p. 209).
24. See D. Barton Johnson's, *Worlds in Regression: Some Novels of Vladimir Nabokov* (Ann Arbor, MI: Ardis, 1985) for an in-depth examination of Nabokov's complex linguistic-formal play and especially his literary development of synaesthesia via a personalised colour alphabet; his frequent use of anagrams; and his construction of plots and themes on the model of chess problems. See also Nabokov's discussion of letters and colours in *Speak, Memory: An Autobiography Revisited* (New York: Putnam, 1966), pp. 34–5.
25. Brian Boyd, *Nabokov's* Pale Fire: *The Magic of Artistic Discovery* (Princeton, NJ: Princeton UP, 2001), pp. 107–26. Boyd provides a comprehensive account of the critical debates between the Shadeans, Kinboteans, and others who attempted for decades to solve the novel's riddle.
26. Boyd's *Nabokov's* Pale Fire: *The Magic of Artistic Discovery* is a fascinating book that argues the case for a hitherto unseen ontological textual element in which ghosts and butterflies covertly prompt various characters – the primary textual evidence being various literary allusions and anagrams of certain butterfly species – to commit certain actions that invisibly link the here and the hereafter, so that the randomness and disconnected nature of life and text are made whole and harmonious in an invisible realm that only Shade's poem [and Nabokov's novel] can speculate upon.
27. Vladimir Nabokov, *Pale Fire* (New York: Vintage, 1989).
28. Vladimir Nabokov, *Strong Opinions* (New York: Vintage, 1989), p. 16.
29. Vladimir Nabokov, 'Preface', in *Bend Sinister* (New York: Time Life Books, 1967), p. xvii.
30. See Gavriel Shapiro's, 'Setting his Myriad Faces in His Text: Nabokov's Authorial Presence Revisited', in Julian W. Connolly (ed.), *Nabokov and His Fiction: New Perspectives* (New York: Cambridge, UP, 1999), pp. 15–35.
31. Nabokov, *Bend Sinister*, p. 94.
32. Nabokov, *Strong Opinions*, p. 40.
33. Ibid., p. 18.
34. Nabokov, 'Preface' in *Bend Sinister*, p. xvii.
35. See Leland de La Durntaye's excellent, 'The Pattern of Cruelty and the Cruelty of Pattern in Vladimir Nabokov', *The Cambridge Quarterly*, 35.4 (2006), pp. 301–26, which explores the critical and reader reaction to the various forms of 'cruelty' in Nabokov's work. I do not wish to perpetuate that myth of Nabokov as merely an unfeeling stylist here but to point out that the cool and arrogant side of Nabokov, while blown out of proportion, nevertheless retains

a few grains of salty truth. Thus while, as William W. Rowe writes, Nabokov's puzzles are based upon an 'honest deception' that is 'scrupulous' because the intentional misleading of the reader is simply what a novel calculated like a chess problem ought to do ('The Honesty of Nabokovian Deception, in Carl R. Proffer (ed.), *A Book of Things About Vladimir Nabokov* (Ann Arbor, MI: Ardis, 1974), pp. 171–81 [pp. 179–80]), this does not foreclose on what Maurice Courturier notes is the 'near tyranny' of Nabokov's godlike 'authorial figure' or his intentional prodding of his readers inability to solve his riddles ('The near-tyranny of the author: *Pale Fire*' in *Nabokov and his Fiction*, pp. 54–72 [p. 71]).

36. Vladimir Nabokov, *Speak, Memory*, p. 35.
37. Briefly, Nabokov's metaphysics, which is expansive and fairly optimistic, recognises the human limits of consciousness and knowledge while accepting the possibility of something – an afterlife or other plane of existence – beyond the known world(s). Since nature and reality are deceptive, full of duplications and duplicity, there is no reason to think that our species, caught up in patterns and designs not of our making, is not subject to a hidden order(er) just as characters in fiction are. As a result, one ought to revel in the particulars and patterns of life rather than accept generalities and pre-made categories, thus embracing the private (experience) over the common(sense). A succinct summary of Nabokov's metaphysics appears in Brian Boyd's *Stalking Nabokov* (New York: Columbia UP, 2011), pp. 57–68. In *Nabokov's* Pale Fire: *The Magic of Artistic Discovery* Boyd writes: 'the generosity of his [Nabokov's] method is more than a matter of method, for it reflects the generosity of his metaphysics, his hunch that the world itself sets before us the possibility and pleasures of endless discovery, inexhaustible excitement, which far from stopping even at death might then merely shift into a higher gear' (p. 247). See David S. Rutledge's *Nabokov's Permanent Mystery: The Expression of Metaphysics in His Work* (Jefferson, NC McFarland, 2011) for a similar defence against the 'mystery' of Nabokov's cosmic vision even as scholars begin to elucidate it.
38. Greenwald Smith's *Affect and American Literature in the Age of Neoliberalism* ends with a consideration of the environment and nonhuman ecologies (pp. 100–130). Vermeulen's *Contemporary Fiction and the End of the Novel* considers the anthropocene and nonhuman scale (pp. 137–52).
39. While Nabokov easily lends himself to Darwinian and evolutionary scientific readings – see Johnson and Coates,' *Nabokov's Blues: The Literary Odyssey of a Scientific Genius* (Cambridge, MA: Zoland, 1999) and Boyd's Pale Fire: *The Magic of Artistic Discovery* (pp. 233–62) – there remains the potential to read Nabokov through chaos theory as well.
40. I owe this point about the book's relation to the ship of Theseus paradox to the editors of this issue, Christopher K. Coffman and Theo Savvas.
41. Doug Dorst and J. J. Abrams, *S.* (New York: Mulholland, 2013), p. 149. (All other references to this edition are given using the abbreviation S. in parentheses).
42. Courtney Jacobs considers *S.*'s move away from postmodern paranoia in 'Rekindling Metaphysical Insight: The Many faces of *S*', *EAPSU Online: A Journal of Critical and Creative Work* (fall, 2014), pp. 47–57.

Disclosure statement

No potential conflict of interest was reported by the author.

Entropology and the end of nature in Lance Olsen's *Theories of Forgetting*

Alison Gibbons

ABSTRACT

In *Tristes Tropiques*, Lévi-Strauss coins the term 'entropology', a lexical blend of 'entropy' and 'anthropology' signifying that the study of humankind is always, necessarily, the study of humankind's transformative (disruptive, corrosive) impact. This article traces entropology as an aesthetic practice through Robert Smithson's Earthwork, particularly the *Spiral Jetty*, and into twenty-first century ecoliterature. At the heart of the article is an analysis of Lance Olsen's contemporary fiction *Theories of Forgetting*, focusing on the interconnected portrayals of human fragility and the environment. *Theories of Forgetting* embodies entropology both in its material poetics and as a thematic trope. By representing the entropological inseparability of the fates of humankind and the natural world, the novel casts contemporary human life paradoxically as both destructive and vulnerable. These affects subsequently require the characteristically metamodern renewal of historical thinking by bringing into focus the impact of humanity's past and present actions on the future.

In his travel memoir *Tristes Tropiques* (originally published in English as *World on the Wane*), Lévi-Strauss documents his encounters with tribes in Brazil. Writing in the midst of the twentieth century, Lévi-Strauss also contemplates the role of the anthropologist, regretful of how contact between cultures is inevitably erosive and mindful of humanity's existence in the universe:

> The world began without man and will end without him. [...] From the time when he first began to breathe and eat, up to the invention of atomic and thermonuclear devices, by way of the discovery of fire – and except when he has been engaged in self-reproduction – what else has man done except blithely break down billions of structures and reduce them to a state in which they are no longer capable of integration? No doubt he has built towns and cultivated the land; yet, on reflection, urbanisation and agriculture are themselves instruments intended to create inertia, at a rate and in a proportion infinitely

> higher than the amount of organisation they involve. As for creations of the human mind, their significance only exists in relation to it, and they will merge into the general chaos, as soon as the human mind has disappeared. Thus it is that civilisation, taken as a whole, can be described as an extraordinarily complex mechanism, which we might be tempted to see as offering an opportunity of survival for the human world, if its function were not to produce what physicists call entropy, that is inertia. Every verbal exchange, every line printed, established communication between people, thus creating an evenness of level, where before there was an information gap and consequently a greater degree of organisation. Anthropology could with advantage be changed into 'entropology', as the name of the discipline concerned with the study of the highest manifestations of this process of disintegration.[1]

Entropy refers in physics – specifically, the second law of thermodynamics – to a directional spread of energy whereby concentrated or localized, and therefore potentially powerful, energy is dispersed or diffused, for instance when ice melts to water or when a hot object (like a saucepan) cools down. Drawing on the language of entropy, Stanley Diamond glosses Lévi-Strauss' comments as the 'prediction of the ultimate thermodynamic leveling of all culture'[2] whilst James Clifford similarly speaks of 'the prophetic disintegration of all real cultural differences'.[3] Still, Lévi-Strauss intends not to extend 'entropy' through the addition of the suffix '–ology' (meaning: the disciplinary study of entropy), but for his coinage, 'entropology', to be understood as a lexical blend of 'entropy' and 'anthropology'. In this way, Lévi-Strauss suggests that the study of humankind is always, necessarily, the study of humankind's transformative (disruptive, corrosive) impact. Thus, the fate of 'the human mind' is intimately intertwined with the fate of local cultures, human civilization as a whole, and the greater cosmos.

Cultural contact and the development of civilisations are certainly Lévi-Strauss's foci, yet his mention of humankind's acts of breathing and eating and of 'urbanisation and agriculture' suggests humanity's draining of the Earth's natural resources whilst 'the invention of atomic and thermonuclear devices' alludes to the fall-out from nuclear testing happening concurrent to his writing. This human impact on the Earth may not have been Lévi-Strauss's primary concern, but his remarks nevertheless prefigure growing anxiety in the late twentieth and early twenty-first centuries about the planetary cost of humanity's development.

Take 1989, often seen as a watershed moment – a transition from a dominant postmodern culture to its emergent aftermath[4]: As the Berlin Wall fell, the Cold War ended, and Communism in Eastern Europe collapsed, cultural commentators – led most prominently by Francis Fukuyama – declared 'the end of History'.[5] Yet at the same time, environmentalists and climatologists were warning that humanity had also reached 'the end of nature'.[6] Just as Fukuyama's declaration did not simply mean that chronological time had expired or that the event was a thing of the past, when Bill McKibben lamented nature's end, he was not suggesting that natural forces would cease or that the Earth's cycles would come to a standstill. Like Fukuyama's, McKibben's argument entailed a fundamental conceptual shift:

> [...] we are at the end of nature.
>
> By the end of nature I do not mean the end of the world. The rain will still fall and the sun shine, though differently than before. When I say "nature," I mean a certain set of human ideas about the concrete changes in the reality around us —changes that scientists can measure and enumerate. More and more frequently, these changes will clash with our perceptions, until, finally, our sense of nature as eternal and separate is washed away, and we will see all too clearly what we have done.[7]

Nature, McKibben argued, could no longer be understood as an autonomous, perpetual force. It could no longer be considered independent of humankind but as having suffered as a consequence of human evolution.

These pronouncements of 'endings' now seem symptomatic of a certain postmodern form of critical thinking: postmodernism entailed the end of history, the end of nature, the end – in Lyotard's conceptualisation – of all metanarratives.[8] Yet, whilst the end of history has since been subject to a rethink,[9] in contrast the end of nature has gathered steam with climate scientists arguing that we have entered a new moment in planetary time. Precisely because of human damage to the earth and its atmosphere, Paul J. Crutzen and Eugene F. Stoermer claim that it is 'more than appropriate to emphasize the central role of mankind in geology and ecology by proposing to use the term "anthropocene" for the current geological epoch'.[10] As climate change demonstrates, humankind's 'central role' has thus far borne out Lévi-Strauss's theory: it has been entropological. The validity of the 'anthropocene' has been widely accepted by climate scientists and humanities scholars alike. Consequently, as a conceptual frame it has become loaded with significance; particularly in cultural studies and the arts, it has come to stand not only for a geological age, but a social age too – a conceptual move facilitated by interconnections between climate change, late capitalism, and global politics.[11] In this respect, the idea of the anthropocene is a vital facet of any conceptualisation of the aftermath of postmodernism.

I interpret the anthropocene, however, not as the *de facto* zeitgeist but as a contributing component within a more complex configuration of contemporary crises – of environment, of financial instability, of social inequality, of political conflict, of terrorism, of technology, and others – that together, relatedly, engender a new cultural sensibility. As such, my thinking develops alongside van den Akker and Vermeulen's paradigm of the metamodern in which climate change plays its part within a socio-political context, brought about by global neoliberalism, where 'wealth is concentrated at the top 1 per cent of the pyramid, while rising sea levels and super storms crumble its base, where the rest of us reside in highly precarious conditions'.[12] Even so, this is not to deny the important role of the environmental crisis: perhaps more than these other afore-mentioned crises, the sense of the end of nature – the fundamental, entropological inseparability of the fates of humankind and the natural world – produce an experience of contemporary human life paradoxically as both destructive and vulnerable. These affects subsequently require the renewal of historical thinking by bringing into focus the impact of humanity's past and present actions on the future.

This article uses entropology as a lens with which to read Lance Olsen's contemporary fiction *Theories of Forgetting*.[13] The analysis concentrates on the interconnected portrayals of human fragility and the environment, demonstrating that *Theories of Forgetting* embodies entropology in both its material poetics and as a thematic trope. Reflecting on the analysis, the article suggests that the novel expresses a metamodern (or post-postmodern) sensibility, largely because the entropological aesthetic of *Theories of Forgetting* regenerates historicity. First, though, the article discusses entropology (including entropy) as aesthetic, starting with its appearance in Robert Smithson's Earthwork and subsequently emerging as a mode of twenty-first century literary ecopoetics.

Entropology as a contemporary aesthetic

Lévi-Strauss's concept of entropology was first taken up as aesthetic theme and practice by twentieth century artist Robert Smithson, who felt that Lévi-Strauss offered 'a good insight'.[14] Entropology became the *raison d'être* of Smithson's work and writings before his untimely death in a plane crash in 1973.[15] Smithson originally discusses the scientific notion of entropy in a 1966 essay – 'Entropy and the New Monuments' – about the minimalist sculpture of Donald Judd, Robert Morris, Sol LeWitt, and Dan Flavin, amongst others. Smithson views their works as a celebration 'of entropy by telling us energy is more easily lost that obtained, and that in the ultimate future the whole universe will burn out and be transformed into an all-encompassing sameness'.[16] He continues:

> Instead of causing us to remember the past like the old monuments, the new monuments seem to cause us to forget the future. Instead of being made of natural materials, such as marble, granite, or other kinds of rock, the new monuments are made of artificial materials, plastic, chrome, and electric light. They are not built for the ages, but rather against the ages.[17]

As a radical reaction against modernism, minimalist art marked – in Hal Foster's words – 'a paradigm shift toward postmodernist practices'.[18] This seems apparent in Smithson's description of sculpture that sits out of time, blacking out the future, and which – in its use of artificial materials – is cold, depthless, and antianthropomorphic. Thus, these works – and

Smithson's interpretation of them – fit neatly within Fredric Jameson's typology of the postmodern as the loss of historicity, the lack of depth, and the waning of affect.[19]

In parallel in the literary sphere, the concept of entropy was an 'all-important' aesthetic strategy of postmodernist fiction between the 1960s-1980s, as Hoffman evidences[20] with reference to the work of Thomas Pynchon,[21] Kurt Vonnegut,[22] and John Barth.[23] To these names can be added William Gaddis who, in 1981, considered entropy 'as the central preoccupation of our time'.[24] Furthermore, Hoffman argues that in *Gravity's Rainbow*, Pynchon presents an 'entropic, beyond-history view of time, a destructive mode of presentism'.[25] Hoffman's analysis of the aesthetics of postmodernist fiction resonates with Smithson's view of minimalist sculpture. Taken together, they demonstrate the prevalence of entropy as a dominant postmodernist sentiment that expresses flatness, fragmentation, and artificiality as well as a lack of futuricity.

Although often categorised as an off-shoot of the minimalist tradition, Earthworks (also known as Land Art or Earth Art) – being made, precisely, *of* natural materials – embody a different aesthetic. Smithson increasingly practiced Earthwork and his most famous piece, the *Spiral Jetty*, tends to be viewed as the 'poster' work of the movement. Smithson's *Spiral Jetty* was built in April 1970 at the Great Salt Lake in Utah. Constructed from mud, salt crystals, water, and black basalt rocks from the shore, the Jetty (originally fifteen-hundred-feet-long and fifteen-feet-wide) moves out from the shoreline before spiralling in an anti-clockwise direction. Its ecological materiality produces a powerful anthropomorphic impact, foregrounding man's place in the physical world by locating the human subject in the centre of its spiral.

Not only does the *Spiral Jetty* emphasise the relationship between man and the environment, the anti-clockwise direction of the spiral places the viewer in an important relationship with time:

> Walking from the shore to the centre, following the spiral of the artwork, the viewer travels in an anti-clockwise direction. This suggests a movement backwards in time. Thus Smithson invites the viewer to ponder geological time as he or she stands on the rocks and earth of the spiral and look out at the lake and the surrounding landscape. The viewer is also invited to think about cosmological time as the shape recalls the spirals of galaxies. In 1970, a year after the first moon landing, outer space and our place within it was at the forefront of consciousness.[26]

Smithson saw the Great Salt Lake as a landscape encapsulating 'prehistory' and the *Spiral Jetty* as creating an 'entropic situation': it 'is physical enough to withstand all these climate changes, yet it's intimately involved with those climate changes and natural disturbances. That's why I'm not really interested in conceptual art because that seems to avoid physical mass' (moments later in this interview, Smithson recalls Lévi-Straus's coinage).[27]

The climate changes to which Smithson refers are the natural rising and falling of water levels at the Great Salt Lake: the Jetty thus develops salt crystals over time and the processes of submergence and re-emergence ultimately produce an erosive effect on its structure. Moreover, despite being built at a remote site (at one time it was only viewable from the air, but it is now possible to drive there, albeit off-road), human visitors who reach and walk across the jetty (kicking up rocks in the process) will inevitably disrupt its shape. The *Spiral Jetty*'s environmental make-up is thus subject to the disintegrating logics of geological time and human time: through the Jetty's materiality and metaphysicality as an endangered artifact, its dual logics simultaneously evoke the past as well as drawing the future into sharper focus.

Earthwork and the aesthetic of entropology seem out of kilter with the dominant culture from which they originate. Rather than sitting neatly within a postmodernist paradigm, they hold contemporary resonance, particularly with regards to historicity and affect. Not only has Levi-Strauss's concept continued to bear critical weight in studies of cultural anthropology in the twenty-first century,[28] but both Earthworks and the aesthetic of entropology have strong on-going artistic and literary traditions. Contemporary Earthwork and environmentally conscious twenty-first century art includes Chris Drury's numerous works outside (for instance, *Heart of Reeds*), Daniel McCormick's *The Watershed: An Ecological Installation*, David Maisel's aerial photographs (particularly the *American Mine* and *The Lake Project*), and James Turrell's *Roden Crater* (although the land was purchased in 1979, the project only came to completion in the twenty-first century).[29]

In literary studies, eco-criticism, eco-literature, and eco-poetics have flourished since the 1980s[30] and, unsurprisingly, it is in this realm that 'entropology' resurfaces. Dissatisfied with 'eco-poetics' as too broad a term, Jonathan Skinner proposes four subcategories, each defined by their relationship to the natural world and by their stylistic traits. Skinner's third category is '*entropological* poetics' (original emphasis) which, acknowledging Robert Smithson as the stimulus, Skinner describes as:

> [A] practice engaged at the level of materials and processes, where entropy, transformation and decay are part of the creative work. Any "concrete" writing focused primarily on procedures of the letter might fall into this category [...] but also other kinds of "writing" that involve marking the land or natural processes and that might more properly be considered under the rubric of visual arts.[31]

These concrete or land-based literary works would, obviously, still need to be thematically interested in the environment. Skinner's category of entropological poetics appears to uphold, relatively faithfully, the sentiment behind

Smithson's aesthetic employment of Levi-Strauss's concept in that form and content, style and substance, are allied in their engagement with ecological concerns. Although *Theories of Forgetting* is a novel (rather than a work of poetry), it most certainly possesses an entropological aesthetic. This is perhaps unavoidable, since Alana, one of the central characters, is making a film about Smithson's *Spiral Jetty*: his Earthwork is therefore an explicit stimulus for Olsen's novel too and the term 'entropology' is presented in Alana's documentation of Smithson's praise for Levi-Strauss's concept.[32]

Olsen's *Theories of Forgetting* is not alone as a contemporary novel inspired by Earthwork, Land Artists, and/or the environment. Rachel Kushner's *The Flamethrowers* (2014), for instance, features a young art school graduate in the 1970s who, impressed by Smithson's *Spiral Jetty*, wants to create her own Earthwork.[33] The Salton Sea—a lake formed accidentally in 1905 from the overflow of water from the Colorado River, which was initially idyllic but now (resulting from rising salt, selenium, and pesticides) seems more like a shrinking toxic soup where sea life and water birds are dying—and the nearby Salvation Mountain appear in novels such as Gayle Brandeis's *The Book of Dead Birds* (2003), Marisa Silver's *The God of War* (2008), and William T. Vollmann's *The Royal Family* (2000) and his non-fiction *Imperial* (2009).[34] Like *Theories of Forgetting*, such works engage with the theme of entropology and, in doing so, can be read as anthropocene fictions[35] – an archetypal metamodern genre (or, at least, a twenty-first century literary trend that resonates beyond the postmodern) – presenting 'challenges to twentieth-century modes of narrative' because they 'successfully reconfigure the historical relationship between fiction and truth-telling; alter assumptions of how humans relate to place; reimagine social and political organisation; or rearticulate the global, mechanised, consumer economies of the twenty-first century'.[36]

In *Theories of Forgetting*, Lance Olsen utilizes both form and content to engage with the environment and human existence. The importance of form for Olsen is evidenced in his decision to take an additional six months to complete *Theories of Forgetting* in order to learn to use the computer programme InDesign so that he could lay out the pages.[37] Furthermore, Olsen views the materiality of the literary text, what he calls its 'architectonics', as politically expressive:

> So-called experimental fiction teaches us a fundamental political lesson over and over again, as much through its structural complications as through its thematics: that the text of the text, the text of our lives, and the text of the world can and should be other than they are.[38]

Both the innovative form of *Theories of Forgetting* as well as its narrative content are crucial to its entropological poetics, as the ensuing analysis demonstrates.

Entropological poetics in *Theories of Forgetting*

The innovative formal design of *Theories of Forgetting* is immediately obvious to readers: you pick up *Theories of Forgetting* and realise that you are looking at the back cover (featuring synopsis, endorsement, author bio, cover credits, and barcode) so you turn it over, only to find on the other side the same identical back cover flipped 180 degrees. Looking at the inside pages offers little clarity: both sides include title, copyright pages, and dedication, leading to the start of the narrative(s) proper. The covers are, ultimately, designed to create confusion and disorientation (manifesting the forgetfulness of the novel's title): it's simply not clear which is the front and which is the back, and therefore at which side of the book you should start reading.

The novel itself is composed of three narratives. There is the first-person diary (presented in Adobe Garamond Pro typeface) of Alana, a middle-aged filmmaker who is making a documentary about Robert Smithson's *Spiral Jetty*, and who is suffering from an epidemic disease; starting at the other side of the book is a third-person narrative (presented in American Typewriter font) of a character referred to as 'the man' but who – through his memories of scenes that also appear in Alana's diary – readers are likely to interpret as Hugh, Alana's husband, who journeys from their home in Utah across Europe and then into the Middle East following his wife's death, as he seems simultaneously to try to remember and to forget. Each narrative starts where the other ends and crosses in the middle, and each page features both (at 180 degree angles to each other).[39] Finally, the third narrative takes the form of blue marginalia throughout the book (realised in Georges typeface, designed to look like handwriting), penned by Alana and Hugh's daughter Aila, an art critic working in Berlin, seemingly addressed to her brother.

Olsen has acknowledged Robert Smithson's 'astounding' Earthwork, *Spiral Jetty*, as the 'formal influence' and 'shape that most influenced the writing of *Theories* both in terms of structure and content'; the placement of the narratives on the pages and the relationships between them therefore 'take the contours of a kind of spiral spinning in on itself'.[40] The book's design, therefore, not only offers readers – as Joe Sacksteder puts it – 'the literary equivalent of walking the Jetty',[41] it is central to the novel's entropological poetics, capturing the integrative and disintegrative nature of human relationships and human life within the book as a metaphorical instantiation of an Earthwork landscape. The three narratives come together in *Theories of Forgetting* to produce a whole, and that whole can be read as a kind of complex system – in this case, a family – but through the course of the novel that system becomes more dispersed, disintegrating: Alana's narrative leads ultimately to her death; Hugh's to his reactionary, mysterious disappearance in Jordan; whilst Aila's marginal comments appear to echo into a silent void as she addresses questions to a brother – about her mother's condition and father's disappearance – who never seems to reply (at least, not in writing within the novel).

Moreover, the concrete realisation of the novel, its material type, also disintegrates: in Alana's narrative, the text and images (such as photos of the *Spiral Jetty*) turn from black to grey at the end; in Hugh's, the type pale from the start perhaps as a result of his grief, fewer and fewer words appear until the final page shows only an incomplete 3-word fragment. Yuriy Taranawsky consequently describes the relationship between Alana and Hugh's narratives as:

> [...] strong and clear contrasting with weak and fuzzy at the beginning and the other way around at the end, alluding to the inevitable process in nature for everything that is born—you start out strong and fade out to nothing in the end.[42]

Another way to put this, of course, is that the book design and narrative structure work together entropologically. Whilst they represent the environment, taking the form of Smithson's Earthwork, they also demonstrate that human life – emotional and physical – is entropic, always in the process of disintegration from birth to inevitable death.

The next two subsections of this article analyse Olsen's portrayal of human fragility and the environment in *Theories of Forgetting*. Whilst treating each theme in turn, the analysis ultimately shows them to be intimately, entropologically, connected.

Human fragility in the world: 'it's just the way it is living inside a human body'

From Alana's first diary entry, *Theories of Forgetting*'s preoccupation with the fragility of the human body and mind is evident:

> 21 June
>
> Something is happening to me.
>
> I wasn't sure at first. Now I am. A glary gray migraine aura. A sheet of plastic lowering between me & me.
>
> The same sort of feeling when you suspect flu has begun scattering through your bloodstream: the peculiar ache behind your eyes, the poisonous ghost at the back of your throat :::: and then again, you say to yourself, maybe you've just worn yourself down lately. It happens. Maybe all you need is a glass of orange juice, some extra sleep, a handful of echinacea.[43]

Lexis relating illness to the body is rife in this opening: 'migraine', 'flu', and 'ache' are complemented by 'bloodstream', 'eyes', and 'back of your throat'. Alana's uncertainty about how to interpret these physical symptoms is communicated by the abstract noun '[s]omething' and by the epistemic modality of the verb phrases 'wasn't sure' and 'suspect' and the repeated adverb 'maybe'. Her uncertainty is, moreover, emphasised by vocabulary that possesses more mystic connotations – such as 'aura' and 'poisonous ghost' as well as the self-estranging metaphor 'A sheet of plastic lowering between me & me' – and these insinuate that Alana may be suffering from a somewhat more ominous illness than 'migraine' or 'flu'. Even so, Alana dismisses such an interpretation, self-reflexively prescribing herself commonplace treatments ('orange juice', 'sleep', 'echinacea'). In this opening passage, then, Olsen emphasises that the human body is an imperfect system, continually struggling to ward off disintegration in the form of disease and sickness, and that experience is fragmented between body and mind.

Also present in Alana's opening diary entry is a strange cluster of four semicolons '::::'. Olsen won a fellowship at the American Academy in Berlin to write *Theories of Forgetting*. At the same time and also published concurrently, Olsen produced a small book, described in its cover synopsis as 'part critical meditation and part trash diary', called *[[there.]]*. In it, Olsen questions 'why we should stop at 14 punctuation marks in English' and goes on to suggest the addition of two new punctuation marks, one of which – '::::' – represents 'what cannot be articulated accurately'.[44] The punctuation mark in Alana's opening diary thus adds to Olsen's representation of psychosomatic fragmentation: the mind is unable to necessarily comprehend or articulate the symptoms experienced by the body.

Over the course of the novel, Alana's health deteriorates. From this strange foreboding of indecipherable illness, Alana's fingertips repeatedly prickle, the tingling sensation spreading to her hands. Trying to make sense of it, she lists various conditions in her diary – Carpal Tunnel Syndrome, Dupuytren's Contracture, Focal Dystonia or Writer's Cramp, Ganglion Cysts, Nerve Injuries, Neuropathy, Tendonitis – eventually telling her husband Hugh and consulting doctors. Alana's preoccupation with her ailing hands extends to the images she includes: x-rays of hands (perhaps her own during the medical testing process), drawings of hands, and sign language instructions. It is, of course, significant that Olsen chose hands as the starting point for Alana's mysterious disease, as another diary entry insinuates:

> 13 July
>
> The hand is the primary organ for manipulating the human environment.
>
> 29 major and minor bones, 29 major joints, 123 named ligaments, 34 muscles responsible for moving the fingers, 48 named nerves, 30 arteries.
>
> Our fingernails are in reality modified hairs.

> Our sense of ~~torch~~ touch is intimately associated with our ~~houn~~ hands, which can form fists, point, prod, emphasize, draw, hold, make, brandish, type, play, pat, signal, stroke, sign, salute, caress, warn, high five, wave hello and goodbye.[45]

This entry similarly links body and mind: it features biomedical information and the list of action verbs, which characterise what hands can physically do, implies a range of human intentions. The final verb in the list – 'wave hello and goodbye' – is perhaps most meaningful since it suggests the role of hands in creating human relationships. Moreover, since the hand is 'the primary organ for manipulating the human environment', Alana's illness can thus be perceived as entropological in that it symbolizes a breakdown not only in human interaction but also in human engagement with the world.

Alana's condition also affects the clarity of her mind, with misspellings and text placed under erasure becoming representative of her state of cognitive disintegration. Initially, these mistakes are few-and-far between, and might appear (as those in the above diary entry) as errors or amendments made during the writing process. However, these slippages increase across the novel with Alana's mortal decline. As such, Olsen's material, concrete-poetic realisation of Alana's deteriorating mental health inscribes a form of neurological realism into the text.[46] At times, Olsen's wordplay also places Alana's condition in relation to the environment, for instance when Alana's diary quotes Hugh's statement 'Wait and see' in error, initially, as '~~Wit and sea~~'.[47] Alana's disease, both in its physical symptoms and cognitive consequences, is, therefore, a metaphor for the entropological relationship between humankind and the Earth.

Alana is not, in fact, suffering alone. Newspaper clippings extracted in Alana's diary contextualise her illness first as an epidemic and eventually as a pandemic – according to the World Health Organization (WHO) – with the widespread contagion of the pandemic made clear from the rising death counts, categorised according to world geography (starting in Canada and moving across the world), also provided by Alana.[48] In her diary, Alana reveals the name for this disease: 'The Frost, they're referring to it as'.[49] Just as the symptoms of the disease stand as an entropological metaphor so, too, does its name. Frost is a process in nature referring to the formation of ice crystals when the temperature drops below freezing (often at night). As the name of the pandemic, 'The Frost' therefore links the health of the human body and mind to natural processes and by extension temperature changes in the environment. Ultimately, then, *Theories of Forgetting* can be read as an example of what Heather Houser calls ecosickness fiction, since it 'deploy[s] affect in narratives of sick bodies to bring readers to environmental consciousness'.[50] Indeed, ecosickness is a recurrent theme within fiction of the anthropocene.

In her marginalia, Aila – Hugh and Alana's daughter – writes that she received an email from her mother 'shortly after she was diagnosed', saying

"Please don't worry too much about my medical news, sweetheart. It's just the way it is living inside a human body."[51] In these lines, Olsen reminds readers that whilst the novel's pandemic 'The Frost' is a dystopic creation[52], human bodies are – by their very nature – entropic. Doing so appears to be a conscious raising scheme: human bodies are fragile and evanescent. The end of nature, the anthropocene, and humankind's entropological relationship with the Earth mean that the planet, too, needs thinking of as fragile and, perhaps, also ephemeral.

The environment around humanity: 'the consummate embrace of the countless quiet catastrophes taking place around us'

One of the central ways in which entropology and the environment surface in *Theories of Forgetting* is through the novel's explicit engagement with Robert Smithson's *Spiral Jetty*. Alana's current film project is described as:

> [...] a short documentary exploring her accuring awareness that Smithson's signature work didn't only change from year to year, season to season, day to day, hour to hour, second to second, an Impressionist's perfection, depending on the texture of the light, how it veils, what it stresses, the level and tincture of the water, the quality of the clouds, the consistency of the atmosphere, the person you were when you observed it then and the person you were when you observed it then, which was, needless to say,
>
> Smithson's specific point: that all experience of his sculpture is by nature ~~braxen~~ brazenly haptic, brazenly full-body sensory involvement with space and place; that you can't so much look at the Spiral Jetty as be in and among it, which is to be in and among landscape.[53]

This description emphasises both the ecological properties of the Earthwork – changing with the natural world – and the human experience of it. Such an experience is physical – 'brazenly haptic, brazenly body sensory involvement' – but also situational, bringing the human subject into a relationship with the Earth, with 'space and place', located 'in and among landscape'.

The syntactic repetition and Alana's underlining of the word 'then' in 'the person you were when you observed it then and the person you were when you observed it then' suggest not only is temporality embedded in the materiality of the Jetty and the dialogue it has with its own site and geological time; the Jetty also produces reflection on the viewer's own changes, changes of self-identity but perhaps also biological cell regeneration, whereby the various cells in the human body move through processes of division, regeneration, and decay. This interpretation is reinforced by Alana's typo, 'accuring', at the start of the passage. Given Alana's illness, Olsen's neologism appears to privilege the word 'cure', that is relief from symptoms of disease. Moreover, because 'accuring' seems to replace 'accruing' (based on its context in the sentence), the typo, similarly to Smithson's Jetty, evokes both material decay (in its neologistic reference to biological wellbeing) as well as a temporal process (of accumulation). In interview, Olsen has said of *Theories of Forgetting*:

> The formalistics of entropology reiterate the thematics of entropology, not only at the level of the biological individual, but at that of the increasingly impoverished planet. Like *Spiral Jetty*, our environment is not-so-slowly sinking into sand, wasting itself away, becoming, in a sense, illegible.[54]

Olsen makes explicit that *Theories of Forgetting* echoes the entropological aesthetics of Smithson's *Spiral Jetty*, in that humanity and the planet are subject to equivalent processes of disintegration, and their fates entwined.

Alana's research for the documentary is manifest in her diary, wherein she includes biological information about Robert Smithson, often quoting him directly or summarising his views. Resultantly, Smithson's voice – his opinions on the relationship between art and environment – is a strong presence in *Theories of Forgetting*'s textuality. For instance, Alana describes a lecture Smithson delivered in 1972, 'advocating a mediation between ecology and industry by means of recycling such culturally dismissed sites as open-pit mines into earthworks.'[55] Additionally, when outlining the debate over the erosion of the *Spiral Jetty* and whether it should be restored and protected – particularly in the face of an application from the Pearl Montana oil company to drill into the site around the Jetty – Alana writes that, for Smithson, it 'would have meant the apotheosis of his aesthetics of entropy, the consummate embrace of the countless quiet catastrophes taking place around us, always and all ways, if only we could be awake enough, brake enough, to pay attention.'[56] Smithson did speak, unambiguously, of entropy relative to the environment:

> One might even say that the whole energy crisis in a form of entropy. The earth is a closed system, there's only a certain amount of resources and of course there's an attempt to reverse entropy through the recycling of garbage.[57]

His reference to 'recycling' implicates humankind's role in the process of geological entropy – both disintegration and potential reintegration. Likewise, Olsen's wordplay in Alana's writing expresses entropology. Olsen's homophonic repetition in 'always and allways' (as with 'accuring') inscribes both temporality and physicality[58]. Moreover, Alana's misspelling of 'brave' as 'brake' not only injects assonantal sound-patterning into the text (rhyming with [eɪ] in 'awake' and 'pay'); in the context of 'be awake enough, brake enough, to pay attention', it also highlights the end of nature. To have any positive impact on climate change, humanity must 'awake' from apathy and 'pay attention', must act to put the 'brake[s]', so to speak, on entropology.

Humankind's response to climate change also arises thematically in Hugh's narrative. After Alana's death, Hugh – in a state of avoidant grief – travels, first across Europe (London, Athens) then, whilst becoming increasingly disorientated and cognitively impaired, to the Middle East where he is recruited, somewhat unwittingly, into a cult: the Sleeping Beauties, so named because their principal action is the taking of powerful barbiturates in order to ignore the destructive nature of humankind's existence on the planet. Essentially, the Sleeping Beauties practice inertia – the very thing Levi-Strauss saw as a consequence of civilisation. Furthermore, in the cult's attempt to indoctrinate Hugh, its spokesperson lists – over the course of fourteen pages – the numerous sins humankind has committed against the planet (including oil consumption, deforestation, the water crisis, factory farming, ocean acidification, amongst others) before highlighting the political, legislative inaction of governments in protecting the environment. The Sleeping Beauties ultimately believe that humanity's characteristic act is 'ecophagy', the destructive consumption of the Earth's ecosystem.[59] Finally, the end of nature is located in history:

> That history's real lesson is how the world is today will absolutely, positively not be how it is tomorrow?
>
> And/or that future humans will therefore someday look back on us, here, now, with a mixture of dumbfounded awe, deep-structure exasperation, and unadulterated loathing in the face of what we allowed to happen?[60]

As Olsen's prose demonstrates, the end of nature forces humans to think historically – to place ourselves within a larger narrative of geological time and of human evolution. For the Sleeping Beauties, the conceptual confrontation with humankind's role in the decline of the planet results in feelings of shame and powerlessness so they treat these 'symptoms' with drugs that obliterate their conscious awareness. In *Theories of Forgetting*, it seems important that Olsen presents such entropological facts as questions: although the Sleeping Beauties hide from the harsh realities of the anthropocene, the questions place the addressee – Hugh, but also the reader – in a position of potential agency: how humanity responds needs to be seen as a choice, both individual and collective.

Hugh, in fact, does not succumb to the Sleeping Beauties' inertia, managing to escape from the confines of the cult. As he flees, he travels into the middle of the desert of the Wadi Rum where his narrative ends. In fact, both Hugh's and Alana's narratives end in entropic landscapes: Hugh in the desert and Alana at Smithson's *Spiral Jetty* (though Alana's presence at the Jetty is probably a memory or hallucination). The desert in Hugh's narrative is a supreme symbol of 'geological exhaustion'.[61] Moreover, describing North America's Great Basin, Alana appears to preempt Hugh's closing experiences, once again interweaving environment with human experience: 'The high desert's combination of severity, immensity, and shock make you conscious of your own breathing, how you negotiate this breath, then this one, then the one after that.'[62]

Olsen's writing implies that the direction of Hugh's escape, from the cult to the desert, is deliberate; that – unable to cope with his grief over his wife's death – Hugh is seeking to obliterate himself. In the final pages, Hugh's narrative is flooded with memories of Alana's illness, of his and Alana's life together. In wandering the desert, Hugh seeks his own inertia – not dissimilar from the practice of the Sleeping Beauties – just as the third-person style of his narrative enacts a psychological distancing from the painful reality of Alana's death. Significantly, in the closing moments, Hugh faces indecision about his own fate and as he does so, the narrative toys with first-person 'I' ('I can manage it'[63]). He realises, though, that 'in the end everything is about oxygen'[64] – for the body, for the planet.

Alana's death is symbolised in the faded closing lines of her narrative as both the endurance of love but the failure of the human body: 'the heart is allways the least to go away'. Hugh's death, in parallel, situates the body in the larger cosmos: 'The stars are the first to go away. And then the—'[65]. As such, the endings of both central narratives of *Theories of Forgetting*, set in entropic landscapes, place humankind at the heart of the decaying natural world, their fates – the possible death or end of humans and nature – entwined. Using ellipsis at the end of Hugh's narrative, moreover, Olsen presents those joint destinies as an unfinished story. Whilst humans today might be in the epoch of the anthropocene, the future is – as yet – unwritten.

Theories of Forgetting, the aesthetics of entropology, and the metamodern

Theories of Forgetting presents the relationship between human life and the environment as entropological – a concept that has travelled from Lévi-Strauss's anthropological reflections through Robert Smithson's Earthwork aesthetic and into contemporary literature as a form of ecopoetics. Expressing the possible 'end of nature', Olsen manifests entropology both in the material substance of the book, its codex form and language, as well as through its narrative themes. *Theories of Forgetting* is, in Olsen's words, 'obsessed with entropology all the way down—from its architectonics to poor Alana and Hugh (which is to say poor you and me) to various linguistic undoings, from failing sentences to crossed-out words and deliberate misspellings.'[66] Just as 'Landmarks create accounts, chronologies'[67], so too does discourse – scientific, philosophical, literary. By emphasising the veracity and urgency of humankind's entropological impact on the environment, Olsen's *Theories of Forgetting* is representative not just of ecoliterature in the epoch of the anthropocene, but also of a metamodern (or post-postmodern) sensibility. This is because novels like *Theories of Forgetting* ask readers to think beyond climate change.

Considering the current dominant culture (as manifest in shopping malls and city design) and the potentialities of science-fiction writing, Fredric Jameson writes:

> I think it would be better to characterise all this in terms of History, a History that we cannot imagine except as ending, and whose future seems to be nothing but a monotonous repetition of what is already here. The problem is how to locate radical difference, how to jumpstart the sense of history so that it begins again to transmit feeble signals of time, of otherness, of change, of Utopia. The problem to be solved is that of breaking out of the windless present of the postmodern back into real historical time, and a history made by human beings.[68]

Theories of Forgetting imagines a near dystopic future in which a pandemic threatens life and the planet's decline has given rise to (cultish) apathy. Its aesthetic of entropology is an assertion of the end of nature and a plea for humanity to reboot (rather than inertly accept the end of) history. Imagining a possible future enables us to retrospectively look back on ourselves in the historical present, to feel the affective force of our predicament, and contemplate how next to act – how, in other words, to complete Olsen's words: 'And then the—'.

Notes

1. Claude Lévi-Strauss, Tristes Tropiques, trans. John Weightman and Doreen Weightman. (London: Penguin, 1973 [1955]), p. 413–414.
2. Stanley Diamond, *In Search of the Primitive: A Critique of Civilization* (New York and London: Routledge, 2009 [1974]), p. 95.
3. James Clifford, 'On Collecting Art and Culture', in Russell Ferguson, Martha Gever, Trinh T. Minh-ha, and Cornel West (eds.), *Out There: Marginalization and Contemporary Cultures* (New York: The New Museum of Contemporary Art; Cambridge, MA; London: The MIT Press, 1990), pp. 141–169 (p. 159).
4. For instance, see Christian Moraru, *Cosmodernism: American Narrative, Late Globalization, and the New Cultural Imaginary* (Ann Arbor: The University of Michigan Press, 2011). The importance of 1989 is also discussed from a planetary perspective by Amy J. Elias and Christian Moraru, 'Introduction: The Planetary Condition', in Amy J. Elias and Christian Moraru (eds.) *The Planetary Turn: Relationality and Geoaesthetics in the Twenty-First Century* (Evanston, IL: Northwestern University Press, 2015), pp. xi–xxxvii.
5. Fukuyama's first thesis on 'the end of history' appeared in his article 'The End of History?', *The National Interest* 16 (Summer 1989), pp. 3–18. It was further developed three years later in his book *The End of History and the Last Man* (London: Penguin, 2012 [1992]).
6. Bill McKibben, *The End of Nature* (New York: Random House, 2006 [1989]).
7. Bill McKibben, *The End of Nature*, p. 41.

8. Jean-François Lyotard, *The Postmodern Condition: A Report on Knowledge* (Manchester: Manchester University Press, 1984).
9. Francis Fukuyama, 'The Future of History: Can Liberal Democracy Survive the Decline of the Middle Class?', *Foreign Affairs* 91.1 (Jan/Feb 2012), pp. 53–61.
10. Paul J. Crutzen and Eugene F. Stoermer, 'The "Anthropocene", *IGBP [International Geosphere-Biosphere Programme] Newsletter* 41 (May 2000), pp. 17–18 (p. 17). Crutzen is generally accredited with having coined the term 'anthropocene', though his article in nature succeeds the aforementioned co-authored piece: see Paul J. Crutzen, 'Geology of Mankind', *Nature* 415 (3 January 2002), p. 23.
11. Timothy Clark traces some of the most forceful accounts of the anthropocene as a cultural age in the humanities in *Ecocriticism on the Edge: The Anthropocene as a Threshold Concept* (London and New York: Bloomsbury, 2015). In particular, he points to work by: Tom Cohen, Claire Colebrook, and J. Hillis Miller in *Theory and the Disappearing Future* (London: Routledge, 2012); Timothy Morton in *Hyperobjects: Philosophy and Ecology after the End of the World* (Minneapolis, MN: University of Minnesota Press, 2013); Tobias Menely and Margaret Ronda in 'Red', in Jeffrey Jerome Cohen (ed.) *Prismatic Ecology: Ecotheory Beyond Green* (Minneapolis, MN: University of Minnesota Press, 2013), pp. 22–41; and Slavoj Žižek in *Living in the End Times* (London: Verso, 2010). See also Theo Savvas's article in this issue.
12. Robin van den Akker and Timotheus Vermeulen, 'Periodising the 2000s, or, the Emergence of Metamodernism', in Robin van den Akker, Alison Gibbons, and Timotheus Vermeulen (eds.), *Metamodernism: Historicity, Affect, and Depth after Postmodernism* (London: Rowman and Littlefield, 2017), pp. 1–19 (p. 17).
13. Lance Olsen, *Theories of Forgetting* (Tuscaloosa, AL: FC2, 2014).
14. Robert Smithson, '" … The Earth, Subject to Cataclysms, is a Cruel Master" (1971): Interview with Gregoire Müller', in Jack Flam (ed.), *Robert Smithson: The Collected Writings* (Berkeley and Los Angeles, CA: University of California Press, 1996), pp. 253–261 (p. 257).
15. Whilst Smithson spoke often of entropy, he explicitly praises Lévi-Strauss's conception of entropology in the above interview (footnote 14) as well as in Paul Cummings, 'Interview with Robert Smithson for the Archives of American Art/Smithsonian Institution (1972): Interview conducted by Paul Cummings July 14 and 19, 1972', in Jack Flam (ed.), *Robert Smithson: The Collected Writings* (Berkeley and Los Angeles, CA: University of California Press, 1996), pp. 270–300 (p. 299).
16. Robert Smithson, 'Entropy and the New Monuments', in Jack Flam (ed.), *Robert Smithson: The Collected Writings* (Berkeley and Los Angeles, CA: University of California Press, 1996), pp. 10–23 (p. 11).
17. Robert Smithson, 'Entropy and the New Monuments', p. 11.
18. Hal Foster, *The Return of the Real: The Avant-Garde at the End of the Century* (Cambridge, MA: MIT Press, 2001 [1996]), p. 38.
19. Fredric Jameson, 'The Cultural Logic of Late Capitalism', in *Postmodernism, or, The Cultural Logic of Late Capitalism* (London; New York: Verso, 1991 [1984]), pp. 1–54. Jameson's three axes of postmodern culture are also considered – as postmodern characteristics as well as contemporary rethinks – in Robin van den Akker, Alison Gibbons, and Timotheus Vermeulen (eds.), *Metamodernism: Historicity, Affect, and Depth after Postmodernism.*

20. Gerhard Hoffman, *From Modernism to Postmodernism: Concepts and Strategies of Postmodern American Fiction* (Amsterdam; New York: Rodopi, 2005), p. 171.
21. Thomas Pynchon, *Gravity's Rainbow* (New York: Viking, 1973) and 'Entropy', in *Slow Learner* (New York: Penguin Press, 2012 [1984]).
22. Kurt Vonnegut, *Cat's Cradle: A Novel* (New York: Dial Press, 2010 [1963]).
23. John Barth, 'Posttape', in *Giles Goat-Boy* (New York: Anchor Books, 2012 [1966]), pp. 697–708, and *LETTERS: A Novel* (Normal, IL: Dalkey Archive Press, 1994 [1979]).
24. William Gaddis, 'The Rush for Second Place: Missed victories in America', *Harper's* 252.1571 (April 1981), p. 35. Gaddis's novel *JR* has been explicitly discussed in relation to entropy, with a focus on the character of Jack Gibbs by Thomas M. Sawyer, '*JR*: The narrative of entropy', *International Fiction Review* 10, pp. 117–22, and by David Buehrer, 'Personal Entropy and Satiric "Incorporation" of Characters in William Gaddis's *JR*', *Critique: Studies in Contemporary Fiction* 53.4 (2012), pp. 366–380.
25. Gerhard Hoffman, *From Modernism to Postmodernism*, p. 301.
26. Robert Shane, 'Rozel Point: Robert Smithson', in Amanda Renshaw (ed.) *Art & Place: Site-Specific Art of the Americas* (London; New York: Phaidon, 2013), pp. 56–57 (p. 56).
27. Robert Smithson, '"... The Earth, Subject to Cataclysms, is a Cruel Master" (1971): Interview with Gregoire Müller', p. 298.
28. For instance, Roberts employs 'entropology' as representative of a 'conscientious' critical approach to the meeting of Western and other cultures (and the inevitable disintegration of each through contact) in Modernist narratives: Kathleen Glenister Roberts, *Alterity and Narrative: Stories and the Negotiation of Western Identities* (Albany, NY: State University of New York Press, 2007), pp. 143–170 (p. 159). Similarly, Michaelsen evokes Levi-Strauss's concept in his consideration of what affective sentiments – particularly empathy, loss, and sorrow – can contribute to anthropological study: Scott J. Michaelsen, 'Our Sentiments', in Scott J. Michaelsen and David E. Johnson (eds.), *Anthropology's Wake: Attending to the End of Culture* (New York, NY: Fordham University Press, 2008), pp. 58–80 ('entropology' is specifically discussed, pp. 78–9).
29. Direct links are drawn between Land Art/Earthwork from the twentieth century and from contemporary art by Oliver Lowenstein, 'Twenty First Century Land Art', *Fourthdoor: Unstructured* 4 (Online: http://www.fourthdoor.co.uk/unstructured/unstructured_04/article4_4.php, 2009). David Maisel's aesthetic is directly compared to Robert Smithson's through entropology by Micah Messenheimer, 'On Entropology', in Thomas Brent Smith (ed.) *Elevating Western American Art: Developing an Institute in the Cultural Capital of the Rockies* (Denver: Petrie Institute of Western American Art, 2012), pp. 174–179. Peter Selz discusses both twentieth and some twenty-first century earthwork artists in 'Toward a Sustainable Earth', in *Art of Engagement: Visual Politics in California and Beyond* (Berkeley and Los Angeles, CA: University of California Press, 2006), pp. 223–246.
30. For a brief overview, see Cheryll Glotfelty, 'Introduction: Literary Studies in an Age of Environmental Crisis', in Cheryll Glotfelty and Harold Fromm (eds.), *The Ecocriticism Reader: Landmarks in Literary Ecology* (Athens; London: The University of Georgia Press, 1996), pp. xv–xxxvii.

31. Jonathan Skinner, 'Statement for the "New Nature Writing" Panel at 2005 AWP (Vancouver)', *Ecopoetics* 4/5 (2004–2005), pp. 128–129 (p. 128).
32. Lance Olsen, *Theories of Forgetting*, p. A241–242. *Theories of Forgetting* has two narratives starting from opposing sides of the book. Both sides have page numbers, so for clarity I use 'A' for Alana's narrative or 'H' for Hugh's in my references.
33. Rachel Kushner, *The Flamethrowers* (London: Vintage, 2014).
34. Gayle Brandeis, *The Book of Dead Birds* (New York: HarperCollins, 2003); Marisa Silver, *The God of War* (New York: Simon & Schuster, 2008); William T. Vollmann, *The Royal Family* (New York: Penguin, 2000) and *Imperial* (New York: Penguin, 2009).
35. Adam Trexler, *Anthropocene Fictions: The Novel in a Time of Climate Change* (Charlottesville and London: University of Virginia Press).
36. Adam Trexler, *Anthropocene Fictions: The Novel in a Time of Climate Change*, p. 14 & p. 16.
37. Christian Schultz, 'Be More Extreme: Interview with Author Lance Olsen', *Slug Magazine*, (Online: https://www.slugmag.com/book-reviews/be-more-extreme-lance-olsen/, 8 April 2017).
38. Olsen speaking in interview with John Domini, 'Lance Olsen with John Domini: *Theories of Forgetting*', *The Brooklyn Rail: Critical Perspectives on Art, Politics, and Culture* (Online: http://brooklynrail.org/2014/05/books/lance-olsen, 6 May 2014).
39. A parallel can be drawn between the graphological layout of Alana's and Hugh's narratives on the page and the layout of Mark Z. Danielewski's *Only Revolutions* (London: Doubleday, 2006), which similarly places the narratives of its two central characters – Sam and Hailey – at 180 degree angles.
40. John Domini, 'Lance Olsen with John Domini: *Theories of Forgetting*', online. Interestingly, as well as being used by Olsen in *Theories of Forgetting*, the spiral shape is also a recurrent figure in Danielewski's *House of Leaves* (London: Doubleday, 2000). Olsen's awareness of the latter is evidenced in his critical work *[[there.]* (Fort Wayne, IN: Anti-Oedipus Press, 2014), in which he writes about 'that enormous spiral staircase in Danielewski's *House of Leaves*' (p. 52).
41. Joe Sacksteder, '*Theories of Forgetting* by Lance Olsen' [Review], *Heavy Feather Review* (Online: https://heavyfeatherreview.com/2014/06/18/theories-of-forgetting-by-lance-olsen/, no date).
42. Yuriy Taranawsky, 'Forgetting Things Present' [Review], *American Book Review* 35.2 (2014), pp. 17 & 29 (p. 17).
43. Lance Olsen, *Theories of Forgetting*, p. A13–14.
44. Lance Olsen, *[[there.]]*, p. 26, p. 28.
45. Lance Olsen, *Theories of Forgetting*, p. A85.
46. The term 'neurological realism' comes from Charles B. Harris, 'The Story of the Self: *The Echo Maker* and Neurological Realism', in Stephen J. Burn and Peter Dempsey (eds.), *Intersections: Essays on Richard Powers* (Champaign and London: Dalkey Archive Press, 2008), pp. 230–259. Two similar genre terms exist. The first is the 'neuronarrative' from Gary Johnson, 'Consciousness as Content: Neuronarratives and the Redemption of Fiction', *Mosaic* 41.1 (March 2008), pp. 169–184. The second is 'Neuronovel' from Marco Roth, 'The Rise of the Neuronovel', *n+1* 8 (online: https://nplusonemag.com/issue-8/essays/the-rise-of-the-neuronovel/, Fall 2009). All three critics identify the

genre using exemplary works of contemporary literature and/or they interpret it as a distinctly contemporary phenomenon.

47. Lance Olsen, *Theories of Forgetting*, p. A168.
48. Lance Olsen, *Theories of Forgetting*. See p. A185 and p. A243 for the two-referenced newspaper clippings; the death counts are given on pages A228, A241, A265, and A299.
49. Lance Olsen, *Theories of Forgetting*, p. A198.
50. Heather Houser, *Ecosickness In Contemporary U.S. Fiction: Environment and Affect* (New York: Columbia University Press, 2014), p. 2.
51. Lance Olsen, *Theories of Forgetting*, p. H47.
52. In this sense, *Theories of Forgetting* is also an instance of 'cli-fi' (sci-fi about climate change), a term that is generally attributed to journalist Dan Bloom; for instance, by Adam Trexler, *Anthropocene Fictions: The Novel in a Time of Climate Change*, p. 8.
53. Lance Olsen, *Theories of Forgetting*, p. A156–158; all emphasis original.
54. John Domini, 'Lance Olsen with John Domini: *Theories of Forgetting*', online.
55. Lance Olsen, *Theories of Forgetting*, p. A143.
56. Lance Olsen, *Theories of Forgetting*, p. A176.
57. Smithson in interview with Alison Sky, 'Entropy Made Visible (1973): Interview with Alison Sky', in Jack Flam (ed.), *Robert Smithson: The Collected Writings* (Berkeley and Los Angeles, CA: University of California Press, 1996), pp. 301–309 (p. 302).
58. The homophonic play of 'always' and 'all ways' resonates with Danielewski's word play – 'allways' – in *Only Revolutions*. Not insignificantly, both novels are interested in temporality whilst their formal design mean that the books must be rotated for both narratives to be read.
59. Lance Olsen, *Theories of Forgetting*, p. H218–232 (p. H223).
60. Lance Olsen, *Theories of Forgetting*, p. H231.
61. Lance Olsen, *Theories of Forgetting*, p. H338.
62. Lance Olsen, *Theories of Forgetting*, p. A26.
63. Lance Olsen, *Theories of Forgetting*, p. H363.
64. Lance Olsen, *Theories of Forgetting*, p. H354.
65. Lance Olsen, *Theories of Forgetting*, p. A357 & p. H365-7.
66. Christian Schultz, 'Be More Extreme: Interview with Author Lance Olsen', online.
67. Lance Olsen, *Theories of Forgetting*, p. A189.
68. Fredric Jameson, 'Future City', *New Left Review* 21 (May-June 2003) pp. 65–79 (p. 76).

Disclosure statement

No potential conflict of interest was reported by the authors.

ORCID

Alison Gibbons http://orcid.org/0000-0001-8912-9350

Typical Eggers: transnationalism and America in Dave Eggers's 'globally-minded' fiction

Bran Nicol

ABSTRACT

Dave Eggers's *What is the What* and *Zeitoun* are transnational works in that their narratives detail a passage between nations and concentrate on the experiences of individuals of 'hyphenated identity'. The sequence of novels Eggers has published in the second decade of the twenty-first century mark a distinctive 'American turn' in his work which offers an alternative but complementary transnational perspective. *Hologram for the King* (2012), *The Circle* (2013), *Your Fathers, Where Are They? And the Prophets, Do They Live Forever?* (2014) and *Heroes of the Frontier* (2016) focus on 'unhyphenated' American protagonists, and examine the United States both as a specific place and as itself typical of a nation in the globalised twenty-first century world. In their post-postmodern ethical approach to fiction and their assumption that fiction's duty is to 'make reality credible', as Philip Roth once put it, these novels are themselves typical of the values and practices of a specifically US historical category, Mark McGurl's Program Era, but also of categories of transnational fiction critics have recently described as 'global' or 'planetary'. Eggers's US quartet critiques globalisation, but is ultimately more interested in asserting the value of connections between human beings in a globalised world.

'He's grappling with what it means to be American right now': Eggers's American 'Quartet'

To describe as 'typical' a novelist with as diverse a body of work as Dave Eggers's requires some qualification. Yet the modest but steadily increasing body of academic criticism devoted to it has tended to regard it as representative of three prominent features of contemporary American fiction. One of these is Eggers's 'one-man zeitgeist' status as a leading cultural entrepreneur and editor, pioneering an alternative 'Generation X' media culture (revolving around a kind of cool, witty, ironic but ethically-conscious brand of short fiction), chiefly through his company McSweeney's Publishing and its promotion of the work of young authors.[1] Another is his concern with the issues of migrant experience and hybrid global identity which are central to both *What is the What* (2006) and *Zeitoun* (2009), and which are complemented by a range of philanthropic 'extra-curricular' ventures which involve lobbying for and directly helping the disadvantaged and unvoiced.[2] A third area is how exemplary Eggers's writing is of a new kind of self-reflexive fictional technique which departs from postmodernism. Critics have contended that the self-reflexivity of Eggers's first three books – *A Heartbreaking Work of Staggering Genius* (2000), *You Shall Know Our Velocity* (2002), and *What is the What* – exemplifies a new kind of metafiction governed by the desire to 'think one's way into a shared space between one being and another', as Peter Boxall puts it in a discussion of *What is the What*, rather than investment in 'the wearily "postmodern" conclusion that all life is a fiction, that we are all fictional characters in search of an author'.[3]

As singular a figure as Dave Eggers would seem to be from one perspective, then, from another he has been regarded as typifying the modes and values of contemporary fiction after postmodernism. In fact these last two features, Eggers's explicit 'globalist' vision of social justice and the newly 'post-postmodern' ethical self-reflexivity in his work, relate to a key context for examining his work, which is central to this essay. Eggers is a transnational writer, and his transnationalism is another dimension of the ethical imperative behind his work noted by critics. Boxall includes him in the 'world community of writers' which he sees as typifying fiction in the early part of this century,[4] while Caren Irr has listed Eggers, along with Christina García, Ha Jin, Rachel Kushner, Jonathan Raban, and Mona Simpson, as part of a group of 'moderately globalist' contemporary U.S. writers (her term to describe faith in an ideal of an 'overlapping international cultural condition').[5] Though he features only fleetingly in Rebecca Walkowitz's *Born Translated: The Contemporary Novel in an Age of World Literature* his work would indeed seem 'born translated', in her memorable phrase, because of the way his stories invite empathy from an international readership. This 'translatability' marks him out as a US counterpart of the writers Adam Kirsch highlights as practitioners of what he terms 'the global novel',[6] such as Haruki Murakami or Orhan Pamuk, writers whose fiction set in specific regions nevertheless can be appreciated easily from a global perspective.

A turn to the global – or to the transnational, or even the planetary (a label I shall return to in due course) – has been pinpointed by a number of theorists as a new context for surveying the contemporary cultural field after postmodernism. Postmodernism was, as David James has said, 'inherently "transnational" from the start' in that it registered the effects of the commercial expansion across the globe, as theorised in landmark studies by Fredric Jameson and David Harvey.[7] However, as a cultural paradigm which purports to describe contemporary culture, it is now widely regarded as fatally compromised by – in the words of Amy Elias and Christian Moraru – its 'ties to late socio-aesthetic modernity, market globalization, and the society of spectacle, simulation, and empty pastiche'[8] and by its function as a totalising, blanket paradigm. Moreover, as a number of recent studies have shown, with their treatment of a remarkably numerous and wide-ranging group of US novelists, there would seem to be sufficient evidence of a significant shift not just in the newly global conditions which go to make up the contemporary novel, but in its outlook and subject matter, to validate a transnational flavour as a definitive characteristic of the contemporary novel after postmodernism.[9]

Eggers's *What is the What* and *Zeitoun* most obviously typify this transnational turn. The former is about a child refugee, Valentino Achak Deng, who flees his country as a result of the Second Sudanese Civil War and eventually immigrates to the United States as part of the Lost Boys of Sudan Program, while the latter tells of a Syrian immigrant, Abdulrahman Zeitoun, who chose to stay and help people in New Orleans during Hurricane Katrina, only to be arrested by the US National Guard under suspicion of terrorism, presumably because of his possession of large sums of money and detailed maps of the city. As both narratives hinge on the literal passage from one nation to another, they thus invite comparison of national differences as well as emphasising the inherently transnational quality of the United States. More precisely, though, the hybrid identities of their eponymous protagonists facilitate the re-imagining of national and postnational identities as a consequence of the kind of contemporary global conditions which give rise to the kind of refugee and migrant crises they detail, and the role of the United States in dealing with these.

In this essay, as a complement to these established critical lines of enquiry, I want to examine four of Eggers's most recent novels, *Hologram for the King* (2012), *The Circle* (2013), and especially *Your Fathers, Where Are They? And the Prophets, Do They Live Forever?* (2014), and *Heroes of the Frontier* (2016). These novels would seem to mark a distinctive shift in Eggers's work away both from the explicitly transnational outlook of *What is the What* and *Zeitoun*, and also from the more postmodernist (that is, metafictional, paratextual, self-deconstructive, ironic) works which began his career, *A Heartbreaking Work of Staggering Genius* and *You Shall Know Our Velocity*. They constitute a distinctive 'American turn' in Eggers's work in that rather than telling the story of individuals of 'hyphenated identity' (to use Boxall's reclamation of Theodore Roosevelt's derogatory phrase)[10] in a way which highlights the role of the United States in a broader global culture, they focus on the stories of individual Americans in a transnational context. This shift of emphasis nevertheless offers a complementary transnational perspective.

While American locations and characters feature in each of Eggers's earlier major works, they cannot be said to be 'about' America in the same way as these recent novels. One enthusiastic reviewer called *Heroes of the Frontier* 'an unlikely state of the nation novel, cleansing the spirit and lifting the heart'.[11] In fact, these novels are *all* 'unlikely state of the nation novels', in that they are preoccupied by – or 'grapple with', to use the phrase chosen by Egger's editor, Jennifer Jackson [12] – what it means to be American in the twenty-first century but resist the grandeur of earlier US state-of-the-nation novels like Philip Roth's *American Pastoral* (1997) or Don DeLillo's *Underworld* (1997), as well as suggesting that, in the twenty-first century, the distinctively American cannot be separated from the global. In fact, the novels seem to go out of their way to present ordinary, that is, typical, characters: all are average, educated, middle-class professionals, and in fact 'unhyphenated' Americans. Alan (*Hologram for the King*) is a businessman, Mae (*The Circle*) a recent graduate, Thomas (*Your Fathers*) an unemployed college drop-out, Josie (*Heroes of the Frontier*) a dentist. Their ordinariness is suggested directly at certain points, such as when Alan catches his reflection in the glass of the next-door balcony and thinks: 'He looked like an average man. When shaved and dressed, he passed for legitimate'.[13]

What is perhaps even more immediately striking about the novels of this recent 'quartet'[14] to those who have kept track of Eggers's output is that by and large they eschew the metafictional techniques (authorial intrusions, double-voiced narration, deconstructive appendices, etc.) which characterise his first three book-length works, and opt instead for a realist mode of writing. Realism, the form Georg Lukács argued best captures the 'organic quality [of a life] which is the aim of biography',[15] might be seen as a complement to the biographical modes Eggers had previously favoured in sustaining the focus on the course of a single individual's life. It also has the appeal of allowing Eggers to remove obvious traces of himself from his work – a perhaps surprising but consistent ambition throughout his career (e.g. as evidenced by the remarkable ventriloquial conceit deployed in *What is the What*, through which Eggers chose to 'write in Val's voice' because it enabled him to 'disappear completely').[16] Traditional unobtrusive realist narration has always been accompanied by the ethical purpose of allowing characters 'freedom' from obvious authorial direction and judgement. This aim seems to be behind the avoidance of self-reflexivity in three of the four novels in question here. The exception is *Your Fathers*, which is an example of the American mini-tradition of the novel in dialogue (with previous examples including William Gaddis's *J R* [1975] and Cormac McCarthy's *The Sunset Limited* [2006]) and which consequently does draw attention to its form. But this is neither the postmodern nor post-postmodern-ethical self-reflexivity identified in Eggers's earlier novels, and the appeal of its 'constrained' mode, Eggers has said, is that it facilitated a kind of authorial withdrawal in requiring him to find 'ways to give direction and background […] without ever leaving the dialogue itself'.[17]

Eggers's focus on ordinary Americans caught up in typical situations does not quite engineer a Lukácsian 'typicality' (the reduced social canvas of his work compared to nineteenth-century historical novels does not lend itself to an analysis of Lukácsian totality) but it does produce a kind of realism which subtly interrogates the notion of typicality in the context of a global culture, and the challenge of capturing what might be typical about America or Americans – a notoriously and definitively *untypical* population. In their clarity and commitment to directly depicting everyday globalised contemporary life, these four novels point to another way Eggers exemplifies the prevailing modes and values of contemporary fiction after postmodernism: a renewed imperative amongst contemporary writers to ensure the novel *responds* to contemporary local and global conditions or specific historical events, encouraging empathy and stimulating debate, and inviting readers to experience the emotions and existential self-questioning they depict in their narratives.

'These sorts of men': making reality credible in *Your Fathers, Where Are They? And the Prophets, Do They Live Forever?*

The challenge of writing fiction that is responsive to the social conditions of contemporary America brings to mind Philip Roth's essay from nearly sixty years ago, 'Writing American Fiction', with its famous complaint that 'the American writer in the middle of the twentieth century has his [*sic*] hands full in trying to understand, describe, and then make *credible* much of American reality'.[18] Roth's real concern in the essay is not, as the standard reading would have it, with how impoverished a form fiction becomes in the face of increasingly outlandish and spectacular reality: a world of violence, political scandal, social conflict, nationalism, riots, and apartheid, etc., all represented via media technology that, in its ability to entertain and immerse its viewers, rivalled the novel. It is with how 'the serious writer' has failed to find an appropriate strategy or form for dealing with the reality of the social and historical world. Roth accuses his contemporaries of failing to respond to the 'distressing communal predicament'[19] they find themselves in because they have been unwilling or unable to approach reality directly. They have tended instead to 'lose heart' and turn either 'to the construction of wholly imaginary worlds', as in the case of Saul Bellow's *Henderson the Rain King*, or 'to a celebration of the self', as in novels by the now largely-forgotten writer Herbert Gold,[20] both solutions beset by the writer's failure to attend properly to 'what is *outside* himself [*sic*] – as subject'.[21] Roth's analysis predates the extraordinary flourishing of US metafiction which began later in the 1960s, and is thus very much a despatch from another era, from a writer working as unwittingly at the cusp of postmodernism as Eggers is writing self-consciously in its wake. However, its principal argument – that writers must find a way of 'dealing with' reality that does not involve simply competing with the extreme situations presented daily in the media nor abdicating the responsibility to do so through the creation of imaginary worlds and introspective, indulgent exercises in style or form – nevertheless sets out some parameters of contemporary fiction which still apply in Eggers's 'quartet'.

To explain this assertion, I shall turn first to *Your Fathers, Where Are They? And the Prophets, Do They Live Forever?* because its outlier status in the quartet helps clarify how these others move beyond the terms of Roth's analysis as well as making clear Eggers's ambitions in all four. Unlike the other three novels in the quartet – and in fact more than any other Eggers work except *Zeitoun*, with its depiction of Hurricane Katrina, this novel takes an extreme event, the kind we encounter via the media, and tries to make it 'credible'. *Your Fathers* is the story of a 34-year-old man, Thomas, who, over the course of a single week, kidnaps seven people, keeping them incarcerated in separate buildings in a disused military base on California's Monterey coast, and interrogates them: an astronaut, a congressman, one of his former teachers, his mother, a policeman, a Director of Patient Access at the local hospital, and a girl on the beach walking her dog whom Thomas thinks – deludedly – destiny has decreed will become his life partner. His aim is to 'stop time and ask questions',[22] to call to account the ones who have let him and his nation down, the leaders and the authority figures, as well as finding out more about a tragic event he has always suspected was also a police cover-up: the death of Don Banh, a half-Vietnamese boy he was at school with, who ended up cornered in his own backyard by twelve policemen and shot dead when he brandished a knife.

Your Fathers suggests that contemporary fiction 'deals with' social reality by replicating it, by presenting readers with the kind of event they might encounter on broadcast media, via their Twitter or Facebook timelines or on TV news, only by permitting them a more direct insight into the mind and the 'back story' of the central character than they would ever get from the news, and guiding them to conclusions which are more elevated than the kind of news media discussion which characterises our age. Eggers is taking on a familiar traumatic event in American society, the young men who become 'school shooters', 'spree killers', or those who 'go postal', taking revenge for what the world has apparently done to them or prevented them from doing. The novel would therefore seem to be working in the same territory Roth explores in 'Writing American Fiction' in its determination to make credible an extreme aspect of American reality. It might also seem that its didacticism causes it to fall into a variation of the problem that Roth identifies: foregrounding the novelist's own motivations. *Your Fathers* is not a work of postmodern metafiction, i.e. it is not designed ironically to undercut its own narrative or deconstruct its message, or even the idea of a message, as postmodernist fiction might. However it is overtly self-reflexive because of how the dialogue form foregrounds the author's manipulative role. Unlike Gaddis's vast *J R*, *Your Fathers* is neat and programmatic, dialogic on the surface yet ultimately delivering a monologue. The novel's formal conceit inevitably draws attention to itself, defamiliarising its very form and drawing attention to the novelist's motivations and composition, and exposing the systematic quality of its structure: chapters are titled 'Building 52', 'Building 53', there are seven kidnappings in seven days, etc., while the meetings with the different abductees, taking place one by one, and with obviously emblematic characters, provides the pretext for discussions about social processes in modern America, such as the government, the police, war, health care, politics, and the space programme. The arresting title of the novel – from *Zechariah 1* in the *Bible* – signals that we should think of both Banh (who, in the backyard siege, 'quoted some line' from the Bible, '[s]omething about missing fathers'[23]) and Thomas as ironic prophets, exposing the malaise of modern society.

This is certainly a didactic novel, a book with a message, and this attempt to make American reality 'credible' by telling the story behind a typical contemporary event hampers its apparent ambition to invite readers to think for themselves through its status as parable. Referring to the Banh killing, the policeman tells Thomas that, somewhere in America, 'This kind of thing happens once a week',[24] while Sara, the girl he kidnaps, says that Thomas reminds her 'of graduate students stuffing their colleagues into crevices, shooting professors, that kind of thing. People like you. Smart but nuts'.[25] Its typicality becomes familiarity, however, leading one reviewer to dismiss the novel by pointing out the link to real-life cases, such as one which actually occurred less than one month before the US publication date of Eggers's novel (on June 17, 2014, when twenty-two-year-old Elliot Rodger killed six people and wounded fourteen before killing himself in Isla Vista in California) and proclaiming: 'Eggers' latest novel should sound familiar. Read yesterday's headlines'.[26] Yet despite its setting, its cast of characters, and list of specifically national social injustices (misdirected government expenditure, institutionalised police racism, etc.) the novel resists a reading of its story as purely American. Eggers responded to one interviewer's assumption that, in *Your Fathers*, 'Thomas's concerns are particular to a young American man' by saying that someone like his protagonist 'could be found anywhere on the globe. And we see desperate acts from these sorts of men every day'.[27]

Furthermore, there is, almost concealed within the main, geometrically-arranged present-day narrative about Thomas's kidnappings, the story of the death of a young man of 'hyphenated identity', Don Banh, the Vietnamese-American. This means that as much as Thomas's kidnapping spree is an act of disillusioned vengeance by another vulnerable young man it also amounts to an act of transnational empathy. Banh's existence at the heart of the narrative is a reminder that determining 'typical Americanness' – or linking 'these sorts of men' to a particular nation – is no easy task, and to attempt to do so at least requires the acknowledgement that America is inherently transnational. The parallel narratives of Don and Thomas (who would seem to be about to suffer a similar fate to his former friend once the police inevitably arrive, an event the novel stops short of describing) underline the shared experience of two very different Americans, reminding us how difficult – and how limited in value – it is to represent Americans as a generality.

'Meaning in motion': nation, globe, and planet in *Hologram for the King, The Circle,* and *Heroes of the Frontier*

Despite its stylistic differences, *Your Fathers, Where Are They? And the Prophets, Do They Live Forever?* resembles the other novels in Eggers's American quartet in that its narrative oscillates between the singular and the typical and the specific and the general. These works do not repeat *Your Fathers*'s attempt to deal head-on with a typical dramatic contemporary event, yet specific, localised, national experience is presented in these works in way which also ultimately reveals it as a symptom of something transnational. Such a veering between poles is inevitable in global fiction beyond simply the work of Eggers, I would contend, as this mode of writing must continually negotiate the boundary between the twin convictions that the world is global and transnational, but that local difference and specificity must be respected. But in Eggers, certainly, each novel focuses on a representative American individual at a moment in time and space in a way which raises the question of what the typical *is* both in the broad context of global culture and the specific context of America. America is thereby presented both as a specific place but as *itself* typical of a nation in the globalised world.

Each of the protagonists in the other three novels is seeking direction in a life made meaningless by the demands of a globalised work environment. Alan is trying to secure the IT contract for the gigantic new Saudi Arabian city, King Abdullah's Economic City. Mae is given the opportunity to work at the sinister social media conglomerate The Circle. Josie has given away her dental practice and is fleeing from Ohio to Alaska with her two children in tow. But at points in each novel there are ironic references to the inapplicability of American hardiness and pioneering spirit to lives made comfortable and secure as a result of decades of national stability and affluence. During a painful procedure to remove a benign growth from his neck by a surgeon, Alan recalls a story his mother would tell him to remind him of how he has benefited from the 'bounty of suburban life' about a distant relative who had witnessed her husband and her children murdered by Native Americans before she herself was abducted.[28] In *The Circle* Mae's confident and successful friend Annie is horrified to discover that her ancestors were slave-owners. The narrative in *Heroes of the Frontier* is punctuated by moments when Josie's son Paul reads aloud to her passages from a feature called 'Trails Grown Dim' in some copies of *Old West* magazine which have been left in their battered rented RV. These mini-narratives about hardship, loss, and death create a comic and ironic parallel between the settlers of the past and Josie's decision to swap Ohio for Alaska.

Such references to the specificity of American national mythology are accompanied, however, by a conviction that contemporary America can only be conceived of in terms of the wider globalised heterogeneity of the world in the twenty-first century. Alan's role, to broker a deal between his US company and a Saudi state so immensely rich from oil money that it can build an entire, gleaming, hi-tech city from scratch in the desert, is typical of the kind of job that Americans of his 'type' do as a result of globalisation. In a discussion with a fellow passenger on a plane, a picture is drawn of how America too, once idealist, pioneering, and singularly powerful in the second half of the twentieth century, has become subsumed by the patterns of globalisation. His neighbour says to him,

> It was good for a while, right? [...] What was it, thirty years or so? Maybe twenty, twenty-two? But it was over, without a doubt it was, and now we had to be ready to join western Europe in an era of tourism and shopkeeping.[29]

This provides further explanation for Eggers's unwillingness to debate how 'American' his novels are. In the same interview that he refuses to narrow the typicality of the story in *Your Fathers* to just the United States, Eggers also insisted that *The Circle* 'is – intends to be – a globally minded book, in the sense that the concerns it addresses profoundly affect everyone's life, across the globe, even though these companies are generally based in California'.[30] He maintained that he wants '[i]deally' to include 'universal things in all of my books', and that what he 'resist[s] [...] is writing a book that takes place in one neighborhood or a single community'.[31] This may be puzzling, for *The Circle* patently does not resist this, providing a rich depiction of an easily recognisable Silicon Valley-type community – part secluded cult hide-away, part forward-looking hi-tech campus, a place which, Mae feels, is quintessentially American. Nevertheless, in the age of neo-liberalism, where multinational corporations are more powerful and influential than nation states, a company like Eggers's Circle is as typical of global developments as US ones. *The Circle* functions as a warning about the powerlessness, indeed the irrelevance, of physical national boundaries in the face of the power to relentlessly control private and public existence wielded by the most aggressively globalist IT companies – real-life counterparts of The Circle such as Google, Amazon and Facebook. *The Circle* thereby inverts *Hologram for the King*'s American-abroad story about the part played by the United States in a broader global economy in focusing on the consequence of globalised economics on American soil.

Eggers's 'global-mindedness', then, combines an interest in a specifically American world with a distinctively globalised one, of which the United States is a representative example. His fiction reminds us that the two things cannot be separated from one another, for the specific is always typical in a globalised world. But what is notable about these four novels is that while globalisation in a context for their individual stories, they stop short of mounting a full-blown critique of globalisation. The explicit introduction of the context of globalisation early in *Hologram for the King* in Alan's meeting on the airplane, as he discusses with his neighbour various topics, such as the pioneer of US globalised trade Jack Welch, how the Chinese are 'making sneakers in Nigeria', and how low wages in Asia and Africa have killed manufacturing on American soil, does not develop into a critique of globalised economics as we might expect it to, nor lead to a climax to the narrative (as it might in an eco-thriller). It merely establishes the backdrop for Alan's personal sense of disillusionment and eventual fulfilment. Ultimately the story is about a moment of personal connection he shares with Dr. Zahra Hakem, a Saudi surgeon. *Hologram for the King* turns out to be a touching transnational love story.

The presence of globalisation in these novels as always there but in the background, to ensure the stories of their protagonists remains central, means that perhaps a more useful term for their outlook is *planetary* rather than global. A suggestive distinction between the global and the planetary has recently been made by Amy Elias and Christian Moraru, building on insights by Gayatri Chakravorty Spivak.[32] They contend that where the global cannot shake off connotations of 'economic, political, and technical administration' the planetary shifts the focus onto a (re)turn to ethical interconnectedness which they term 'relationality'. By this model any category of the global novel (and this is indeed consistent with Adam Kirsch's definition of this genre)[33] denotes fiction which is both produced as a result of globalised practices in publishing and transmission, and also contains a critique of or a focus on the effects of globalisation (economic, political, etc.). Planetary fiction, by contrast, places the emphasis on 'new models of transnationality, internationality, or multinationality', and 'our moment [...] measuring time, space, and culture [..] on the planet at large'.[34] As Elias and Moraru insist, focusing on the planet means an emphasis not simply on human practices and their effects the world over, but on the position of the human being on a planet which, by definition, turns and changes. Planetarity is thus a de-territorializing perspective on the global, opening up spaces and crossings between places and people at various points in the globe.

Eggers's novels explore planetarity more implicitly even than they confront globalisation. They do not concentrate specifically on ecological issues, such as climate change. Yet in their concern with the experience of typical human beings in a globalised world, their emphasis is on the significance of a broader 'relationality', or (in Elias's and Moraru's terms) human beings 'coming together, or "worlding"'.[35] Underpinning each of the stories in *Hologram for the King*, *The Circle*, and *Heroes of the Frontier* is faith in the importance of a community of human beings learning about, respecting and loving one another – being connected in a more traditional sense than via technology. This ethical imperative most clearly drives *Heroes of the Frontier*. This novel is the part of the quartet which, even more so than *The Circle*, is geared up to providing a detailed portrait of a specific region of the United States: Alaska. The peculiarities of Alaska – its scenery, its remoteness, its local names and customs – are detailed evocatively throughout, and from the defamiliarizing perspective of an outsider, Josie. This sense of regional singularity is strengthened by the fact that Alaska is such an *untypical* part of the United States, both geographically and culturally (though it would be difficult to designate any place as typical in so vast and diverse a nation as the US). *Heroes of the Frontier* is another Eggers story of movement, one of the recurring narrative tropes of his fiction as whole. His characters travel restlessly, internationally, as in *You Shall Know Our Velocity*, *What is the What* and *Hologram for the King*. Josie's travels may only be within the United States, but her literal exploration of Alaska parallels her own attempt to decide what she should do next. The questions she is asking herself (who is she? why has her marriage failed? what should she do next?) are the standard everyday existential crises of average suburbanites not just in America but across the globe.

Josie's perpetual mobility underscores the novel's comparison – which is picked up from the three previous novels – between contemporary Americans and their forebears. In an echo of Alan's reflections on the incompatibility of heroism and suburbia, Josie wonders, when arriving in Alaska, 'So where were the heroes? All she knew where she had come from were cowards'.[36] Throughout the story she and her children travel restlessly to different part of Alaska, staying with new friends, sleeping in their RV, squatting in an unoccupied cabin, in a way that calls to mind two key American myths of mobility and escape. The first is, of course, the Western. While the comparison is treated ironically, as we have seen, at a deeper level, the refrain of tales from 'Trails Grown Dim' points to a meaningful continuity between Americans in the nineteenth century and Americans in the twenty-first, a history of people upping sticks and moving on, often as a result of domestic hardship, just as Josie has done. The second foundational myth is *Walden*. This is not referenced directly in the novel, but the role in the story played by a cabin in the woods, and the fact that Josie's escape is a journey of independence and spiritual discovery inevitably brings Thoreau to mind. Her escapade involves removing herself and her children from their twenty-first century comforts in order to live a simpler life. Settling in the borrowed cabin, her children begin to sleep better, to no longer fear the dark, to perform happily regular chores such as washing their clothes, until she has the sense that 'they were immeasurably better now than they were in Ohio'. [37] She arrives at an epiphanic recognition about what she has achieved as a parent: 'All along she had been looking for courage and purity in the people of Alaska. She had not thought that she could simply – not simply, no, but still – create such people'.[38]

The singularity of Alaska as a pastoral haven in the contemporary United States enables Josie to achieve a universal relationality, with her children, with people in the same state, with earlier generations of Americans, but also – by implication – with other humans elsewhere in the world. In this respect it is notable how frequently Josie's meditations involve putting her own experiences in a much broader perspective than her life story, indeed one of planetary scale. The word planet features regularly throughout the novel, used metaphorically, as in Josie's description of the best parents as those who 'circle with the predictability of planets', or when reflecting on environmental crisis:

> The world is running out of water. [...] We are exceptional, our planet singular in its ability to sustain life. No, there are billions of Earth-like planets, most of them bigger than ours, most of them likely to be far better developed.

Together these references confirm Josie's understanding of her status as part of a system much bigger than herself. In the exciting climax to the novel –created, significantly, not by any human interaction but by an electrical storm which causes an avalanche – Josie has to guide herself and her children to safety. As they prepare to run, 'Above, a planet popped like a balloon'.[39] Josie has indeed accomplished something heroic after all, something pioneering on a personal level, albeit modest and small-scale compared with the drama of the Western. It is nevertheless the kind of interconnection which approximates the planetary rather than the global. She recognises that although it may have been a mistake to flee to Alaska, people like her – 'every mother, every father' – must understand that leaving is an option, a right, and a necessity: 'without movement there is no struggle, and without struggle there is no purpose, and without purpose there is nothing at all. [...] There is meaning in motion'.[40] With its protagonist's epiphany Eggers's novel reaches a genuinely uplifting, heroic, note.

Crucially, however, this is not the end of *Heroes of the Frontier*. The novel concludes with a single-line chapter which creates an open-endedness which is in keeping with Eggers's ethical approach to the relation between author and reader: 'But then there is tomorrow'.[41] The line suggests that Josie's positive conclusion about their adventure is only temporary. It can plausibly be read as focalised through Josie's consciousness, but could just as easily be taken for a final, solitary but decisive, act of authorial intervention. It shows that the story is not complete with the novel's ending, but that life continues. The planet continues to turn and this has not only spatial consequences but temporary ones too. 'But then there is tomorrow' can be both optimistic or ominous. Life will go on. We have learned by this stage that Josie's husband has tracked her down and is trying to serve her a writ, and so all future possibilities remain open: continued flight, lasting happiness, a return to the mundane struggles of divorce. Which it will be is not suggested by the novel, and the author himself refuses to speculate. Instead, the impression is that Eggers himself has no idea what the outcome will be. He is simply presenting what happens in Josie's world at this moment in time and place and leaving it up to the reader to decide.

'Impressively typical': Eggers, the Program Era, and transnational ethics

Eggers's most recent novels, and their negotiation of the ideas of typical American and typical global or planetary experience, validates Boxall's inclusion of him as part of the 'world community of writers' which typifies fiction in the early part of this century, and who are distinguished by their 'novelistic response to our twenty-first century contemporaneity'.[42] But their values and style also suggests a connection with another, more specific but still broad-ranging, community to have been identified in modern American writing, the one which comes together under the banner of Mark McGurl's term for the extraordinary influence of creative writing programmes in United States universities on modern and contemporary fiction since their establishment in the 1960s: the Program Era. Like Eggers's treatment of American experience, the Program Era is both singular, as it develops from a range of social and cultural factors peculiar to the United States in the mid- to late-twentieth century (such as the rise of the Creative Writing programme, and the American reception of modernist aesthetics), and typical, for it prescribes a set of literary values and techniques which shape writing beyond the confines of the United States and are evident in the international contemporary-fiction community identified by Boxall. McGurl's *The Program Era* is at the same time a study of a distinctively national tradition (there is no other nation about which a similar story of the impact of creative writing tuition could have been told, except perhaps for the United Kingdom, though this story would be shorter and begin much more recently) and one which has a transnational core. Central to McGurl's analysis of the development of programme-fiction is its dissemination of the values of what he calls 'high cultural pluralism', a kind of writing which binds 'the high literary values of modernism with a fascination with the experience of cultural difference and the authenticity of the ethnic voice'.[43] The distinctively American development of The Program thus reflects the inherently transnational nature of the United States.

In his study McGurl commends the 'impressive typicality' of Philip Roth as a Program-Era writer.[44] Even though Roth was less integrated in university writing programmes than many of his contemporaries, he nevertheless strikes McGurl as entirely representative of what he considers the foundational practice of Program-Era fiction, what he calls 'autopoesis', the reflexive awareness of what it means to be a writer while doing the work of a writer, which shapes the work produced, most obviously though self-reflexive technique.[45] Eggers is similarly both untypical and yet quite representative of what McGurl calls the third phase of the Program Era, the period from the mid-1970s to the present day, when even books written outside the academy become absorbed into the ethos of the Program because this ethos has spilled so powerfully outwards. Eggers was not himself schooled in creative writing programmes, nor has he taught creative writing regularly in the academy, as many of his contemporaries do. Yet McGurl acknowledges the impact of his 'impressive cultural entrepreneurship [...] with its literary magazines and publishing ventures and community centers'.[46] Amy Hungerford has recently developed this insight further, arguing that, more than any other figure, Eggers embodies the expanded notion of 'the school' which is part of this third phrase of McGurl's Program Era, as he 'schools', directly or indirectly, a generation of young writers.[47]

Eggers might therefore be regarded as both the product of and a disseminator of the values of the Program Era. We might develop a case that his writing throughout bears the hallmarks of Program-Era values and techniques, with *What is the What* clearly an example of 'high cultural pluralism', *A Heartbreaking Work of Staggering Genius* not as late postmodernism but an exercise in autopoesis, and *Your Fathers* the kind of Program-endorsed creative writing exercise designed to trigger debate about a particular topic. But most typical of the Program Era in Eggers seems to me the way his writing – like that of Roth, as different as it is in terms of historical location, ethnic identity, and favoured styles and subject matter – exemplifies the 'response-mode' in contemporary writing. Both Eggers and Roth, impressively typical exceptions to the rule, assume, in different ways, that the duty of contemporary fiction is to respond to reality, to detail what is typical of the age, whether this is extreme (as in the examples in Roth's essay or *Your Fathers*) or a state of being (Eggers's other three American novels). What is clear from a comparison between the two writers, and in particular the time of Roth's 'Writing American Fiction' and Eggers's quartet of 'American' novels, is the fact that contemporary fiction has in the intervening years become global, and the role of US fiction in this shift has had much to do, somewhat ironically, with the specifically American development of the Program. Where

Roth's definition of 'American reality' *is* something peculiar to the United States (because he observes a profound change in his country due to an increase in extreme behaviour and the media fascination with it), Eggers regards it as symptomatic of broader global conditions.

But both writers assume that the fictional response must be presided over by a properly committed writer. While Roth sketches out a portrait of this figure, referring to positive examples (Salinger and Bellow) and negative ones (Gold), Eggers himself seems to typify the kind of professional writer this figure has evolved into in the twenty-first century: one who is aware of himself as rooted in the social world, performing a social function he reflects on continually, and producing a socially committed kind of fiction. The awareness of the message of his fiction Eggers reveals in interviews, its capacity to respond to broader social issues, underlines the impression that his political awareness and activism are not supplements to his career as a writer of fiction and biography but part of the same socially-engaged mission. This mission has been shaped by Eggers's status as a global author and his sensitivity to transnational relationality, factors that make him, for all the diversity of his work, a writer as typical as he is singular.

One final point, or note of caution, is to acknowledge that the high-point of globally-minded Western writing, which Eggers's fiction exemplifies, coincides with the moment at which global politics is witnessing a turn inwards, *away* from global or planetary concerns. In the same years as literary fiction is shaped by a transnational or planetary turn (as evidenced by the appearance of studies between 2013 and 2015 which cite a vast range of evidential authors and texts),[48] politics in the United States, and also in the UK and in Europe, sees a fomenting of the conditions that would in 2016 result in a decisive turn away from neoliberalism and towards the assertion and redefinition of national identity. The publication of a warm-hearted, expansive, 'planetary' novel like *Heroes of the Frontier* in this very year seems completely out of kilter with the contemporaneous nationalist socio-political climate. Indeed, the overall tenor of literary fiction now seems at odds with a political world dominated by an aggressive nationalism, which places the emphasis on economic isolationism, closing borders and controlling immigration. To account for this disjunction between literary practice and politics, to decide whether (for example) it is do with the persistence of the deep connection between literary (as opposed to popular) fiction and liberalism, even neoliberalism, and the role played by the US Program in this, is a task far beyond the scope of this article. But the fact that social reality and literary fiction are in some ways now worlds away from each other adds an extra vitality to the transnational ethics which are so central to Dave Eggers's recent interrogations of what it means to be an American in the second decade of the twenty-first century.

Notes

1. Caroline D. Hamilton, *One-Man Zeitgeist: Dave Eggers, Publishing and Publicity* (London: Continuum, 2010). See also Sarah Brouillette, 'Paratextuality and Economic Disavowal in Dave Eggers's *You Shall Know Our Velocity*', *Reconstruction: Studies in Contemporary Culture*, 3, no. 2 (2003). http://reconstruction.eserver.org/issues/032/brouillette.htm; and Amy Hungerford, 'McSweeney's and the School of Life', *Contemporary Literature*, 53, no. 4 (Winter, 2012), pp. 646–680.
2. Michelle Peek, 'Humanitarian Narrative and Posthumanist Critique: Dave Eggers's *What is the What*', *Biography*, 35, no. 1 (2012), pp. 115–136; Valorie Thomas, '"Dust to Cleanse Themselves": A Survivor's Ethos: Diasporic Disidentifications in *Zeitoun*, *Biography*, 35, no. 2 (2012), pp. 271–285.
3. Peter Boxall, *Twenty-First-Century Fiction: A Critical Introduction* (Cambridge: Cambridge University Press, 2013), p. 111, p. 116. See also: Liesbeth Korthals Altes, 'Sincerity, Reliability and Other Ironies – Notes on Dave Eggers' *A Heartbreaking Work of Staggering Genius*', in Gunther Martens and Elke D'hoker (eds.), *Narrative Unreliability in the Twentieth-Century First-Person Novel* (Berlin: De Gruyter, 2008), pp. 107–128; Adam Kelly, 'David Foster Wallace and the New Sincerity in American Fiction', in David Hering (ed.), *Consider David Foster Wallace: Critical Essays* (Los Angeles, CA/Austin, TX: Sideshow Media Group Press, 2010), pp. 131–46; James Clements, 'Trust Your Makers of Things!: The Metafictional Pact in Dave Eggers's *You Shall Know Our Velocity*', *Critique*, 56 (2015), pp. 121–137.
4. Boxall, *Twenty-First Century Fiction*, p. 6.
5. Caren Irr, *Toward the Geopolitical Novel: U.S. Fiction in the Twenty-First Century* (Columbia University Press, 2013), p. 19.
6. Adam Kirsch, *The Global Novel: Writing the World in the 21st Century* (New York, NY: Columbia Global Reports, 2017).
7. David James, 'Transnational Postmodern and Contemporary Literature', in Yogita Goyal (ed.), *The Cambridge Companion to Transnational American Literature* (Cambridge University Press, 2017), pp. 122–140, p. 123.
8. Amy Elias and Christian Moraru, 'Introduction: The Planetary Condition', in *The Planetary Turn: Relationality and Geoaesthetics in the Twenty-First Century* (Evanston, IL: Northwestern University Press, 2015), p. xi–xxxvii, p. xi.
9. See Paul Jay, *Global Matters: The Transnational Turn in Literary Studies* (Ithaca, NY: Cornell University Press, 2014); Rebecca Walkowitz, *Born Translated: The Contemporary Novel in an Age of World Literature* (New York, NY: Columbia University Press, 2015); Christian Moraru, *Reading for the Planet: Towards a Geomethodology* (University of Michigan Press, 2015).
10. Boxall, *Twenty-First Century Fiction*, p. 173.
11. Alex Preston, '*Heroes of the Frontier* Review: Dave Eggers Finds Utopia in Alaska', *The Guardian*, 17th July 2016: https://www.theguardian.com/books/2016/jul/17/heroes-of-the-frontier-dave-eggers-review-utopianism
12. Alexandra Alter, 'Dave Eggers Journeys Into Alaska in *Heroes of the Frontier*', *The New York Times* (April 4 2016): https://www.nytimes.com/2016/04/05/books/dave-eggers-journeys-into-alaska-in-heroes-of-the-frontier.html
13. Dave Eggers, *A Hologram for the King* (London: Penguin, 2013), p. 12.
14. I use this term loosely to determine the sequence of four novels on similar themes, while acknowledging that Eggers has not applied this term to them nor referred to them as a sequence.

15. Georg Lukács, 'From The Theory of the Novel: A Historico-Philosophical Essay on the Forms of Great Epic Literature', in Michael McKeon (ed.), *Theory of the Novel: A Historical Approach* (Baltimore, MD, & London: Johns Hopkins University Press, 2000), pp. 185–218, p. 198.
16. Dave Eggers, 'Interview with Dave Eggers and Valentino Achak Deng'. http://www.vadfoundation.org/interview-with-the-creators/
17. Dave Eggers, [no interviewer identified] 'A Short Q&A With Dave Eggers About his New Novel *Your Fathers, Where Are They? And the Prophets, Do They Live Forever?*', *McSweeney's Internet Tendency*, June 11, 2014. https://www.mcsweeneys.net/articles/a-short-q-a-with-dave-eggers-about-his-new-novel-your-fathers-where-are-they-and-the-prophets-do-they-live-forever.
18. Philip Roth, 'Writing American Fiction' [1961, 1965], in Malcolm Bradbury (ed.), *The Novel Today: Contemporary Writers on Modern Fiction* (London: Fontana, 1977), pp. 27–43, p. 29.
19. Roth, 'Writing American Fiction', p. 42
20. Ibid., p. 42.
21. Ibid., p. 39.
22. Dave Eggers, *Your Fathers, Where Are They? And the Prophets, Do They Live Forever?* (London: Penguin, 2014), p. 194.
23. Eggers, *Your Fathers*, p. 161.
24. Ibid., p. 165.
25. Ibid., pp. 198–199.
26. Don Oldenburg, 'Disturbed Young Man All Too Familiar in *Fathers*', *USA Today*, June 15, 2014. http://www.usatoday.com/story/life/books/2014/06/15/your-fathers-where-are-they-and-the-prophets-do-they-live-forever/10251431/
27. Dave Eggers, 'A Short Q&A'. https://www.mcsweeneys.net/articles/a-short-q-a-with-dave-eggers-about-his-new-novel-your-fathers-where-are-they-and-the-prophets-do-they-live-forever.
28. Eggers, *Hologram*, p. 270.
29. Ibid., p. 12.
30. Ibid., p. 552.
31. Ibid., p. 552.
32. Elias and Moraru, 'Introduction: The Planetary Condition', pp. xi–xxxvii; Gayatri Chakravorty Spivak, *The Death of a Discipline* (New York, NY: Columbia University Press, 2005).
33. Kirsch, *The Global Novel.*
34. Elias and Moraru, 'Introduction: The Planetary Condition', p. xvii, p. vii.
35. Ibid., p. vii.
36. Dave Eggers, *Heroes of the Frontier* (London: Vintage, 2016), p. 5.
37. Ibid., p. 307.
38. Ibid., p. 308.
39. Ibid., pp. 150, 126–7, 375.
40. Ibid., p. 363.
41. Ibid., p. 385.
42. Boxall, *Twenty-First Century Fiction*, p. 6.
43. Mark McGurl, *The Program Era: Postwar Fiction and the Rise of Creative Writing* (Cambridge, MA & London: Harvard University Press, 2009), p. 32.
44. Ibid., p. 56.

45. I am distinguishing here between 'reflexive', the kind of 'reflex' behaviour (involving continual self-assessment, verification, checking, etc.) associated with 'reflexive modernity', the sociological theory which underpins McGurl's perspective in *The Program Era*, and 'self-reflexivity', the more deliberate practice of referring to oneself associated with aesthetics, e.g. postmodernism.
46. McGurl, *The Program Era*, p. 29.
47. Hungerford, 'McSweeney's and the School of Life', p. 661.
48. Boxall, *Twenty-First Century Fiction* (2013); Irr, *Toward the Geopolitical Novel* (2013), Jay, *Global Matters* (2014), Walkowitz, *Born Translated* (2015), Moraru, *Reading for the Planet* (2015).

Disclosure statement

No potential conflict of interest was reported by the author.

Making it long: men, women, and the great American novel now

Kasia Boddy

ABSTRACT

In 2010, following the publication of Jonathan Franzen's fourth novel, *Freedom*, a furore briefly emerged in the literary media about whether the Great American Novel, so-called since 1868, is 'coded male'. This essay briefly explores the history of novelistic claims to national spokesmanship, and, latterly, spokeswomanship. It considers the influence on Don DeLillo on contemporary fiction, and particularly, his importance for women writers such as Jennifer Egan, Dana Spiotta, Rachel Kushner and A.M. Homes. The bulk of the essay offers a reading of Homes's 2013 novel *May We Be Forgiven*, which simultaneously critiques the macho posturings of the GAN and asserts its place within that tradition.

He said he would make a long story short. Then he made it long. He entertained the men, why not?[1]

'There comes a time in the mid-life of every male American writer when he feels compelled to make his big statement about the state of the union.'[2] Thus the conventional wisdom goes. This particular formulation is by Tim Adams, reviewing Ethan Canin's *America America* in 2008. Adams argues that by choosing such a 'hubristic' title for his 'fat' novel Canin was announcing a 'self-conscious' connection to the long-standing tradition of the Great American Novel (GAN). It was a move that demonstrated 'undeniable guts', Adams suggests, for it invited reviewers like him to measure the novel against the canon of 'big ones'; and some of those reviewers inevitably concluded that it didn't 'quite earn its grand double-barrelled title'.[3] That verdict – not *quite* a GAN but 'a Very Good American Novel' – was, of course, also conventional.[4] Since its initial formulation in the 1860s, the GAN idea has always been more about inspiration than achievement; the very fact that it has been attempted but remains 'unwritten' providing a spur to future engagement with both nation and national literature.[5] The partial failure of a novel like *America*

America was therefore nothing to be ashamed of, but rather a testimony to its author's effort, ambition, and assumption of authority. It is those qualities, pointed out Katha Pollitt, that are usually 'coded male' and that glean rewards, both financial and in the 'economy of prestige'.[6]

Pollitt was contributing to the 'Franzenfreude' debate that briefly dominated the literary press in 2010 after the publication of Jonathan Franzen's fourth novel, *Freedom*. The widespread press coverage given to *Freedom* spurred two other bestselling novelists, Jodi Picoult and Jennifer Weiner, to comment on the paucity of book reviews, particularly in the *New York Times*, afforded to fiction by women and to commercial fiction (the two categories were often conflated).[7] The 'fracas' had wide ramifications, drawing attention to data on gender disparity in the US literary press.[8] But Weiner also made another, rather different, point: 'when a man writes about family and feelings, it's literature with a capital L, but when a woman considers the same topics, it's romance or a beach book'.[9] 'Novels about suburban families,' echoed Pankaj Mishra, 'are more likely to be greeted as microcosmic explorations of the human condition if they are by male writers; their female counterparts are rarely allowed to transcend the category of domestic fiction.'[10] When Franzen's *The Corrections* appeared in 2001 the *New York Times* entitled its review 'A Family Portrait as Metaphor for the '90s'.[11]

By focusing on 'topics', however, Weiner ignores the conscious signalling that works like *Freedom* do to indicate capital L, or capital GAN, status. The most obvious paratextual 'password' comes in the form of a title such as *America America* or *American Pastoral* or, more circumspectly or emblematically, *Independence Day* or *Freedom*.[12] Would Franzen really have been showcased on the cover of *Time* magazine as 'Great American Novelist' if he'd entitled his 550-page 'bromance' of Walter and Richard *Not Best Friends Forever*?[13] Although he initially disavowed the GAN tag – 'I always hated the expression' – he then qualified that dissociation: 'mostly because I encountered it in stupid or sneering contexts.'[14] Franzen knew exactly what he was doing.

Titles are not the only means by which novelists seek to 'transcend the category of domestic fiction'. Carefully chosen allusions also allow an author to choose 'his [or her] peers and thus his [or her] place in the pantheon.'[15] After dissecting the recent plethora of books with titles of 'faintly nationalistic simplicity' – 'American anything, really' – Chad Harbach modestly called his own first novel, *The Art of Fielding*.[16] But Harbach had other means to signal his ambition. As a 'topic', baseball offered an easily recognisable 'American' link to Don DeLillo's *Underworld* (1997), as well as to Philip Roth's *The Great American Novel* (1973). Moreover, like *Freedom* itself, *The Art of Fielding* makes much of its allusions to the masterpieces of the 'American Renaissance'. Reviewers dutifully acknowledged, and praised, its 'echoes of the nineteenth-century greats' and concluded that they 'lend' the novel an 'unexpected richness' which raises it 'high in the standings'.[17] While Harbach went to considerable lengths to avoid using the phrase 'Great American Novel', preferring to talk in institutional terms of the 'New York "canon"', journalists reviewing, or interviewing, him were less coy.[18]

Moi Aussi, Perhaps

'A whale-ship was my Yale college and my Harvard', says Ishmael at one point in *Moby-Dick*, but Harbach's Harvard actually was Harvard.[19] The same college introduced the same novel to Norman Mailer half a century earlier, albeit through a different critical lens. Both writers rework Melville's story of men together, 'federated along one keel', but while *The Naked and the Dead* (1948) interprets this in the light of F. O. Matthiessen's emphasis on 'the defects of individualism', *The Art of Fielding* looks to early-1990s queer theory.[20] Allusion is always critically filtered, even if its purpose seems to remain largely the same. Convinced that 'everyone would know' his 'biggest influence', Mailer, like Harbach, wanted educated readers to recognise his own education.[21]

But Mailer was also signalling something that Harbach, in 2012, didn't really have to worry about: what might be called his right to allusion. Lynne Tillman recently described the 'gan' [sic] that emerged after the Second World War as a 'cultural product of America's new role as a dominant world power', akin to Abstract Expressionism in its relentless masculine self-assertion.[22] While there is something to be said for this, Tillman's argument fails to acknowledge that at the time writers such as Mailer and Saul Bellow and, one she doesn't mention, Ralph Ellison, were hardly self-evident spokesmen for all-American masculinity. Rather, each assumed that role precisely to avoid an expected 'minority tone'.[23] In the early 1950s, Ellison and Bellow each published a *Bildungsroman* in which a young man, seemingly on the periphery of America, becomes its spokesman. When Bellow's *The Adventures of Augie March* (1953) came out, reviewers compared him to John Dos Passos and Thomas Wolfe, although one complained that he was 'aiming too early and too directly at the Great American Novel'.[24] Bellow was certainly forthright about his intention. 'I am an American,' announces his protagonist (initials AM) in the novel's opening line, and its final word is 'America'.[25] The opening of Ellison's *Invisible Man*, published a year earlier, would seem to undercut this stance: 'I am an invisible man,' the protagonist declares. But when, after telling a tale that allegorises black history by riffing on Twain and Melville, the novel concludes with the challenge, 'Who knows but that, on the lower frequencies, I speak for you?', it transpires that he also means 'I am an American'.[26] 'Whatever my role as "race man",' Ellison liked to say, 'I am as a writer … a custodian of the American language'.[27] Bellow was Jewish, from Chicago; Ellison was black, living in New York: each keen to assert directly, and through his allusions, that he spoke not simply as a Jewish writer or a black writer or a New York writer or a Chicago writer. The strategy worked. In 1953 *Invisible Man* won the National Book Award, and 1954 the prize went to *The Adventures of Augie March.*

Since then, allusion's signal of 'cultural entitlement' has seldom faltered in what Jonathan Freedman dubs the 'assimilation-by-culture' project.[28] Women writers, of whatever race or ethnicity, have, as we have seen, faced an additional problem – the almost axiomatic understanding of the GAN as a particularly male enterprise. This was largely a twentieth-century invention. In its original formulation, argues Lawrence Buell, 'the GAN idea was seldom explicitly framed as a gendered concept'; indeed, it was widely accepted that the 'nearest approach to the desired phenomenon' was Harriet Beecher Stowe's *Uncle Tom's Cabin* (1851–52).[29] After the Civil War, however, as the United States embraced 'bigness and greatness in all their forms' – imperial expansionism, corporate consolidation, aesthetic style – a connection was increasingly made between size and masculinity.[30] Increasingly, then, novels claimed national significance by dint of the amount of logistical work they did – their assiduousness in collecting, organising and then representing data in the name of 'complete and whole articulation'.[31] It was in this particular context that Gertrude Stein temporarily abandoned a long novel called *The Making of Americans*, writing to a friend,

> I am afraid that I can never write the Great American novel. I dn't [sic] know how to sell on a margin or to do anything with shorts and longs, so I have to content myself with niggers and servant girls and the foreign population generally.[32]

The suggestion here is that these groups somehow belong to the short story, to local colour, rather than to the national epic, and that Stein, as a woman, a Jew, and a lesbian, also belonged to the modest margins of representation. But Stein, perhaps because she considered herself a 'masculine type', soon regained her confidence. In the notebooks for *The Making of Americans*, she wrote of Picasso, Matisse, and the 'maleness that belongs to genius', adding 'moi aussi, perhaps'.[33] What better way to demonstrate that affinity than by writing a 925-page novel? It's true that *The Making of Americans* offers a 'satirical view' of the GAN, but its 'antidote to patriarchy', its 'patricide', is nonetheless enacted in masculine terms.[34] When Stein said that George Washington 'began a novel, the novel the great American novel', she was identifying the first president as 'a crucial prototype of her own original American genius'.[35]

The evolution of modernism into postmodernism did little to shift the gender, and ethnic, identity of the Great American 'novelist-as-giant'; in the familiar narrative of Pynchon begetting DeLillo begetting Wallace, masculinity has remained 'constitutive of the genre'.[36] Since the emergence of second-wave feminism in the 1970s, however, the giants have become rather self-conscious about their big books, worried that by playing the 'GREAT AMERICAN GAME' they might simply be indulging in a rarefied form of adolescent 'showing off'.[37] At first, men published confessions about their youthful GAN delusions, about how they fooled themselves that 'Thoreau-Emerson' could be used expose the 'crucial facts of the age' (things like 'Americans are lonely'; 'Americans are greedy'; 'the Bomb is bad') until consciousness-raising revealed that, rather than performing a 'patriotic duty', all that they had 'really wanted' was 'literary stallionship.'[38] The next generation, the 'post-boomers' born or raised in the 1960s and 1970s, were even more anxiously ambivalent about their desire to present 'the American Century as Seen Through a Brick' of a novel.[39] Updike, Mailer, and Roth ('the Great Male Narcissists who've dominated post-war realist fiction') became whipping boys for many male writers. They found it more difficult, however, to shake off the 'dangerously attractive' 'boy-novel phallicism' of Gaddis and Pynchon.[40]

But, despite all the embarrassment, there has been no shortage in the twenty-first century of male-authored long novels filled with canonical allusions and titles that hint at state-of-the-nation reflections. Business as usual in the 'genre of "genius"' then, except perhaps for the inclusion of a humorous, and self-inoculating, line or two about a writer-character's 'searing ambition to write the Great American Novel' and eventual realisation that he was doing it for 'all the wrong reasons', such as a desire to feature on 'the cover of *Time*'.[41] Appearances to the contrary, these novels insist, the author himself is *not* a misogynist and indeed is well aware of the masculine posturing *usually* involved in the '*big* book' – a work whose 'thickness' and 'length' will translate into 'muscularity and febrility', as well as, of course, hard cash.[42] 'Literature could turn you into an asshole', but not if you took sufficient care with your 'arrogance problem'.[43]

The position of post-boomer women writers is rather different from both that of their male peers, and that of the generation of women writers born in the 1930s and 1940s, writers such as Toni Morrison, Marilynne Robinson, Jane Smiley, Joyce Carol Oates, and Lynne Tillman, who freely used American history and 'classic American literature', reimagined 'from a female perspective', in order to diagnose the 'national disease' but who shied away from the GAN cliché.[44] If the narrator of Tillman's *Motion Sickness* (1991), for example, wonders if her friend might 'secretly … be hard at work on the Great American Novel', she quickly corrects herself, since 'no woman I've ever known has used that phrase, one that's ridiculous to me.'[45] 'I don't think that way at all,' insists Joyce Carol Oates; 'I don't have any friends who think that way.'[46] For both, the 'gendered' nature of the Great American Novel is 'constitutive of the genre': 'this means a woman could write it, but then it wouldn't be the gan'.[47]

The next generation of women writers have been more equivocal. On winning the British Costa Prize in 2013 for *May We Be Forgiven*, A.M. Homes was asked if she thought she had written a GAN. She said that she did, although, she insisted, the word 'great' should not be understood as a term of 'critical judgment' nor, it seemed, to express quantity; rather she was thinking of 'great as in expansive, and far reaching, and so in that sense, absolutely, very much, I think of myself, in positive and negative ways, as a very American writer.'[48] There is perhaps something a little disingenuous in Homes's gloss here, especially since she'd just won a prize for her longest book to date. Did the judges think it 'great' in the first sense because it was 'great' in the second? Did she win the 'women's prize for fiction' despite, or because, the novel was narrated by a man and was, in Homes's own phrase, a 'guy book'?[49]

Once more allusion is a vital component in the mix. *May We Be Forgiven* is filled with authorial name-checks and references. *Moby-Dick* gets a passing mention, but Homes's focus is squarely on those post-war American novels that, as Tillman argued, were 'part of the cultural ascendancy of America after the war'.[50] Homes identified, as particular 'literary mentors', Joseph Heller's *Catch-22* (1961) and *Something Happened* (1974), and John Cheever's *Falconer* (1977).[51] Both were writers who had considered the GAN – Heller had been happy to accept, 'in modest deference to many people who hold that view', that *Catch-22* was '*a*' if not 'THE' Great American Novel, while Cheever's appearance on the cover of *Newsweek*, to celebrate the publication of 'A Great American Novel' was in many ways the culmination of a life worrying about his place 'in the big league'.[52] But while Cheever's ghost makes a brief appearance in 'an old tan corduroy jacket', the biggest walk-on part in *May We Be Forgiven* is given to Don DeLillo; like Cheever, and the novel's protagonists, he is a resident of Westchester County.[53] DeLillor is first spotted buying tea and lemon pound cake in Starbucks, and the narrator initially thinks he looks like 'a cross between a guy who might change your flat and Clint Eastwood'. A little later, he shows up at a hardware store to buy 'duct tape and dust masks and a flashlight'. The salesman wonders if he 'putting together [his] disaster kit', but it's just 'spring cleaning'. When he appears a third time, in the mall, 'coming out of one of the stores', the narrator thinks it's a conspiracy, but DeLillo protests. 'I live here,' he says.[54]

While Cheever and Heller are rarely discussed by contemporary novelists, Homes is far from alone in paying homage to DeLillo and the 'paranoid Seventies' novel.[55] 'No writer of his era,' it is often asserted, 'has had anything close to his influence on American fiction.'[56] What's more surprising, perhaps, given the 'crammed maleness' of his writing, is how many of his 'heirs' are women.[57] Dana Spiotta's first novel, *Lightning Field* (2001) featured a DeLillo blurb on its jacket, while Christian Lorenz described her second, *Eat the Document* (2006), along with Rachel Kushner's *The Flamethrowers* (2013) and Jennifer Egan's *Look at Me* (2001) and *Welcome to the Goon Squad* (2010), as written 'under the spell of *Underworld*'.[58] All three writers have appeared on stage with DeLillo and eagerly acknowledge his importance for their own development. Kushner says he is her 'favourite living author' and that he taught her to be 'worldly'.[59] Egan praises his 'ambition' in showing how 'the pressure within ordinary humans collide with the pressures of politics and history'.[60] This echoes DeLillo's own formulation of his legacy as 'taking the novel out of the realm of the domestic and into that of history'.[61] There are, of course, many forms that the political or historical novel can take. What DeLillo offered both male and female writers, I would suggest, was a way of using 'ordinary humans' *and* history allegorically in novels of 'big ideas' about 'American consciousness'.[62] Like Ellison, Bellow and the others, DeLillo had written his way 'out of a certain narrowness' and into 'the broader culture' by doing just this: '*Americana* – the title itself says something', he admitted of his first novel.[63] When an interviewer asked whether he was a post-modern writer, he replied that he'd 'prefer not to be labelled. I'm a novelist, period. An American novelist'.[64] DeLillo made it acceptable for twenty-first century women writers to identify themselves in the same way.[65]

'A Very American Writer'

May We Be Forgiven, A.M. Homes's sixth novel, pulls together different strands of her earlier work: the black suburban humour of *The Safety of Objects* (1990) and *Music for Torching* (1999); the exposure of sexual abuse that first appeared in *The End of Alice* (1996); and the middle-aged-reinvention fable of *This Book Will Save Your Life* (2006). Homes has consistently described the concerns of these books as 'very American'.[66] In *May We Be Forgiven*, she underlines that point with references to Richard Nixon as well as Don DeLillo.

On one level, these are easily ignored. This is a fast-paced cultural comedy of vacations, hospital visits and trips to the mall; it involves Googling, sexting and cats having kittens; bugs are killed, dogs walked and, in an explicit nod to DeLillo's *Underworld*, the 'magical' qualities of multi-coloured Jell-O are celebrated.[67] The TV is always on, prompting the narrator to reflect on how 'television binds us as Americans – we are what we watch', and to ask such questions as 'is it still "real" if it's not documented and delivered back to us in the media?'[68] This sense of 'myth being born right there in our living room' is familiar from *White Noise* (1984), but DeLillo's novel also seems to have taught Homes that, in fiction as well as on screen, 'an occasional catastrophe' helps to 'break up the incessant bombardment of information' and 'the other-worldly babble of the American family'.[69]

The novel begins with two brothers, George and Harold Silver, living very different lives.[70] George is a TV executive, with a wife, Jane, two children, Nate and Ashley, a cat, a dog, and a house in the Connecticut suburbs; Harold is an academic historian who lives a semi-detached Manhattan life with his wife Claire. Within forty pages everything changes. George has a car accident, killing a Hispanic couple and orphaning their son, Ricardo; shortly afterwards, on finding Jane in bed with Harold, he clocks her with the bedside lamp; Jane dies, George is incarcerated, and Harold, divorced by Claire, moves to the suburbs to look after the kids. After this, the plot doesn't slow down – for example, Ashley is sexually abused by her teacher; George gets involved with an Israeli arms dealer; and Harold is briefly abducted by some children, then shadowed by a seventies-style conspiracy theorist – but the novel becomes more interested in pursuing the 'possibility of repair'.[71] Although he laments his 'despicable descent into adultery and murderous familial fellowship', Harold's occasional reports of an 'overwhelming sense of dread' feel more gestural than real.[72]

Homes says she was attracted to the works of Heller and Cheever because of their balance of seriousness and comedy, darkness and light.[73] But *May We Be Forgiven* has little of the profound existential angst that lies behind the jokes in a novel like *Something Happened*. 'Is this *all* there is for me to do?' asks Heller's protagonist, Bill Slocum, 'Is this really the *most* I can get from the few years left in this one life of mine? And the answer I get, of course, is always … *Yes*!'[74] *May We Be Forgiven*, however, is a book about 'second chances'. We never think that the children's lives have been 'ruined'; on the contrary, we watch their gradual transformation, under Harold's care, from 'lumps' who sit at the table with 'eyes focused on their small screens' into responsible young citizens. For Heller, the consequences of parenthood are tragically absurd; for Homes, adoptive parenting provokes a 'better version' of Harold.[75] A lot rests on structure. Although the novel has no chapters, perhaps to suggest Harold's sense of 'free fall', we never really doubt his ability to 'get a grip on the runaway world'.[76] Moreover, both Harold and the novel find order in the rituals of Jewish mourning, coming of age – his nephew's Bar Mitzvah, but also his niece's first menstruation – and, as the title suggests, atonement. If these signal that this is Homes's 'Jewish book', we should not forget that the novel begins and ends at Thanksgiving, one of the annual civic rituals that connect family to national life.[77] The year has been lurid but rarely dull.

Harold also approaches his job as a historian through the structures of ritual and atonement. Although his students believe that their attention should be 'perpetually present', or even 'future-forward', he insists that knowledge of the past is needed for 'growth, progression or forgiveness'.[78] This is a resolutely 'therapeutic model of history', interested less in retrieving or dissecting what has happened than in purging oneself of it, seeking 'redemption from the past for the present'.[79] A similar drive toward reconciliation characterises *Underworld* and *Eat the Document*, but Homes associates this approach with her beliefs as 'a Jewish Buddhist': 'I'm constantly trying to feel like, How do we let go of things? How do we not let our future be completely tainted by the past, but also be cognisant of that past?'[80] In *May We Be Forgiven*, letting go is rendered literally: a physical purge (involving special South African teas) is what Harold needs to expel the 'foul' thing, the 'rusty sense of disgust' that has accumulated over the many years he's been working on a book about Richard Nixon.[81]

Coming to terms with Nixon requires Harold to eschew an analysis of his political career and instead focus of his own 'psychic connection' to the President – his 'relationship to stuff', his 'love of bowling' or 'his favourite candy, Skittles'.[82] The more we hear the more we recognise Nixon's 'dark' and 'complicated' personality as an amalgam of Harold, a junk-food-loving depressive with a relationship to China (or at least a Chinese-American woman) who likes 'to think of himself as decent', and George, an imaged-obsessed 'paranoid bully' who is frightened of being alone.[83] In reconciling the two 'sides of the coin' that is Nixon – 'integrity and deceit [... and] moral superiority and arrogance' – Harold is able to forgive the former President, and, in doing so, to forgive his brother and himself.[84]

But history is not only an allegory of family. Harold also wants his readers to think of Nixon as 'the bridge between our prewar Depression-era culture [when Nixon was young and 'just coming into himself'] and the postwar prosperous American-dream America', which ended with his resignation.[85] The American Dream that Nixon first encountered in the 1930s wasn't about individual success but encapsulated the belief that 'life should be better and richer and fuller for everyone, with opportunity for each according to ability or achievement regardless of social class or circumstances of birth'.[86] Nixon's change of perspective – coming to privilege personal over social ambitions – was also, and has remained, America's. Writing elsewhere, Homes has decried the twenty-first-century's 'upsizing of the American Dream': 'inflated [...] as if to distract us from an underlying depression – emotional and economic; as though we are consuming, stuffing, and spoiling ourselves to avoid our fear of failing, of falling, of having nothing at all'.[87] This analysis, which seems to be the starting point for both *This Book Will Save Your Life* and *May We Be Forgiven*, builds on Christopher Lasch's 1979 diagnosis of 'the culture of narcissism'. Both novels deal with the ongoing impact of 'the proliferation of images, therapeutic ideologies, the rationalisation of the inner life, the cult of consumption' and 'the waning of the sense of historical time'.[88]

When Harold first arrives in Westchester he finds a 'big history of Thomas Jefferson' by George's bedside, a nod to the post-war suburban version of 'the Jeffersonian ideal of a house on a private piece of land'.[89] Gradually, Harold transforms the single-family home into something more than a 'boarding house' but less than a commune, 'adopting' Ricardo, the Hispanic child orphaned by George's car accident, and later the aged parents of a woman he meets in the mall.[90] Repopulating the Dream's 'primary symbol', Harold is refuting popular 1990s jeremiads about the 'innately introverted' suburb, as well as more recent calls for a 'digitised version' of communitarian life.[91] By the end of the novel, Harold tells us that, for the 'first time' in his life, he feels both 'part of a community' and mindfully 'here, in the moment'.[92]

On this reading, the novel ends with the completion of a superior kind of self-help programme, one that rejects Nixon-era 'inward-turning self-cultivation' in favour of the millennial 'self-development' that comes from 'attachments beyond the self'.[93] While novelists in the 1970s worried about 'individualism and sexual liberation', David Foster Wallace said, his contemporaries feared 'the prospect of dying without even once having loved something more than yourself'.[94] These ideas, which are also at the heart of *This Book Will Save Your Life*, are given a more overt political resonance in *May We Be Forgiven.* The community that Harold creates within his home exists within a nexus of other communal spaces, including a prison, cemetery, boarding school, mall, psychiatric hospital, and nursing home, all of which experiment with different ways of living. Together they suggest the recovery of some approximation of the 1930s Dream that had 'gone underground'.[95] It was not unreasonable, Barack Obama declared in 2006, to think about 'Reclaiming the American Dream'.[96]

While few cultural theorists used this kind of language, it can be connected to an early twenty-first-century revival in what was variously described as 'anti–anti-Utopianism', 'iconoclastic utopianism', 'post-utopian utopianism, or utopian post-utopianism'.[97] The last two are Marianne DeKoven's formulations, and she connects the mood to the 'current postmodern ... moment'. What makes post-utopia postmodern, she argues, is its awareness of its limitations: what it offers is necessarily 'muted, partial, local, diffuse, multiple, sceptical' and always aware of its own, unavoidable 'complicity'.[98] Post-utopian thinking, she insists, reminds us that 'we are always within the given of global, multinational, corporate consumer capitalism' and the best that can be done is to 'ironize, distance, critique, subvert, resist those configurations from within them.'[99]

The repurposed suburban home and family (the 'little country' that stands for the big one) offers a good example of a utopianism 'from within', and Homes goes some way to ironize its practices. Whenever anyone seems to be 'thinking all too well' of himself and his beneficence, someone else appears to pull him up short. For example, Harold thinks of his trip with Ricardo to the Plaza's Oak Room as 'the most fun he's had in years', until Ricardo tells him about the hard life of his cousin who worked at the hotel. And when he finds himself 'almost crying' alongside Ricardo's aunt, she challenges his claim to empathy: 'What do you have to cry about? You're a big white guy with a big house'. Self-consciousness about philanthropy only increases when Harold and the kids raise money for the South African village of Nateville (the narcissism of the name alerts us to the problem). When Nate criticises the South African beneficiaries for not using the money wisely, Harold reminds him that 'they live in the same world as we do'.[100]

And yet, in a novel about atonement and 'reparations', this kind of inoculating irony is sporadic at best. Like self-help, gifts are good only if they are the right kind. At the start of the novel, Harold is married to someone who 'asked very little' of him but who also 'gave very little back'. His initial response to any kind of trouble is to look for a 'gift shop' while preserving a 'life of [his] own'. While this is immediately an improvement on George (who believes himself 'a gift of the gods'), shopping is not enough. Harold needs to learn to treat his own 'life as currency', and then to work out where to 'spend it': 'What's the best value?' These thoughts lead to further reflections on the need for 'some larger idea, some sense of enhancing the lives of others'.[101] In some ways Homes seems to be responding directly to the remark in DeLillo's *Cosmopolis* (2003), another novel of information, catastrophe, and atonement, that 'money has lost its narrative quality', and 'is talking to itself'.[102] While the trajectory of DeLillo's novel is toward self-punishment and self-destruction, *May We Be Forgiven* is about rich people giving money back its narrative power. When Harold becomes a 'human cash machine', keeping track of what comes in and what goes out of the family coffers, he begins to value the way that money can inscribe history as well as shape the future.[103]

In formulating these ideas, Homes seems to be drawing on Lewis Hyde's *The Gift*, a book begun in the late 1970s, published in 1983 and, following its gradual rise to cult status, reissued in 2006.[104] Building on earlier anthropological work on gift economies, Hyde emphasises their social and spiritual functions. Gifts, he argues, are 'agents of transformation' which 'bespeak relationships', connecting people to each other and also 'to the gods'. He discusses atonement ('to atone is to reunite') and emphasises that 'human life is a gift'.[105] In *May We Be Forgiven*, we are meant to see a corollary between the organ donation that has enabled Jane to continue to 'save the lives of others' and Harold's own 'gift of life'.[106]

The Gift of the GAN

Homes has always confronted assumptions about what women are 'supposed' to write. In *The End of Alice*, for example, she adopted the perspective of a fifty-three year old paedophile in jail, rather than that of either of the young female protagonists, because 'women are not supposed to do things that are not very, very nice'.[107] *May We Be Forgiven* marks another stage in her challenge to the premise that only 'male writers … write broad social novels. The great American novels'.[108] And yet Homes is not 'passing' as a writer of 'guy books', nor even attempting (as Franzen thinks he is) to overcome 'the sexual division of labour in American fiction'.[109] Rather, just as *The End of Alice* challenged us to reread works like *Lolita*, *May We Be Forgiven* brings the whole 'Great Literary American Novel Syndrome' into sharp relief.[110]

On the face of it, Harold is a familiar figure from GAN mythology. He has spent fifteen years working on his book, dragging around a canvas bag containing a 'thirteen-hundred page manuscript, covered with an elaborate system of Post-its and flags that seem entirely undecipherable'.[111] We can think of many similar figures. Recent examples include: a schoolteacher who keeps his novel in two large manuscript boxes in the boot of his car (the 2004 movie *Sideways*); a baker who refuses to be separated from his 'collection of worn notebooks, legal pads, typing papers, all of it scribbled on and marked up, bound into a single passage with elastic bike cords' (Tracy Letts's 2010 play *Superior Donuts*); or, closest to Harold, a historian with a 'beige metal file cabinet' containing 'the makings of his multivolumed history of Rockford, Illinois, a work that would be unprecedented in scale and ambition (he hoped, on good days)' (Jennifer Egan's *Look at Me*).[112] These hopeful if shambolic authors are themselves descendants of DeLillo's ubiquitous men in small rooms: Jack Gladney, from *White Noise*, a 'harmless, ageing, indistinct' guy who finds Hitler a 'fine, solid, dependable' object of study; Nicholas Branch, from *Libra*, a retired CIA analyst, who, at the novel's start, is 'in his fifteenth year' in a 'room of documents' – 'legal pads and cassette tapes are everywhere … a massive file cabinet stuffed with documents so old and densely packed they may be ready to ignite spontaneously'; and the novelist Bill Gray, from *Mao II*, who wants 'to live like other people' but instead spends 'twenty-three years' sitting amid 'drifts of paper' and 'charts … covered with scrawled words, boxes, lines connecting words', 'making changes', 'whiting out and typing in'.[113] Branch's struggle to complete his 'secret history' of Kennedy's assassination is perhaps most relevant, for, like Harold, his problem is when 'to stop assembling data' and how to turn that 'data-spew', 'notes in three-foot drifts', into 'actual finished prose'.[114] The important point is that, unlike all these other writers, Harold does finish his book, and, although he strips to Maileresque shorts and feels as if he's in a 'boxing gym', he does so without much fuss. 'There is no more need for perfection', he concludes; writing is simply a chore to be completed before 'the children come home'. And once the book is 'cooked', he can get back to looking after the family.[115]

But Homes is not only interested in what it means to take novel out of the realm of history and reinsert it into the domestic sphere, nor simply in subverting what Reno, the artist-protagonist of Rachel Kushner's *The*

Flamethrowers, calls the 'long-winded narcissism' and 'burning need for others to *listen*' characteristic of an 'old American novelist'.[116] Rather she is trying to imagine how the GAN fits into what Hyde would call the 'female commerce' of 'gift aesthetics'.[117] On the one hand, this means abandoning the Oedipal displacements needed to reach the top of Cheever's 'big league' and thinking instead of allusion as a kind of acknowledgement of the ways in which another author's gift 'leaves us altered'.[118] While *May We Be Forgiven* makes its fair share of jokes at the expense of heavyweight 'champs', it also makes 'eye contact' with numerous friends and colleagues, including Lynne Tillman, Grace Paley, Rick Moody, and David Remnick.[119] But there is a limit to what can be achieved with eye contact. If Homes enjoys building a community, inviting everyone into her suburban novel, she also knows what is needed to write herself into 'the broader culture' of bestseller lists and book awards. By exploring the nation's key concerns with a framework that stretches from Jefferson to Nixon, Homes fulfils the Great American brief of effort, ambition and the assumption of authority. Like Harold Silver, and all the other compromised post-postmodernists and post-utopians, she has allowed her gifts to make 'peace with the market'.[120]

Notes

1. Don DeLillo, *Underworld* (London: Picador, 1997), p. 192.
2. Tim Adams, 'How America Sold Its Soul to the Devil', *The Observer*, July 13, 2008. https://www.theguardian.com/books/2008/jul/13/fiction.reviews3.
3. John Updike, 'An Upstate Saga', *The New Yorker*, June 23, 2008. http://www.newyorker.com/magazine/2008/06/23/an-upstate-saga.
4. Robert Epstein, '*The Art of Fielding*, by Chad Harbach', *The Independent*, January 15, 2012. http://www.independent.co.uk/arts-entertainment/books/reviews/the-art-of-fielding-by-chad-harbach-6289666.html.
5. T. S. Perry, 'American Novels', *North American Review* (October 1872), pp. 366–78 (378).
6. Katha Pollitt, 'Franzenfreude, Continued', *The Nation*, September 15, 2010. https://www.thenation.com/article/franzenfreude-continued/; James English, *The Economy of Prestige: Prizes, Awards and the Circulation of Cultural Value* (Cambridge, MA: Harvard University Press, 2005).
7. Franzen's quarrel with women's popular fiction dated back to 2001 when he withdrew *The Corrections* from the Oprah Book Club because he had 'some hope of actually reaching a male audience'. Terry Gross, 'Novelist Jonathan Franzen', *NPR*, October 15, 2001. http://www.npr.org/templates/story/story.php?storyId=1131456.
8. Ruth Franklin, 'The READ: Franzen Fallout', *The New Republic*, September 7, 2010. https://newrepublic.com/article/77506/the-read-franzen-fallout-ruth-franklin-sexism. On gender data, see Double X Blog, 'Fact-Checking the Franzenfreude: Is the *New York Times*' book section really a boys' club?', *Slate*, September 2, 2010. http://www.slate.com/articles/double_x/doublex/2010/09/factchecking_the_franzenfreude.html?from=rss. On the annual 'Count'

undertaken since 2010 by VIDA: Women in the Literary Arts, see http://www.vidaweb.org/the-count/.

9. Jason Pinter, 'Jodi Picoult and Jennifer Weiner Speak Out on Franzen Feud', *The Huffington Post*, August 28, 2010. http://www.huffingtonpost.com/jason-pinter/jodi-picoult-jennifer-weiner-franzen_b_693143.html. Franzen responded with remarks about the 'Jennifer Weinerish self-promotion' demanded by contemporary literary culture and, in his 2015 novel *Purity*, with a jibe about the *NYTBR*'s belief that 'Jonathan' was 'synonymous with talent, greatness. Ambition, vitality'. Karl Kraus, *The Kraus Project*, translated and annotated by Jonathan Franzen (London: Fourth Estate, 2014), p. 274; Jonathan Frazen, *Purity* (New York: Farrar, Straus and Giroux, 2015), p. 207.
10. Cheryl Strayed and Pankaj Mishra, 'Is There a Double Standard for Judging Domestic Fiction?' *New York Times*, May 17, 2015. http://www.nytimes.com/2015/05/17/books/review/is-there-a-double-standard-for-judging-domestic-themes-in-fiction.html?_r=0.
11. Michiko Kakutani, 'A Family Portrait as Metaphor for the '90s', *New York Times*, September 4, 2001. http://www.nytimes.com/2001/09/04/books/books-of-the-times-a-family-portrait-as-metaphor-for-the-90-s.html.
12. Gérard Genette, *Paratexts: Thresholds of Interpretation*, trans. Jane E. Lewin (Cambridge: Cambridge University Press, 1987), p. 160. The novel by a woman that Weiner felt did fulfil the paratextual brief is Anne Tyler's *Digging to America* (2006). Twitter, Aug 23, 2010. https://twitter.com/jenniferweiner/status/21930482445.
13. *Best Friends Forever*, Weiner's sixth novel, was published in 2009 and spent eighteen weeks on the bestseller list. The Oprah Book Club asked whether 'Richard and Walter [were] having a "bromance"'. '*Freedom* Book Club Discussion: Producer Jill's 3rd Post', http://www.oprah.com/oprahsbookclub/oprahs-book-club-producer-jills-freedom-discussion-3.
14. Lev Grossman, 'Jonathan Frazen: Great American Novelist', *Time*, August 12, 2010: http://content.time.com/time/magazine/article/0,9171,2010185,00.html.
15. Genette, *Paratexts*, p. 160.
16. Chad Harbach, 'MFA vs NYC', in Harbach (ed.), *MFA vs NYC: The Two Cultures of American Fiction* (New York: n+1/ Faber, 2014), pp. 9–28 (25).
17. Dennis Drabelle, 'Review of Chad Harbach, *The Art of Fielding*', *Washington Post*, September 5, 2011. http://www.washingtonpost.com/entertainment/books/book-world-chad-harbachs-the-art-of-fielding-reviewed-by-dennis-drabelle/2011/07/18/gIQAN3C14J_story.html].
18. Harbach, 'MFA vs NYC', p. 19.
19. Herman Melville, *Moby-Dick* (Oxford: Oxford University Press, 1988 [1850]), p. 124.
20. Melville, *Moby-Dick*, p. 122; F.O. Matthiessen, *From the Heart of Europe* (Oxford: Oxford University Press, 1948), p. 37. 'Gay studies had really taken off' when Harbach took a Melville seminar at Harvard. Frederick McKindra, 'The Strategies of Baseball, Friendship and Love', *LAMBDA Literary*, February 8, 2012. http://www.lambdaliterary.org/features/02/06/chad-harbach-the-strategies-of-baseball-friendship-and-love/. On Mailer's reading of Matthiessen's *American Renaissance* (1941), see J. Michael Lennon, *Norman Mailer: A Double Life* (New York: Simon and Schuster, 2013), p. 31.

21. Harvey Breit, 'Talk with Norman Mailer' (1951), in J. Michael Lennon (ed.), *Conversations with Norman Mailer* (Jackson: University Press of Mississippi, 1988), pp. 15–17 (15).
22. The acronym is usually capitalised, but Tillman prefers a deflating lower case. Lynne Tillman, 'A Fictional Past: The Myth of the "Great American Novel"', *Frieze*, 163 (May 2014). https://frieze.com/article/fictional-past.
23. Saul Bellow, 'Man Underground' (1952), in John Hersey (ed.), *Ralph Ellison: A Collection of Critical Essays* (Englewood Cliffs: Prentice-Hall, 1974), pp. 28–29 (29).
24. James Atlas, *Bellow: A Biography* (London: Faber, 2000), pp. 193, 198, 211.
25. Saul Bellow, *The Adventures of Augie March* (New York: Viking, 1960), pp. 3, 536.
26. Ralph Ellison, *Invisible Man* (New York: Vintage, 1995), pp. 3, 581.
27. Ralph Ellison, 'The World and the Jug', in John F. Callahan (ed.), *The Collected Essays* (New York: Modern Library), p. 172.
28. John Guillory, *Cultural Capital: The Problem of Literary Canon Formation* (Chicago: University of Chicago Press, 1993), p. 121; Jonathan Freedman, *The Temple of Culture: Assimilation and Anti-Semitism in Literary Anglo-America* (New York: Oxford University Press, 2000), p. 13.
29. Lawrence Buell, *The Dream of the Great American Novel* (Cambridge: Harvard University Press, 2014), p. 31; [John W. De Forest], 'The Great American Novel', *Nation*, January 9, 1868, pp. 27–29 (28).
30. William James, Letter to Mrs. Henry Whitman, 7 June 1899, in Henry James (ed.), *The Letters of William James* (Boston: Atlantic Monthly Press, 1926), vol. 2, p. 90. On 'the culture of size in America, 1865–1930', see Michael Tavel Clarke, *These Days of Large Things* (Ann Arbor: University of Michigan Press, 2007).
31. Thomas Wolfe, *The Story of a Novel* (New York: Charles Scribner's Sons, 1936), p. 92.
32. Patricia Wald, *Constituting Americans* (Durham: Duke University Press, 1995), pp. 239–40.
33. Lisa Ruddick, *Reading Gertrude Stein* (Ithaca: Cornell University Press, 1990), p. 65.
34. Buell, *The Dream of the Great American Novel*, p. 39; Marianne DeKoven, *A Different Language: Gertrude Stein's Experimental Language* (Madison: University of Wisconsin Press, 1983), p. xvii; Ruddick, *Reading Gertrude Stein*, Ch. 2.
35. Gertude Stein, *Four in America* (New Haven: Yale University Press, 1947), p. 169; Barbara Will, *Unlikely Collaboration: Gertrude Stein, Bernard Faÿ, and the Vichy Dilemma* (New York: Columbia University Press, 2011), p. 58.
36. Norman Mailer, *Cannibals and Christians* (London: Sphere, 1969), p. 122; Lynne Tillman, 'A Fictional Past'.
37. Charles McGrath, 'The Souped-Up, Knock-Out Total Fiction Experience', *New York Times*, April 17, 2005. http://www.nytimes.com/2005/04/17/weekinreview/the-soupedup-knockout-total-fiction-experience.html?_r=0; Robert Coover, *The Universal Baseball Association* (1968) (New York: Plume, 1971), p. 19.
38. Bill Henderson, 'My Great American Novel', *Chicago Review*, 26, no. 1 (1974), pp. 52–64 (pp. 52–3). Although GAN debunking began almost as soon as the phrase was coined, it was only in the 1970s that machismo became its main component.

39. David Foster Wallace, *Infinite Jest* (Boston: Little, Brown, 1996), p. 989. For a more recent portrait of a male writer who prefers books by dead, white men but worries 'whether he was a bit misogynistic', see Adelle Waldman, *The Love Affairs of Nathaniel P.* (London: William Heinemann, 2013), p. 57.
40. David Foster Wallace, 'Certainly the End of *Something* or Other, One Would Sort of Think', in *Consider the Lobster* (New York: Little, Brown, 2005), pp. 51–59 (51). Franzen has written about his youthful ambition to 'save the American novel', his anxiety about *Gravity's Rainbow*, and his eventual coming round to Roth and Updike. *The Kraus Project*, pp. 229, 181, 120–21. See Michael Kalisch, 'Correcting Philip: Reading Franzen Reading Roth', *Philip Roth Studies* (Fall 2017), 21–38.
41. Amy Hungerford discusses the 'masculine cultural shape' of that genre in *Making Literature Now* (Stanford: Stanford University Press, 2016), p. 153; Garth Risk Hallberg, *City on Fire* (London: Vintage, 2016), pp. 5, 867.
42. Franzen, *Purity*, pp. 186–87. This is another joke about the *New York Times Book Review*.
43. Harbach, *The Art of Fielding*, p. 328; David Foster Wallace quoted in D.T. Max, *Every Love Story is a Ghost Story* (New York: Viking, 2012), p. 199.
44. Elaine Showalter, *A Jury of Her Peers* (London: Virago, 2010), p. 578; Roth, 'On *The Great American Novel*', in *Reading Myself and Others* (London: Penguin, 1985), pp. 75–92 (92).
45. Lynne Tillman, *Motion Sickness* (London: Serpent's Tail, 1991), p. 14.
46. Katy Guest, 'Joyce Carol Oates', *The Independent*, August 23, 2007. http://www.independent.co.uk/arts-entertainment/books/features/joyce-carol-oates-a-teacher-academic-and-one-of-the-most-prodigious-novelists-of-all-time-462721.html.
47. Tillman was born in 1947, Homes in 1961. Tillman, 'A Fictional Past'; Jane Ciabattari, 'A.M. Homes on Her New Novel *May We Be Forgiven*', *Daily Beast*, Sept 29, 2012. http://www.thedailybeast.com/am-homes-on-her-new-novel-may-we-be-forgiven. I discuss Tillman's engagement with the 'genre', focusing on *American Genius: A Comedy* (2006), in 'Lynne Tillman and the Great American Novel', *electronic book review* (July 2011). http://www.electronicbookreview.com/thread/fictionspresent/american.
48. Kira Cochrane, 'A.M. Homes Interview', *The Guardian*, June 7, 2013. https://www.theguardian.com/books/2013/jun/07/am-homes-interview-womens-prize-fiction.
49. Richard Wolinsky, 'Out of the Darkness: Interview with A.M. Homes', *Guernica*, November 15, 2012. https://www.guernicamag.com/out-of-the-darkness/.
50. Tillman, 'A Fictional Past'.
51. A.M. Homes and Yuka Igarashi, 'A.M. Homes Interview', *Granta*, 124, Online Edition, June 6, 2013. https://granta.com/interview-am-homes/.
52. George Mandel, 'Literary Dialogue with Joseph Heller' (1970), in Adam J. Sorkin (ed.), *Conversations with Joseph Heller* (Jackson: University Press of Mississippi, 1993), pp. 61–77 (pp. 67–68). As young man, Cheever had been 'impressed' particularly by the 'size' of *The Naked and the Dead* and had got the 'heaves' reading reviews of *The Adventures of Augie March*. He fantasised about writing a book so 'massive' that 'you'll be able to lift it to the sound of outboard motors'. John Cheever, *The Journals* (London: Vintage, 1993), pp. 13, 33; Robert Cromie, 'Book Beat', in Scott Donaldson (ed.), *Conversations*

with John Cheever (Jackson: University Press of Mississippi, 1987), pp. 44–57 (52). Homes has said that *Falconer* 'may, in fact, be The Great American Novel – or at least the greatest American novel of the last 30 years.' 'Introduction' to John Cheever, *Falconer* (London: Penguin, 2005), pp. vii–x (vii).

53. Homes, *May We Be Forgiven* (London: Granta, 2012), p. 471. 'The train ride from midtown Manhattan to the picture-book Westchester suburb where DeLillo lives,' wrote Anthony De Curtis, 'offers a capsule view of virtually the entire spectrum of American life.' '"An Outsider in This Society": An Interview with Don DeLillo', in Thomas DePietro (ed.), *Conversations with Don DeLillo* (Jackson: University Press of Mississippi, 2005), pp. 52–74 (54).
54. Homes, *May We Be Forgiven*, pp. 62, 298, 339.
55. Nicholas Dames, 'Seventies Throwback Fiction', *n+1*, 21 (Winter 2015). https://nplusonemag.com/issue-21/reviews/seventies-throwback-fiction/.
56. Charles Finch, 'Buying a Way Past Death: *Zero K* by Don DeLillo', *Chicago Tribune*, April 28, 2016. http://www.chicagotribune.com/lifestyles/books/ct-prj-zero-k-don-delillo-20160428-story.html.
57. DeLillo, *Underworld*, p. 34; Christian Lorentz, 'The Genius of Don DeLillo's Post-*Underworld* Work', *Vulture*, May 2, 2016. http://www.vulture.com/2016/04/genius-of-don-delillos-post-underworld-work.html.
58. Lorentz, 'The Genius of Don DeLillo's Post-*Underworld* Work'. Consistently praised for the 'ambition' of *Look at Me*, particularly when compared to her 'circumscribed' first novel, Jennifer Egan mentioned *Underworld* ('Not that I'm saying my book's as good as that, but they're similar in that they're both complicated books with multiple plotlines'). 'Briefly Noted', *New Yorker*, October 29, 2001. http://www.newyorker.com/magazine/2001/10/29/look-at-me-3; Ron Hogan, 'Interview with Jennifer Egan', *IndieBound*. http://www.indiebound.org/author-interviews/eganjennifer.
59. 'Rachel Kushner: By the Book', *New York Times Book Review*, February 6, 2014. https://www.nytimes.com/2014/02/09/books/review/rachel-kushner-by-the-book.html?_r=0; Sophie De Rosee, 'The World of Rachel Kushner', *The Telegraph*, January 14, 2014. http://www.telegraph.co.uk/culture/books/authorinterviews/10589332/The-world-of-author-Rachel-Kushner.html.
60. Jennifer Egan, Introducing DeLillo, NBA Distinguished Contribution to American Letters, 2015. https://youtu.be/1XiSC3ozVBQ.
61. Maria Nadotti, 'An Interview with Don DeLillo', in DePietro (ed.), *Conversations with Don DeLillo*, pp. 109–18 (115).
62. 'A.M. Homes, winner of the women's prize for fiction, talks to Jeanette Winterson', *The Guardian*, June 10, 2013. https://youtu.be/SEIIv6cyHx0; Kevin Connolly, 'An Interview with Don DeLillo', in DePietro (ed.), *Conversations with Don DeLillo*, pp. 25–39 (28).
63. Kim Echlin, 'Baseball and the Cold War', in DePietro (ed.), *Conversations with Don DeLillo*, pp. 145–51 (148).
64. Nadotti, 'An Interview', p. 115.
65. Of course, not every woman writer has followed this pattern. While the title of Chimamanda Ngozi Adichie's *Americanah* (2013) might suggest a homage to *Americana*, its heroine, a Nigerian immigrant who 'hungered to understand everything about America', remains unconvinced by the books recommended by her Princeton boyfriend, 'novels written by young and youngish men and packed with *things*, a fascinating, confounding accumulation of brands and music and comic books and icons, with emotions skimmed over, and each

sentence stylishly aware of its own stylishness.' *Americanah* (London: Fourth Estate, 2014), pp. 135, 11–12.

66. Kasia Boddy, Unpublished Interview with A.M. Homes, 1999.
67. Homes, *May We Be Forgiven*, p. 444; DeLillo, *Underworld*, pp. 513–14.
68. Homes, *May We Be Forgiven*, pp. 257, 213.
69. Don DeLillo, *White Noise* (London: Picador, 1986), pp. 51, 66, 101.
70. Homes locates the inspiration for this in Cheever's 'Goodbye, My Brother' as well as *Falconer*. Ciabattari, 'A.M. Homes on Her New Novel *May We Be Forgiven*'.
71. Homes, *May We Be Forgiven*, p. 230.
72. Ibid., pp. 298, 468.
73. 'What I did not understand,' reflects one of Cheever's narrators, 'was how a world that had seemed so dark could, in a few minutes, become so sweet.' 'The Housebreaker of Shady Hill'. *The Collected Stories* (London: Penguin, 1982), pp. 253–69 (268).
74. Joseph Heller, *Something Happened* (London: Vintage, 1995), p. 36.
75. Homes, *May We Be Forgiven*, pp. 293, 49, 2, 414. Homes shares DeLillo's belief in the resilience of children, in their ability to 'find a way.' *Underworld*, p. 673.
76. Homes, *May We Be Forgiven*, p. 261; Don DeLillo, *Libra* (London: Penguin, 1988), p. 211.
77. Wolinsky, 'Out of the Darkness'. Richard Ford also uses Thanksgiving to connect the personal, the suburban and the national, although more pessimistically, in *The Lay of the Land* (2007).
78. Homes, *May We Be Forgiven*, pp. 97, 277.
79. Christopher Colvin, '"Brothers and Sisters, Do Not Be Afraid of Me": Trauma, History and the Therapeutic Imagination in the New South Africa', in Katharine Hodgkin and Susannah Radstone (eds), *Memory, History, Nation: Contested Pasts* (New York: Routledge, 2003), pp. 153–68 (158).
80. Wolinsky, 'Out of the Darkness'.
81. Homes, *May We Be Forgiven*, pp. 447, 418.
82. Ibid., pp. 182, 76, 169. This again follows DeLillo's mandate for fiction which 'slips into the skin of historical figures. It gives them sweaty palms and head colds and urine-stained underwear and lines to speak in private and the terror of restless nights.' 'The Power of History', *New York Times*, September 7, 1997. http://www.nytimes.com/library/books/090797article3.html.
83. Wolinsky, 'Out of the Darkness'; Homes, *May We Be Forgiven*, p. 448.
84. Homes, *May We Be Forgiven*, pp. 188, 446.
85. Ibid., pp. 202, 264.
86. Ibid., p. 264, quoting James Truslow Adams, *The Epic of America* (Boston: Little, Brown, 1931), p. 405. On Nixon as one of the Dream's 'most avid spokespersons', see Lawrence R. Samuel, *The American Dream: A Cultural History* (Syracuse: Syracuse University Press, 2012), pp. 81, 77–78.
87. A.M. Homes, *Los Angeles* (Washington: National Geographic, 2002), p. 17.
88. Christopher Lasch, *The Culture of Narcissism: American Life in An Age of Diminishing Expectations* (New York: W.W. Norton, 1979), pp. 32, 3. Early twenty-first-century reworkings of these themes include David G. Myers's *American Paradox: Spiritual Hunger in an Age of Plenty* (New Haven: Yale University Press, 2000).
89. Homes, *May We Be Forgiven*, p. 12; Samuel, *The American Dream*, p. 6. Homes has described *Music for Torching* as 'very much about the American Dream, which I think came out of World War 2 and into the development of suburbia

and the notion of prosperity, and kind of fell apart in the sixties and seventies.' Boddy, Unpublished Interview, 1999.

90. Homes, *May We Be Forgiven*, p. 477. 'To be adopted,' Homes wrote of her own experience, 'is to be adapted, to be amputated and sewn back together again.' *The Mistress's Daughter* (London: Granta, 2007), p. 54.
91. Homes, *May We Be Forgiven*, p. 294; Robert Putnam, *Bowling Alone: The Collapse and Revival of American Community* (New York: Simon and Schuster, 2000), p. 210.
92. Homes, *May We Be Forgiven*, pp. 433, 478.
93. Marianne De Koven, *Utopia Limited: The Sixties and the Emergence of the Postmodern* (Durham: Duke UP, 2007), p. 255; Rachel Greenwald Smith, *Affect and American Literature in the Age of Liberalism* (Cambridge: Cambridge University Press, 2015), 41.
94. Wallace, 'Certainly the End of *Something*', p. 54.
95. Homes, *May We Be Forgiven*, p. 264.
96. Barack Obama, *The Audacity of Hope: Thoughts on Reclaiming the American Dream* (New York: Crown/Three Rivers Press, 2006).
97. Fredric Jameson, *Archaeologies of the Future* (London: Verso, 2005), p. xvi; Russell Jacoby, *Picture Imperfect: Utopian Thought for an Anti-Utopian Age* (New York: Columbia University Press, 2005), p. 85; De Koven, *Utopia, Limited*, p. 269.
98. De Koven, *Utopia, Limited.*, pp. 272, 25.
99. Ibid., pp. 15–16.
100. Homes, *May We Be Forgiven*, pp. 463, 387, 337, 462.
101. Ibid., pp. 31, 11, 25, 1, 463, 435–6.
102. Don DeLillo, *Cosmopolis* (London: Picador, 2004), p. 77.
103. Homes, *May We Be Forgiven*, p. 463.
104. Hyde's fans include Zadie Smith, David Foster Wallace and Jonathan Lethem. See Lee Konstaninou, 'Lewis Hyde's Double Economy', *ASAP/Journal*, 1.1 (2016), pp. 123–49.
105. Lewis Hyde, *The Gift: How the Creative Spirit Transforms the World* (Edinburgh: Canongate, 2007), pp. 139, 71, 60, 69, 97.
106. Homes, *May We Be Forgiven*, pp. 49, 454.
107. Kasia Boddy, Unpublished Interview with A.M. Homes, 1996.
108. Jennifer Gilmore, 'A.M. Homes' Novel Addresses '70s Childhood', *Forward*, October 23, 2012. http://forward.com/culture/164618/am-homes-novel-addresses-70s-childhood/.
109. Wolinsky, 'Out of the Darkness'; Jeremy Green, *Late Postmodernism: American Fiction at the Millennium* (New York: Palgrave, 2005), p. 103.
110. Laura Miller, 'Why Can't a Woman Write the Great American Novel?', *Salon*. http://www.salon.com/2009/02/24/elaine_showalter/.
111. Homes, *May We Be Forgiven*, p. 59.
112. Tracy Letts, *Superior Donuts* (New York: Theatre Communications Groups, 2010), p. 31; Jennifer Egan, *Look at Me* (London: Corsair, 2011), p. 133.
113. DeLillo, *White Noise*, pp. 83, 89; *Libra*, p. 14; Don DeLillo, *Mao II* (London: Jonathan Cape, 1991), pp. 55, 51, 36, 35, 53, 55.
114. DeLillo, *Libra*, pp. 59, 15.
115. Homes, *May We Be Forgiven*, pp. 453, 446.

116. Reno also feels 'a sudden tenderness' for the heavy-drinking, ping-pong-playing, misogynistic author 'and the burden he bore'. Rachel Kushner, *The Flamethrowers* (London: Vintage, 2014), pp. 222, 251.
117. Hyde, *The Gift*, pp. 105, 143.
118. Ibid., p. 46.
119. Homes, *May We Be Forgiven*, pp. 383, 84, 53, 438. In her acknowledgements, Homes also thanks Yaddo, a writers' retreat committed to 'culture as a gift'. Micki McGee, 'Creative Power and the Making of American Culture', in McGee (ed.), *Yaddo: Making American Culture* (New York: Columbia University Press, 2008), pp. 1–16 (1).
120. Hyde, *The Gift*, p. 278.

Disclosure statement

No potential conflict of interest was reported by the author.

Index

Note: Footnotes are indicated by "n" and the note number after the page number e.g., 33n32 refers to footnote number 32 on page 33.

For Product Safety Concerns and Information please contact our EU representative GPSR@taylorandfrancis.com
Taylor & Francis Verlag GmbH, Kaufingerstraße 24, 80331 München, Germany

www.ingramcontent.com/pod-product-compliance
Lightning Source LLC
Chambersburg PA
CBHW071527100726
47908CB00004B/1309

* 9 7 8 0 3 6 7 6 4 0 1 1 8 *